Heritage and Globalisatio

C000134399

This volume analyses the politics, policy and practice of cultural heritage at the global level, identifying the major directions in which international heritage practice is moving, and exploring the key issues likely to shape the cultural heritage field well into the 21st century. It examines the tensions between the universal claims of much heritage practice, particularly that associated with the World Heritage system, and national and local perspectives. It explores the international legal framework developed since World War Two to protect heritage, particularly at times of war, and from theft, showing how contemporary global problems of conflict and illicit trade continue to challenge the international legal system.

Heritage and Globalisation critiques the incorporation of heritage in the world economy through the policies of international development organisations and the global tourism trade. It also approaches heritage from seldom-considered perspectives, as a form of aid, as a development paradigm, and as a form of sustainable practice.

The book identifies some of the most pressing issues likely to face the heritage industry at a global level in coming decades, including the threat posed by climate change and the need for poverty reduction. Providing a historically and theoretically rigorous approach to heritage as a form of and manifestation of globalisation, the volume's emphasis is on contemporary issues and new fields for heritage practice.

Sophia Labadi is a consultant for the European Cultural Foundation and UNESCO. She is a heritage specialist with wide interests in culture and development, cultural industries and immigrants' histories. She has published on various issues related to culture and edited *World Heritage: Challenges for the Millennium* (2007). She has been the recipient of a number of scholarships and awards, most recently the 2008 Cultural Policy Research Award.

Colin Long lectures in Cultural Heritage at Deakin University, Australia. A historian with interests in Southeast Asian history and heritage, Australian urbanism, and post-communist heritage, his recent publications include an analysis of tourism and World Heritage in Havana and a history of the Lao capital, Vientiane.

Key Issues in Cultural Heritage

Series Editors:
William Logan and Laurajane Smith

Heritage and Globalisation

Edited by
Sophia Labadi and Colin Long

LONDON AND NEW YORK

First published 2010
by Routledge
2 Park Square, Milton Park, Abingdon, Oxon OX14 4RN

Simultaneously published in the USA and Canada
by Routledge
711 Third Avenue, New York, NY 10017

*Routledge is an imprint of the Taylor & Francis Group, an informa
business*

Typeset in Garamond by Taylor and Francis Books
Printed and bound in Great Britain by CPI Antony Rowe,
Chippenham, Wiltshire

British Library Cataloguing in Publication Data
A catalogue record of this book is available from the British Library

Library of Congress Cataloguing in Publication Data
Heritage and globalisation / edited by Sophia Labadi and Colin Long.
    p. cm.
  1. Heritage tourism. 2. Sustainable tourism. 3. Culture and
tourism. 4. Culture and globalization. I. Long, Colin, 1966- II. Labadi,
Sophia. III. Title: Heritage and globalization.
  G156.5.H47H46 2010
  338.4'791–dc22
                                    2010011860

ISBN 13: 978-0-415-57111-1 (hbk)
ISBN 13: 978-0-415-57112-8 (pbk)
ISBN 13: 978-0-203-85085-5 (ebk)

ISBN 10: 0-415-5711-1 (hbk)
ISBN 10: 0-415-57112-X (pbk)
ISBN 10: 0-203-85085-8 (ebk)

Contents

Illustrations

Contributors

Marc Askew is a Senior Fellow in the Anthropology Program at the University of Melbourne and an ethnographer and historian with major research interests in the cultural dynamics of urban life in Mainland Southeast Asia, the politics of cultural representation, and social change in that region, particularly in Thailand, Laos, and Cambodia.

Olwen Beazley, an archaeologist and cultural resource manager, has worked both in Australia and the UK. Olwen has written and published on issues relating to the implementation of the World Heritage Convention and has been involved in the work of the Convention both as a public servant and academic.

Chiara Bortolotto is a postdoctoral researcher at the Laboratoire d'Anthropologie et d'Histoire de l'Institution de la Culture (Paris) and teaches a course on International Organization of Cultural Heritage at IULM University (Milan).

Sophia Labadi is a consultant for the European Cultural Foundation and UNESCO. She is a heritage specialist with wide interests in culture and development, cultural industries and immigrants histories. She has published on various issues related to culture and edited *World Heritage: Challenges for the Millenium* (2007). She has been the recipient of a number of scholarships and awards, most recently the 2008 Cultural Policy Research Award.

Kathryn Lafrenz Samuels is a PhD Candidate at Stanford University and writing her dissertation on international heritage management projects in North Africa. Her research interests include the political economy of archaeology and heritage, archaeological ethnography, value, development, rights, cultural property, governmentality, transnationalism, and critical engagements with temporality and materiality.

Colin Long is the Director of the Cultural Heritage Centre for Asia and the Pacific at Deakin University. He is an urban historian with interests in Vietnamese, Lao and Cambodian history and heritage, Australian urban and labour history, and heritage in post-communist societies.

Lynn Meskell is a Professor at the department of Anthropology at Stanford University and at Rock Act Research Institute, University of the Witwatersrand, Johannesburg, South Africa. She holds a PhD from Cambridge University. Her current research and teaching interests include a broad range of fields, including Egyptian archaeology, ethnography in South Africa, identity and sociopolitics, gender and feminism, and ethics.

Noel B. Salazar obtained his PhD from the University of Pennsylvania (USA) and is a Marie Curie Fellow (7th European Community Framework Programme) and Postdoctoral Fellow of the Research Foundation Flanders (FWO) at the Faculty of Social Sciences, University of Leuven (Belgium). He is also a Visiting Research Associate at the Centre for Tourism and Cultural Change, Leeds Metropolitan University (UK).

Anita Smith is Charles La Trobe Research Fellow, Archaeology, La Trobe University. She is an archaeologist specialising in the cultural heritage of the Pacific with current research interests in built heritage in Fiji and the cultural landscapes of Eastern Polynesia. Since 2002 she has been an advisor to the UNESCO World Heritage Centre on Pacific Island heritage and capacity building for cultural heritage management in the region.

Fiona Starr is completing a PhD at the Cultural Heritage Centre for Asia and the Pacific, Deakin University, Australia, examining the intersection of World Cultural Heritage site conservation and Corporate Social Responsibility.

Juliette van Krieken-Pieters is a freelance researcher affiliated with both the Roling Foundation and Webster University in the Netherlands, and is an expert on international law related to theft of cultural heritage.

Tim Winter is Senior Research Fellow, Centre for Cultural Research at the University of Western Sydney. He is author of *Post-conflict Heritage, Postcolonial Tourism Culture, Politics and Development at Angkor*, Routledge, 2007, and editor of *Asia on Tour: exploring the rise of Asian Tourism*, Routledge, 2008, and *Expressions of Cambodia: the Politics of Tradition, Identity and Change*, Routledge, 2006. Tim is also Production Editor of the ICOMOS Australia journal *Historic Environment*.

Series General Co-Editors' Foreword

The interdisciplinary field of Heritage Studies is now well established in many parts of the world. It differs from earlier scholarly and professional activities that focused narrowly on the architectural or archaeological preservation of monuments and sites. Such activities remain important, especially as modernisation and globalisation lead to new developments that threaten natural environments, archaeological sites, traditional buildings and arts and crafts. But they are subsumed within the new field that sees 'heritage' as a social and political construct encompassing all those places, artefacts and cultural expressions inherited from the past which, because they are seen to reflect and validate our identity as nations, communities, families and even individuals, are worthy of some form of respect and protection.

Heritage results from a selection process, often government-initiated and supported by official regulation; it is not the same as history, although this, too, has its own elements of selectivity. Heritage can be used in positive ways to give a sense of community to disparate groups and individuals or to create jobs on the basis of cultural tourism. It can be actively used by governments and communities to foster respect for cultural and social diversity, and to challenge prejudice and misrecognition. But it can also be used by governments in less benign ways, to reshape public attitudes in line with undemocratic political agendas or even to rally people against their neighbours in civil and international wars, ethnic cleansing and genocide. In this way there is a real connection between heritage and human rights.

This is time for a new and unique series of books canvassing the key issues dealt with in the new Heritage Studies. The series seeks to address the deficiency facing the field identified by the Smithsonian in 2005 – that it is 'vastly under-theorized'. It is time to look again at the contestation that inevitably surrounds the identification and evaluation of heritage and to find new ways to elucidate the many layers of meaning that heritage places and intangible cultural expressions have acquired. Heritage conservation and safeguarding in such circumstances can only be understood as a form of cultural politics and that this needs to be reflected in heritage practice, be that in educational institutions or in the field.

It is time, too, to recognise more fully that heritage protection does not depend alone on top-down interventions by governments or the expert actions of heritage industry professionals, but must involve local communities and communities of interest. It is critical that the values and practices of communities, together with traditional management systems where such exist, are understood, respected and incorporated in management plans and policy documents if heritage resources so that communities feel a sense of 'ownership' of their heritage and take a leading role in sustaining it into the future.

This series of books aims then to identify interdisciplinary debates within Heritage Studies and to explore how they impact on the practices not only of heritage management and conservation, but also the processes of production, consumption and engagement with heritage in its many and varied forms.

William S. Logan
Laurajane Smith

Acknowledgements

The editors would like to thank the Series Editors, Bill Logan and Laurajane Smith, and Lalle Pursglove at Routledge, for their patience and encouragement. The book is partly the outcome of an Australian Research Council Discovery Grant, *UNESCO – Agent of Cultural Globalisation? Analysis of the Conflict between Universal Values and Local Cultural Identity in the Asia-Pacific Region.*

Introduction

Colin Long and Sophia Labadi

> Constant revolutionizing of production, uninterrupted disturbance of all social conditions, everlasting uncertainty and agitation distinguish the bourgeois epoch from all earlier ones ... All that is solid melts into air, all that is holy is profaned, and man is at last compelled to face with sober senses, his real conditions of life, and his relations with his kind.
>
> (Karl Marx and Friedrich Engels, *Manifesto of the Communist Party*)

The words of Marx and Engels described the great disruptive transformation of the industrial revolution, but could just as easily be used today to describe the era of neo-liberal globalisation, an era that covers the last three decades. Recent shocks make the future of this form of globalisation uncertain: the continued integration of the nations and regions of the world, however, is likely to continue apace, even if only because of economic necessity and environmental crisis. Both of these phenomena leave no part of the world untouched. The industrial revolution, as Marx and Engels described, involved not just the 'revolutionizing of production': the dynamism of capitalism is not just creative, but also profoundly disruptive to 'all social conditions'. The current process of globalisation is driven not by steam and colonialism, as industrialisation was in Marx's time, but by information technology, multinational corporations and multilateral institutions (one continuity between both periods is the role of a political and military hegemon prepared to use or threaten violence to foster the spread of its vision of global integration, although the country itself is no longer the same). Marx and Engels knew, as we know today, that the revolutionising of production and the spread of the relations of capitalism around the world affect more than just the sphere of economics. All social relations, including culture, are drawn inexorably into capitalism's influence. Indeed, culture is at once shaped by processes of exchange and helps to shape them. The forces of production act on culture, but culture can also be a force of production in itself – as the creative industries so powerfully demonstrate. This may not be an entirely new phenomenon, but the *importance* of culture in processes of exchange today almost certainly is.

When thinking about the role of culture in contemporary processes of globalisation, there are many facets that we could have considered: the role of television or other forms of popular culture; the impact of globalisation on traditional cultures; the fate of culture in the digital age; and so on. Many of these aspects have been covered in some detail elsewhere (see for instance Storey 2003 on popular culture or Tomlinson 1999 on globalisation and identity). Instead, this book seeks to examine one aspect of culture at a global level that does not receive the attention it deserves: cultural heritage. Because cultural heritage crosses national boundaries, is subject to legal and illegal international trade, is a key component of the world tourism industry, and is subjected to destruction in conflicts, it has for a long time been a global issue. Since the end of World War II, and particularly since the establishment of the World Heritage system, the United Nations Educational, Scientific and Cultural Organisation (UNESCO) has played an important role in encouraging a global perspective of cultural heritage. UNESCO has also played an important role in defining that perspective. In recent decades new developments have reinforced the intertwining of cultural heritage and global processes of political and economic interaction: climate change, concerns about loss of cultural diversity, poverty and sustainable development.

As the varied chapters in this volume show, cultural heritage has become increasingly important across a diverse range of fields: it plays a vital role in discourses about human rights; it is increasingly seen as important to strategies to mitigate or cope with climate change; it is integrated in tourism and other economic development strategies, or is viewed as a means of making development strategies more socially and environmentally sustainable; it is frequently in the news as the victim of political instability, wars and poverty. Cultural heritage practice long ago – or so we hope – moved way beyond the popular notion of protecting old buildings. In fact in the 21st century it is clear that it is asked to do an increasing amount. While heritage protection has never been simply about the past, it seems more than ever to be seen as a strategy for the future.

This volume analyses the politics, policy and practice of cultural heritage at the global level, identifying the major directions in which international cultural heritage practice is heading, and exploring the key issues likely to shape the cultural heritage field into the 21st century.

Globalisation as context

While globalisation – if we take this to mean the greater interaction of the nations of the world – is not a new phenomenon, the intensity, extent and character of its current form is. Previous waves of globalisation included the great imperial expansions of the European powers in the eighteenth and nineteenth centuries, particularly the British and French, as well as the earlier interventions by those nations and, more substantially, Spain and Portugal in Asia and the Americas. The linking of often very distant lands by trade routes goes back even further, as the Silk Road attests, and the movement of populations over vast distances, often in the form of military conquest – think of Chinggis Khan's invasion of Europe, or the Muslim incursions into Spain and other parts of the European continent – is by no means a new phenomenon.

The current wave of globalisation commenced at the end of World War II, with the establishment of the United Nations and the so-called Bretton Woods institutions – the International Monetary Fund and the International Bank for Reconstruction and Development (now part of the World Bank). These institutions were intended to stimulate global political and economic integration as well as greater understanding between cultures, in an effort to avoid the recurrence of the calamities of the previous fifteen years – economic crisis and war. It is often argued that the collapse of the Soviet Union and the socialist bloc at the end of the 1980s removed the last roadblock on the path to a fully globalised world. The reality is that when Stalin decided not to involve the USSR in the Bretton Woods institutions – it had been invited to participate in them – at the end of the War (Gaddis 1997), and when a broader pattern of East–West animosity hardened into the Cold War, there were, for several decades, two main competing forms of globalisation. The competition between the two superpowers and the blocs that they dominated (but did not control) was ideological, cultural, economic, political and, not least, military. Rather than operating as a roadblock to greater world integration, the Cold War encouraged and facilitated unprecedented interaction – often, as with the case of the American War in Vietnam, in a forced way – between nations. The very fact that nations were asked to choose sides – or, in the case of the Non-Aligned Movement, forced to *not* choose sides – indicates the extent to which it was no longer possible to avoid involvement in broader global processes. Because of the all-encompassing nature of Cold War competition, and because of its deeply *ideological* nature, engagement in one or other of the competing globalisations entailed, in most cases, more than superficial political or military cooperation acceded to through the signing of treaties. It also meant accepting economic integration and cultural influence, in the case of the latter seldom uncritically, although the room for manoeuvre in the Soviet bloc was always much less than in the Western, where the winning of converts was much more reliant on enticement and attraction than brute force.

The collapse of the Soviet Union did not mean the clearing of the last barrier to globalisation: it represented the triumph of one of the competing globalisations, free market capitalism, over the other, state socialism. Once victorious, the former was free to expand its reach and to intensify its influence, encountering in opposition only a weakened left, an incipient but largely disorganised 'anti-globalisation' movement whose focus on symbolic politics – rather than who does or doesn't control the levers of economic power – is both its strength and its weakness, and conservative religious movements of one stripe or another, most noticeably, of course, Islamic fundamentalism.

It is this free market capitalist globalisation that is what most people think of today when we speak of globalisation, and its fundamental characteristics are well known: free trade, liberalisation of the international flow of capital, an enhanced role for the financial sector, deregulation of, and increased use of the coercive powers of the state in support of, the activities of business (but, especially in the English-speaking world, stricter and punitive regulation of labour), privatisation, reduction in the direct role of government in the economy, a winding back of the welfare state, and a greatly expanded role in social and economic policy for unfettered market forces. Note our exclusion here of liberal democracy as a key characteristic of this form of globalisation: China and Singapore, amongst others, show that states can be fully active – indeed very successful – participants in current globalisation processes while maintaining authoritarian political regimes. Although the collapse of communism led some incautious commentators to claim that this mode of production represented the pinnacle of human achievement (Fukuyama 1992), the economic crisis that has gripped the United States since the end of 2007 and the rest of the world since late 2008 has demonstrated the folly of such claims. While global integration will continue, it is likely to take quite different forms, and have different emphases. Indeed, as the chapter by Long and Smith in this book shows, even if economic integration were to grind to a halt, the global environmental crisis will demand even more thorough international cooperation than ever before.

Much of the commentary – both in the media and in academic circles – has tended to focus on the economic aspects of globalisation. However, as we have already argued, both the Soviet and Western forms of globalisation were heavily imbued with ideological and cultural manifestations. While the death of the Soviet alternative has reduced the overtly ideological nature of current Western globalisation, the latter's cultural aspects remain integral. Indeed, culture has played an important role in stimulating demand in the debt-fuelled expansion of consumption that has driven contemporary globalisation, by, for instance, the portrayal of desirable lifestyles through Hollywood movies and the international television industry, or through the appropriation of cultural performances or cultural heritage by the tourism industry.

Nationalism, universalism and heritage

The post-World War II world was, nevertheless, more than just an arena for the struggle between the two superpowers and their competing globalisations. Of almost equal importance, and intersecting with this struggle in complex ways, was the effort to overcome a *previous* form of globalisation, that is, the fight by nationalist organisations to free their nations from the yoke of colonialism. Again, because of the omnipresent nature of the Cold War, these struggles for national independence became, rather paradoxically, caught up in the larger competition, and few post-colonial nations indeed were allowed to opt, without some form of negative consequence, for real neutrality. Fewer again were able to choose an economic path completely independent of the two competing models on offer. Yet nationalism remained a difficult force to integrate into the different globalisations. The lack of political and ideological flexibility of the Soviet model did not serve it well in this regard, and national sentiment in its satellites in Eastern Europe and even in its allies – or sometime allies – in Asia frequently chafed against Russian strictures. In Western Europe cultural nationalism – think of French cultural policy or British popular culture – has managed to coexist with increasing supra-national integration, a testament to the power of the essence of the Western globalising process – that nations would be more prosperous and peaceful if they cooperated more. (It needs to be recognised, of course, that systems dominated by hegemons – as the Soviet Union and the USA were – are prone to losing sight of these essential aims, and that what might have started out as an effort towards greater international cooperation can become much more like an imperial system in which the hegemon's power becomes oppressive: such became the case at various times during the Cold War and even more so since the implosion of the Soviet hegemon, and the concomitant release of restraints on the USA.)

Nationalism, to return to our point, has not disappeared as a result of globalisation. Indeed the collapse of the Soviet Union and its empire in Eastern Europe led to an efflorescence of nationalism, with positive and negative results, which continues to this day. This is one of the superficial paradoxes of globalisation – superficial because on closer inspection it is obvious why this should be the case. Globalisation's chief effect – as the term itself suggests – is to expand horizons, to open up different political, geographical and economic layers to new influences and opportunities. Enhanced Scottish autonomy within the United Kingdom – to take an arbitrary example – is now possible because the UK is no longer Scotland's only point of reference – there is now also the European Union and, beyond it, the world. Some cities – New York, London, Tokyo are the most commonly cited – are called 'global cities' because many of their primary relationships are with the rest of the world, rather than their own nations (we should be careful not to over-state this: London and Tokyo, for instance, as political capitals, continue to play important roles within their respective countries, not least for symbolic purposes, a purpose also served by New York). Nationalism continues to shape the way countries interact with global processes, and with global institutions such as the World Bank and, in particular, the United Nations.

What is striking is that between the two competing forms of globalisation another institution of global cooperation managed to persist and, at least in some fields, flourish: the United Nations. Unlike the Bretton Woods institutions, the UN engaged both blocs. Because of the tensions between the two, the institutional structure of the UN – which reflects power relations and political expediencies that were relevant at the time of its creation, but not necessarily now – and the very fact that it brings together sovereign governments, the UN has, of course, not always run smoothly or without controversy. Rather than a forum for international cooperation it has on too many occasions been a forum for demonstrations of national, regional or alliance interests at the expense of others. But it is perhaps through its constituent bodies, such as UNESCO, the United Nations Development Program (UNDP), the United Nations Environment Program (UNEP) and others, that the UN has had its greatest influence and most success. Although the UN's peace-keeping missions have been possibly the most publicly prominent of its activities – often because of their problematic nature rather than resounding success – it may be the case that its 'soft power' – its social and cultural programs – has been more effective in communicating its goals of peace, international cooperation, cultural respect and universality. In this regard the Convention Concerning the Protection of the World Cultural and Natural Heritage (the World Heritage Convention) has been singularly popular with UN member states, with 186 of them having acceded to it since its adoption by UNESCO in 1972. This makes it one of the most popular of the UN's instruments.

As Logan (2002) has argued, the Convention has been very important in spreading heritage consciousness and particular heritage practices around the world. This has not been without problems, unforeseen consequences or controversy. Yet what is truly remarkable is that despite the international political context that we outlined in the first part of this introduction the World Heritage Convention has been popular with states on both sides of the Cold War divide and at very different levels of economic development.

The reasons for this popularity are multifold. We must be careful, though, not to assume that the Convention has managed to overcome the great divisions in the world, to unite nations in a shared and altruistic appreciation of cultural diversity beyond the reaches of nationalism: the recent military clashes between Thailand and Cambodia over Preah Vihear temple after it was added to the World Heritage List, examined by Winter in this volume, should put paid to that fantasy. Indeed, one of the key reasons why there is such enthusiastic engagement with the Convention is because it enables nations to promote certain national and cultural identities. In other words, as Askew argues in this volume, nations use the alleged universalism of the World Heritage Convention for their own nationalistic ends.

Nations use World Heritage listing as a form of soft power, a means of communicating their cultural, social and even environmental credentials to the world. The enthusiastic embrace of heritage as a resource for tourism development is, of course, entirely symptomatic of broader globalisation processes. As we have already argued, tourism is a form of globalisation *par excellence*. For nation-states its economic benefits are several. It brings in foreign earnings (it is thus counted in the national accounts as exports), a fact of great importance for nations that otherwise struggle with balance of payments problems. Tourism developments are often attractive to foreign investors, which makes tourism a viable development strategy even in nations where indigenous capital formation potential is low (although the downside of this is the large flow of tourism income out of the host country to the home countries of the foreign investors). Both natural and cultural heritage represent important 'free' resources (in the sense that they already exist, even if they must be maintained at some cost, rather than requiring substantial capital to establish) that can be employed to generate revenue. This is very important in the poorer nations of the world, where natural and cultural heritage may sometimes represent the main form of income-generating resource. In wealthier countries tourism is frequently seen as an important contributor to the growth of the post-industrial economy, helping to replace income lost from the decline of industry in the face of competition from the newly industrialised countries of Asia or from the decisions taken by multinational corporations to move production to sources of cheaper labour. Tourism, especially cultural heritage tourism, has been integral to numerous revitalisation strategies in old industrial areas in Europe (see, for instance, European Association of Historic Towns and Regions 2007), and to place-marketing efforts that seek to re-brand cities and regions as socially and culturally (and hence economically) vibrant nodes in the global service and consumer economy (see Landry 2002; Landry et al. 1996; Couch et al. 2003). Tourism is also a major provider of low-skill jobs and is relatively labour-intensive, which makes it attractive to poor and rich countries alike.

Of no less importance is the use of World Heritage as a form of tourism-advertising strategy. This is one of the reasons for its sustained popularity over the years. World Heritage sites are seen as major tourist attractors, and for some countries may indeed become important sources of income. The inscription of sites on the World Heritage List, in particular those that are not well known, often leads to their increased visibility through incorporation in key guidebooks as well as the mainstream and specialised press.

Reliance on tourism has, nonetheless, its downsides, the most obvious being the tension between tourism development and heritage protection. Unsustainable tourism development is one of the most frequent threats affecting World Heritage sites, some of which are particularly fragile, and methods for regulating tourism, including strict controls of tourist numbers (as in the case at the Hal Saflieni Hypogeum in Malta) as well as measures to minimise tourist impact on properties (as is the case at the Taj Mahal in India for instance), have had to be introduced (see Bandarin and Labadi 2007). The extent to which nations seek to engage in tourism development, even in often quite inappropriate ways (see Long and Reeves 2009 on the Cambodian effort to develop the former Khmer Rouge stronghold of Anlong Veng as a tourist attraction), reveals another aspect of globalisation: it is a deeply unequal process, and the options for poorer nations or regions are very limited, and often only seem to amount to an attempt to attract tourists. It is not only wealthy European nations or the USA that have found it hard to maintain industries in the face of the rise of China as an industrial super-power. Even countries such as Japan and South Korea, or poor countries such as Cambodia or Laos, find it difficult to compete with China to produce industrial goods. All too often it seems that the only alternative to industrial development that is considered is tourism.

Tourism strategies are not entirely dependent on natural or cultural heritage, of course, although even mass sun and sea tourism still requires the preservation of usable and at least minimally attractive beaches. But heritage is increasingly recognised as an important attractor for more sophisticated and high-spending tourists, and in some countries (such as Laos) is the predominant component of its national heritage strategy (Lao National Tourism Administration c. 2005). Heritage is also seen as an important element, as we indicated above, in place marketing strategies, not only to attract tourists but also to help in the re-creation of local identities as cities and regions seek new, post-industrial futures and compete for foreign investment and the location of business enterprises, or even government or supra-government agencies (for instance, European Union institutions). In this context heritage sites – particularly World Heritage sites – play multiple roles: they are extremely effective symbols of cultural vibrancy that help to create a certain image of a place or region, while also functioning as economic development resources for tourism and the attraction of business investment. In this sense it is important to acknowledge that the international heritage movement with UNESCO at its pinnacle does not stand outside or counter to processes of globalisation; it is inherently implicated with them.

The complex interactions of tourism and heritage are explored in two chapters in this book, by Winter and Salazar, indicating the importance that we think this topic should be given. Winter shows that we need to revise our ideas about tourists, where they come from, what heritage means to them and how they interact with it, if we are to generate a more accurate impression of heritage and tourism in the twenty-first century. The characteristics of mass tourism as it developed in the second half of the twentieth century – it was dominated by relatively well-educated and relatively well-off Westerners – are no longer so salient, Winter argues. The rise of Asian tourism, that is tourists *from* Asian countries, particularly China, is already having substantial ramifications for the tourism industry as a whole, as well as for individual tourist destinations. This can be seen, more broadly, as symptomatic of the growing significance of Asian nations, particularly China and India, in global economic and political processes. Salazar explores the complexities of tourism through the prism of the phenomenon of glocalisation, that is, the way that heritage destinations worldwide are adapting themselves to the homogenising standards of global tourism at the same time as trying to maintain, or even increase, their local distinctiveness. He argues that thinking of globalisation and local differentiation as being opposed to each other is not very helpful in understanding and explaining contemporary tourism. The constant (re)shaping of local heritage is in many respects part of and simultaneously occurring with the globalising process itself. Indeed, heritage destinations worldwide may be adapting themselves to the homogenising trends of global tourism, but, at the same time, they have to commodify their local distinctiveness in order to compete with other destinations. This is epitomised in the daily practices of local guides and the way they (re)present and actively (re)construct local culture for a diversified audience of global tourists. Through analysing these daily practices, Salazar argues, we can learn a lot about how processes of globalisation and localisation are intimately intertwined and how this glocalisation is transforming culture through tourism and other channels.

The popularity of the World Heritage Convention, already mentioned in relation to tourism, is also a symptom of the influence of nationalism in the heritage field. On the one hand, the World Heritage system seems to obey rational, objective, universal and professional criteria that exclude political and nationalist considerations. This is embodied in the ten universal criteria that sites have to meet to be of 'outstanding universal value' and included on the World Heritage List. This is reinforced by the discourse of apolitical universalism employed by UNESCO, the International Council on Monuments and Sites (ICOMOS) and the International Union for Conservation of Nature (IUCN; the latter two are the agencies responsible for assessing for World Heritage listing nominated cultural and natural sites respectively).

In a very real sense this is an important function of the system: there would perhaps be no listing of sites if the process were entirely politicised (Long 2003). On the other hand, it is this very universalised and de-politicised veneer that seems attractive to nation-states, since their nationalistic and political intentions are easily obscured behind the façade of objectivity that is resolutely maintained by all involved. This is one of the reasons why the World Heritage system flourished during the Cold War and continues to do so today: nominated sites are chosen by national governments (often for nationalistic reasons) and assessed according to 'objective' criteria that exclude political and nationalistic considerations (of course we acknowledge the politics involved in the World Heritage Committee's deliberations).

The complex interactions between the universal and rational objectives of the World Heritage system and their nationalistic uses by States Parties have been addressed in this volume primarily by Askew and Beazley. Askew suggests that UNESCO sees its activities as a beneficent form of globalisation that protects and promotes the different cultures of the world against the negative and homogenising effects of market capitalism. He then argues that, 'despite the laudable universalist ideals of many dedicated intellectuals and practitioners involved in UNESCO's array of heritage conservation programs today, the globalised and institutionalised heritage system has not overcome nation-state-based power structures and nationalist agendas, but has rather enhanced them, and this severely compromises the ideal of forging a countervailing meta-national zeitgeist evoked by the term "World Heritage"'. Beazley, using the example of the Hiroshima Peace Memorial (Genbaku Dome) in Japan, unravels the deeply political and contested terrain of heritage narratives at international, national and local levels, especially when sites representing difficult or traumatic heritage are involved. She details the diplomatic wrangling that takes place on the World Heritage Committee over the listing of sites and explains how World Heritage is being used to sanction a specific version of national memory while at the same time disempowering and subjugating the memories and heritages of minority groups.

Whilst globalisation is often associated with homogenisation, analyses of the implementation of the World Heritage Convention also reveal a certain 'incredulity toward metanarratives' (Lyotard 1984), that is, a resistance towards universalised principles. Indeed, one of the most cogent recent criticisms of the World Heritage system is that what are supposed to be universal principles are actually deeply Eurocentric and developed for European contexts. This acknowledgement of the Eurocentric nature of the World Heritage Convention is reflected in the adoption by UNESCO of the 1994 Global Strategy for a Balanced, Credible and Representative World Heritage List, which aims to ensure that the diversity of the world's heritage is better represented (see Labadi 2005). The Nara Document on Authenticity of 1994 is another attempt to move beyond the Eurocentric criteria used to assess the state of conservation of sites for inclusion on the World Heritage List. Labadi's chapter in this volume provides a genealogy of the changes of definitions and understandings of the concept of authenticity at the international level of the World Heritage Committee, and at the national level, as represented in nomination dossiers. She deconstructs the notion of authenticity, demonstrating that the so-called 'objective' definition used by the World Heritage Committee and nations for the past thirty years did not reflect the reality of the state of authenticity of sites. She introduces the notion of 'post-authenticity' to critique this unreal and untruthful definition of authenticity and to better reflect the decentralising of the definition reflected in the Nara Document on Authenticity.

UNESCO's move away from a Eurocentric conception of cultural heritage to one that embraces the diversity of culture is not limited to the World Heritage Convention. It is also reflected in the UNESCO Convention for the Safeguarding of the Intangible Cultural Heritage, which was partially devised to represent cultural expressions that were not adequately captured by the World Heritage Convention (Smith and Akagawa 2009). In her chapter, Bortolotto analyses the concept of intangible heritage, explaining its non-European roots and the difficulties in making it fit into Western cultural heritage models. In doing so, she draws parallels between the translation of foreign and European categorisations of arts into Japanese language at the end of the 19th century and the translation of the concept of intangible heritage from the Japanese to a Western context. She details a number of key differences between the World Heritage and Intangible Heritage Conventions, including the removal of the concept of authenticity and the replacement of 'outstanding universal value' by the more inclusive and relativist idea of 'representativeness'.

Hence, as explained by Labadi and Bortolotto, UNESCO has attempted to move away from a Eurocentric conception of culture and cultural heritage to one that truly recognises, protects and promotes the diversity of the world's cultures. However, as Bortolotto suggests, these efforts might be undermined by the very nature of the UN system, which gives nomination power over sites or cultural expressions to national governments alone. In essence, the system gives the power to determine representative and authentic cultural expressions to governments. As Freeman (2000: 47) argues, however, it is not at all beyond question that governments are 'morally and epistemologically competent to interpret the diverse cultures of the world':

> We cannot respect cultures unless we have reliable knowledge of what those cultures are, and we cannot have reliable knowledge of cultures unless the voice of the people is clearly heard. Many individuals and groups throughout history have claimed to speak for 'the people', but we have theoretical and empirical grounds for being quite skeptical of such claims. Theoretically, elites may well lack the capacity to understand the culture of the people and may also lack the incentive to understand it. Empirically, we know that elites have commonly been unconcerned with, or hostile to, the culture of the people.
>
> (Freeman 2000: 49)

From this perspective, one of the problems of the World Heritage and Intangible Heritage systems is that they narrow cultural diversity by restricting it to official conceptions. However, the obligation to involve local communities in the nomination of intangible heritage for inclusion on the UNESCO list might be a first step towards a better representation of cultural diversity.

Globalisation, heritage and ethics

The globalisation processes of the post-WW2 period have had two important ramifications for cultural practices and heritage. First, the extension of market relationships into almost all geographical and social spaces has been deeply disruptive to cultures at many levels, from the local up to the national scale, and to traditional cultures in particular. This disruptiveness is, of course, not new. Colonialism and imperialism, as earlier forms of globalisation, were also profoundly disruptive forces. As with contemporary globalisation, these involved, especially in their nineteenth-century manifestations, the extension of capitalist relations as well as the overt exertion of political and ideological power through real or threatened violence. Second, increasing economic and, to a lesser extent, political integration have brought local, regional and national cultures into closer proximity than ever before, a process that has been intensified by radical time-space compression facilitated by revolutions in information technologies and transport (Castells 1996; Harvey 1990). This has had effects which are apparently contradictory: there is growing pressure for cultural homogeneity at the same time as significant, sometimes violent, expressions of cultural difference. Both of these developments – the intensified pressures on cultures from the spread of market relationships, and the increasing global interaction between cultures – have placed culture squarely at the forefront of contemporary processes of globalisation, both as 'participant' and in resistance. As we have seen already, culture, particularly cultural heritage, has been mobilised by governments in tourism and urban development strategies that explicitly accept its commodification. On the other hand, culture and cultural heritage are increasingly being seen as useful resources to either ameliorate the effects of development, to make it more culturally and environmentally sensitive, or to resist it altogether.

Several of the chapters in this book specifically examine the role that cultural heritage is playing or might play in key global problems. Long and Smith examine what is probably the most profound challenge facing the world today – climate change – and suggest that understanding 'how local communities, heritage preservation, sustainable development and climate change intersect' enables the redirection of 'attention away from climate change as a threat to buildings and structures to climate change as a threat to the livelihoods and cultures of the people who give those buildings, structures and other cultural expressions life'. Long and Smith argue that climate change is not only a danger to numerous heritage sites around the world, including a large number of World Heritage sites, but that it also represents a profound challenge to the continuity of intangible practices, knowledge systems and even entire societies. It can be viewed, indeed, as a major threat to human rights. At the same time, they make the case for recognition of the power of these practices and systems – these manifestations of cultural heritage – as tools to combat climate change and to adapt to its effects. Ultimately, they conclude, a sustainable cultural heritage practice can contribute to an 'alternative way of viewing resources and their use … [and] by doing so … will not only improve heritage practice, but contribute to the broader effort of creating a sustainable society'.

The idea of cultural heritage as a key element in a new model of sustainable development sees heritage as important in the fight against poverty and in the protection of the environment, and as a source of capital for local populations as well as a source of pride, social cohesion and collective identity. This approach is based not on a restricted view of poverty as being only about a lack of money, but also recognises the importance of a capacity approach that focuses on the well-being of individuals, households or communities through the provision of a decent living environment, social stability and cohesion, *as well as* decent incomes. Of course, achieving a balance between poverty reduction, human development and cultural heritage protection remains a real challenge (see Bandarin and Labadi 2007).

The positioning of cultural heritage within poverty-reduction strategies implicates it thoroughly in global processes since these strategies are often developed by or related to international or regional organisations such as the World Bank or the Aga Khan Foundation. As demonstrated by Lafrenz's in-depth analysis of the World Bank's projects on cultural heritage and poverty reduction in the Middle East and North Africa (MENA) region in this book, such development strategies are not neutral but are caught up 'in a constellation of Western concerns – security, terrorism, failed states, and the promotion of democracy' – that, it is believed, can be resolved by economic growth. Lafrenz takes as an example the project of cultural heritage preservation and poverty reduction in the Fez Medina in Morocco. She highlights the numerous reasons for the 'failure' of this project, including the imposition of Western values and perceptions of heritage and private property that clashed with those of the local population. She also rejects the claim that the failure was solely due to the local population, the main stakeholder group in the process of poverty reduction, arguing that a broader approach, taking into account webs of influence, the politics of the past and processes of (de)colonisation, would have been more appropriate.

Lafrenz demonstrates the complexity and difficulty of identifying new models of sustainable development based on heritage preservation. Moreover, finding sustainable solutions for caring about cultural heritage and transmitting it to future generations remains a real challenge. Indeed, the phenomenon of tourism, as argued above, has put strains on our environment and on cultural heritage. In view of these increased strains and related costs of preservation of the environment and cultural heritage, new innovative partnerships need to be found. This includes, for instance, a greater role for the private sector, a theme explored in Fiona Starr's chapter. The World Monuments Fund's actions to preserve the most precious and often most fragile cultural heritage sites, for instance, have been primarily financed by American Express. However, the involvement of the private sector can raise ethical questions since the aims of companies might not always be compatible with site preservation. Some companies might try to improve their public image and reputation through investing in heritage conservation whilst at the same time engaging in commercial activities that are unethical or damaging to people and the environment. Moreover, the involvement of companies might also imply profit-oriented decisions in relation to the preservation, management and interpretation of sites. This can result, for instance, in revised interpretation of sites so as to attract a maximum of visitors, new visitor policies, a focus on 'blockbuster' exhibitions or the introduction of obtrusive shops selling tacky tourist products. Above all, private companies might make money from association with a site without returning any revenue to the local population or to site preservation. This is often the case with restaurant and bar chains located at the heart of heritage properties.

In order to minimise the potential problems of corporate engagement in heritage preservation Starr looks to the principles of Corporate Social Responsibility (CSR) to guide the interaction of companies with heritage places. CSR calls for the activities of companies to be guided by economic, social and environmental considerations, rather than just the profit motive. Starr's chapter analyses the role played by CSR as a regulator of the complex relationships between cultural heritage and the private sector, insisting that 'through responsible behaviour, companies can potentially achieve a range of important business benefits, including improved public image and reputation, increased profitability, access to new markets, sustainability, greater consumer loyalty, licence to operate, higher employee morale, market positioning, risk profile management, ability to attract top job candidates, and improved investor relations'. However, she stresses the difficulty in obtaining appropriate private support for the conservation of cultural heritage since it tends to be overshadowed by more popular causes, such as wildlife or environmental protection. Unfortunately, she reminds us, CSR is 'still often regarded with cynicism, being criticized as a costly, public-relations-focused activity that does not address business objectives'. Thus greater commonalities need to be found between CSR and the ethical agenda of companies on the one hand and that of heritage conservation on the other.

The ethical implications of dealing with heritage at local and international levels, as well as of the actions of diverse stakeholders, such as representatives of international and regional organisations or local authorities and local populations, are key themes running through this book.

Ethics is a key lens through which one can analyse the relationships between heritage and conflict. Unfortunately, heritage is too often a target in conflicts, for iconoclastic reasons for instance, as testified by the destruction of the Bamiyan Buddhas in Afghanistan. Meskell's chapter unravels the difficult ethical considerations related to cultural heritage and conflict. Taking the case of the Bamiyan Buddhas in Afghanistan as one of her examples, she highlights the diverging opinions of the international community and the local populations. On the one hand, the international heritage constituencies considered the Buddhas 'global patrimony and their erasure subsequently stood for symbolic violence, loss, and the intolerance and "barbarity" of the Taliban regime'. On the other hand, at the local level, some voices denounced what could be perceived as a Western imposition of values related to heritage and its conservation as well as a lack of attention paid to the hardships of the Afghans and a respect for religious difference. Hence the importance of a holistic approach, as stressed in other chapters of this volume, that integrates heritage conservation with sustainable human development strategies centred around local population needs and views. Meskell, through her second example of Qurna, Egypt, details the conflict between a local population that believes it has a right to live on the site of the Tombs of the Nobles and the local officials who want to remove the settlement to present a pristine site to tourists and visitors. This sad case is not isolated and reveals conflictual representations and uses of the past by local, national and international constituencies. As a conclusion, Meskell calls for a serious reflection on the translatability of terms such as 'access' or 'preservation', taking into account the diversity of sites, locations and stakeholders.

Meskell also alludes to another ethical issue that has taken on global proportions in the last decades and which is the focus of the chapter by Juliette van Krieken-Pieters: illegal plundering of archaeological sites and museums, in particular in conflict zones. The illicit trade in antiquities is considered to be the second largest illegal business in the world; according to Interpol and Saving Antiquities for Everyone, it is estimated to be worth as much as $4 billion a year (http://www.savingantiquities.org). These figures reveal the weaknesses of the international legal system for the protection of movable heritage against illicit trade. The UNESCO Convention on the Means of Prohibiting and Preventing the Illicit Import, Export and Transfer of Cultural Property, adopted in 1970, is, with 117 countries signatory to it (as of May 2009), the most widely ratified legal text on this issue. But as van Krieken-Pieters argues, the relative success of this Convention reflects its non-constraining nature. Thus the importance of the 1995 UNIDROIT Convention, which should be understood as complementing the 1970 Convention and which imposes much stricter rules on its ratifying parties, but which has had a rather limited success, with only 29 countries signatory to it (as of May 2009). According to Kaufman (2000: 416), this discrepancy relates to the fact that 'many of the Convention's provisions are inconsistent with numerous art market countries' internal law or policies'. It might also reflect a lack of awareness and of political willingness. Van Krieken-Pieters' chapter explains the complexity and ethical dilemmas she faced when helping to protect some of the artefacts from the National Museum in Kabul, Afghanistan. In the mid-1990s, this museum fell victim to civil war, with the theft of many of its precious artefacts. The Society for the Preservation of Afghanistan's Cultural Heritage (SPACH), of which van Krieken-Pieters is a leading member, faced a dilemma: to seek to protect as many artefacts as it could by purchasing them, even on the black market, or to refuse to engage in the ethically dubious and potentially criminal activity of black market purchase, but thus lose the artefacts to unscrupulous buyers. In the end SPACH, in its role as a 'safe haven' for Afghan heritage, decided to buy some of the pieces that had been looted from the National Museum in Kabul and that were available on the black market and then hand them over to the Musée Guimet in Paris, to ensure their safekeeping until the return of some stability and peace in Afghanistan.

One of the great challenges for the twenty-first century will be the resolution of the tension between universalism and exceptionalism, particularly in the realm of political, social and cultural rights: the rise of China and its forceful assertion of its own distinctive model of development, not to mention the divisions even within the so-called 'West' between Continental Europe's model of social democracy and the Anglo-Saxon model of free market individualism, will ensure that.

In this context it is easy for culture and heritage to be stripped of the universalist aspirations given to them by organisations such as UNESCO and enlisted in the assertion of localist particularity. We have seen such strategies employed in varying cultural contexts.

It seems to us entirely reasonable to predict that as the twenty-first century unfolds and the great challenges – economic restructuring, economic injustice and environmental crisis – play out, that cultural heritage will be brought to the fore in ways that will often be problematic, and in ways that will sometimes see it in tension with other global processes. But it need not always be so. Paying attention to the distinctiveness of cultural contexts has become the accepted basis of good development practice, and we hope that it would become even more firmly entrenched in the ideological and practical processes of international agencies of all kinds in the difficult years ahead.

This volume is part of a series, *Key Issues in Cultural Heritage*. Because of space restrictions and a desire to minimise repetition between volumes in the series, we have not included a chapter on indigenous heritage, surely one of the most important and dynamic fields in global heritage practice today. This topic is analysed in detail in two other books in the series: *Intangible Heritage*, edited by Laurajane Smith and Natsuko Akagawa, and *Cultural Diversity, Heritage and Human Rights: intersections in theory and practice*, edited by Máiréad Nic Craith; Michele Langfield and William Logan.

Finally, just as we make a strong claim for respect for cultural diversity, the aim of an edited collection like this should be to provide a diversity of views. It should be taken as a given that the views of the various authors are not necessarily those of the editors.

References

Bandarin, F. and Labadi, S (eds) (2007) *World Heritage: Challenges for the Millennium*, Paris: World Heritage Centre.

Cassar, M. and Hawkings, C. (eds) (2007) *Engineering Historic Futures*, Stakeholders Dissemination and Scientific Research Report, London: University College London, Centre for Sustainable Heritage.

Castells, M. (1996) *The Rise of the Network Society*, Oxford: Blackwell.

Cordes-Holland, Owen (2007) 'The sinking of the Strait: the implications of climate change for Torres Strait Islanders' human rights protected by the *ICCPR*', *Melbourne Journal of International Law*, vol. 9 (2).

Couch, C., Fraser, C. and Percy, S. (2003) *Urban Regeneration in Europe*, Oxford: Wiley-Blackwell.

Donnelly, J. (1989) *Universal Human Rights in Theory and Practice*, Ithaca: Cornell University Press.

European Association of Historic Towns and Regions (EAHTR) (2007) *Inherit: Investing in Heritage*, Norwich: EAHTR.

Freeman, M. (2000) 'Universal rights and particular cultures', in Michael Jacobsen and Ole Bruun (eds) *Human Rights and Asian Values: Contesting National Identities and Cultural Representations in Asia*, Richmond: Curzon.

Fukuyama, F. (1992) *The End of History and the Last Man*, New York: Free Press.

Gaddis, J. L. (1997) *We Now Know: Rethinking the Cold War*, New York: Oxford University Press.

Harvey, D. (1990) *The Condition of Postmodernity*, Oxford: Blackwell.

IPCC (2007) *Climate Change 2007: Synthesis Report. Summary for Policymakers*. http://www.ipcc.ch/pdf/assessment-report/ar4/syr/ar4_syr_spm.pdf.

Jacobsen, M. and Bruun, O. (eds) (2000) *Human Rights and Asian Values: Contesting National Identities and Cultural Representations in Asia*, Richmond, Surrey: Curzon.

Kaufman, R. (ed.) (2002) *Art Law Handbook*, New York: Aspen Law and Business.

Labadi, S. (2005) 'A review of the Global Strategy for a Balanced, Representative and Credible World Heritage List 1994–2004', *Conservation and Management of Archaeological Sites* 7.2.

Landry, C. (2002) *Imagination and Regeneration: Cultural Policy and the Future of Cities*, Strasbourg: Council of Europe.

Landry, C., Greene, L., Matarasso, F. and Bianchini, F. (1996) *The Art of Regeneration: Cultural Development and Urban Regeneration*; Pub. Comedia in Association with Civic Trust Regeneration Unit, London and Nottingham City Council.

Lao National Tourism Administration (c. 2005) *Lao National Ecotourism Strategy and Action Plan 2005–2010*, Vientiane: Lao National Tourism Administration.

Logan, W. S. (2002) 'Globalising Heritage: World Heritage as a Manifestation of Modernism and the Challenge from the Periphery', in D. S. Jones (ed.) *Twentieth Century Heritage – Our Recent Cultural Legacy: 2001 Australian ICOMOS National Conference*, School of Architecture, University of Adelaide, Adelaide: 51–57.

Long, C. (2003) 'Feudalism in the Service of the Revolution', *Critical Asian Studies*, Vol. 34, No. 4: 535–58.

Long, C. and Reeves, K. (2009) '"Dig a hole and bury it": reconciliation and the heritage of genocide in Cambodia', in W. Logan and K. Reeves (eds), *Places of Pain and Shame: Dealing with 'Difficult' Heritage*, Abingdon: Routledge.

Lyotard, J-F. (1984) *The Postmodern Condition: A Report on Knowledge*, trans. Geoff Bennington and Brian Massumi, Minneapolis: University of Minnesota Press.

Marx, K. and Engels, F. (1888) *Manifesto of the Communist Party*. Online. Available http://www.marxists.org/archive/marx/works/1848/communist-manifesto/index.htm (accessed 23 September 2009).

Roberts, S., Keeble, J. and Brown, D. (2002) 'The Business Case for Corporate Citizenship', Arthur D. Little. Available online. HTTP: <http://www.adlittle.com/insights/studies/pdf/corporate_citizenship.pdf > (accessed 7 January 2008).

Smith, L. J. and Akagawa, N. (2009) *Intangible Cultural Heritage*, London: Routledge.

Storey, J. (2003) *Inventing Popular Culture: From Folklore to Globalisation*, Oxford: Wiley-Blackwell.

Tomlinson, J. (1999) *Globalisation and Culture*, Cambridge: Polity Press.

Trend, D. (ed.) (2001) *Reading Digital Culture*, Oxford and Malden, MA: Blackwell.

Part I

Global and local tensions

Chapter 1

The magic list of global status
UNESCO, World Heritage and the agendas of states

Marc Askew

The fate of good intentions: UNESCO, nation-states and the globalising of heritage

In a world populated by global signifiers, paradigms and buzz words, 'heritage' (with locally equivalent terms in non-English-speaking countries) stands out as conspicuous in its normative resonance, particularly when linked to the expressions 'cultural heritage', 'natural heritage' or 'world heritage'. These terms stand for an array of normative as well as commercialised values attaching to the preservation, restoration and display of history, culture and nature. For various purposes, heritage in its multifarious guises is endorsed simultaneously by a global bureaucratic apparatus (the United Nations Education, Scientific and Cultural Organisation, UNESCO), a global tourist industry, and national governments. In the 1960s and 1970s 'heritage' was the catchcry for strident campaigns to save the endangered material and natural world from depredation, culminating at the global level in UNESCO's adoption of the World Heritage Convention in 1972. As David Lowenthal (1998) has evocatively shown, the contemporary cult of heritage was a result of the successes of these movements, and the term is fully institutionalised and commercialised as a condensed label for the valorised past – or, as one critic has defined it: 'a mode of cultural production that gives the endangered or outmoded a second life as an exhibition of itself' (Kirshenblatt-Gimblett 2006: 168). Such is the iconic status of the heritage trope that although 'heritage' and its associated assumptions have been subject to continued interrogation and refinement, most professionals and academics who critique its application and definitions ultimately rely on the term, whether because there is no adequate alternative, or because they have a key stake in the term's preservation as a carrier for their own alternative models (see, e.g., Tunbridge and Ashworth 1996; Smith 2006).

Although UNESCO was neither the originator nor sole custodian of the leitmotif 'heritage' and its associated ideas, none could dispute that it is today the indisputable global-level instrument which mobilises resources, reproduces dominant arguments and rationales, establishes program agendas and policies, and dispenses status surrounding the conservation and preservation of the thing called 'heritage'. For at least a decade UNESCO's leadership, assemblies and associated organisations have pronounced that its expanding cultural programs aim towards mitigating the destructive effects of 'globalisation', particularly the cultural globalisation represented by the commodifying and homogenising culture industries of capitalism. The rhetoric of UNESCO's key texts (its conventions and declarations) position the organisation outside the threatening globalising processes of the world ('bad' globalisation), but UNESCO itself is a prime expression of a countervailing form of beneficent (or 'good') globalisation, as expressed in its advocacy of world-wide protection of cultures and their valued tangible and 'intangible' past by means of protocols, declarations of universal principles and, most crucially, the compilation of inventories. Moreover, 'World Heritage', which UNESCO promotes and numerous cultural and tourism industries rely on, has emerged from the process of globalisation: 'World Heritage, like world's fairs and museums, are [*sic*] part of a world system, within which the world is to be convened, a world image projected, and a world economy activated' (Kirshenblatt-Gimblett 2006: 163).

To many, stating that UNESCO is a global instrument may seem trite and unremarkable. The heritage movement that has become channelled and appropriated by UNESCO reflects a long history of internationalism, with its origins in late-eighteenth-century romanticism, enlightenment universalism, and a missionary zeal among intellectuals aiming for human betterment by cooperating across national boundaries. This was consolidated in the post-World War Two period by a widely shared determination to overcome the destructive forces of racism, exploitation and international strife, represented by the formation of the United Nations and its agencies, including UNESCO. It is thus understandable that UNESCO's supporters are offended or perplexed when the institution's programs are critiqued, since this implies a flaw in their undoubtedly good intentions for the world and the fuzzy but evocative founding rubric of UNESCO: 'Since wars begin in the minds of men, it is in the minds of men that the defences of peace must be constructed'. My point here is that despite the laudable universalist ideals of many dedicated intellectuals and practitioners involved in UNESCO's array of heritage conservation programs today, the globalised and institutionalised heritage system has not overcome nation-state-based power structures and nationalist agendas, but has rather enhanced them, and this severely compromises the ideal of forging a countervailing meta-national zeitgeist evoked by the term 'World Heritage'. As Michael Herzfeld has recently remarked with specific reference to UNESCO and cultural heritage programs: 'while global mobilization may in some respects be an attempt to supersede nationalism, it can also foment it', a point made by other critics as well (Herzfeld 2008: 146). The most conspicuous recent example of this has been the nationalist-infused confrontation between Thailand and Cambodia, which exploded in early 2008 following the nomination of the Preah Vihear temple site to UNESCO's World Heritage List.

This chapter addresses the influence of UNESCO's global reach and functions, not by pointing to a Foucauldian-style dominance at the level of 'discourses' of heritage or the imposition of a world cultural regime, as some critics have done, but rather by drawing attention to the organisation's authorising role in assigning 'World Heritage' as a status, one that is crystallised in the instrumental-symbolic function

Figure 1.1 Demonstrators of the People's Alliance for Democracy demand the prosecution of the Thai cabinet for endorsing Cambodian nomination of Preah Vihear temple as a World Heritage site, July 2008 (Photo courtesy *Bangkok Post*)

of the World Heritage List and its generally unintended and uncontrollable consequences. UNESCO's influence with respect to heritage signification lies far less in its institutional powers, which are relatively weak in formal legal terms. Thus, though the World Heritage Convention is nominally binding on member state signatories, the obligations on states concerning conservation do not override domestic laws or states' sovereignty, and effectively amount to 'non-binding political or moral ideals' (Atherton and Atherton 1995: 637–38). UNESCO's power in the sphere of heritage resides in the application of normative pressure and the harnessing of symbolic capital for a variety of constituencies, including professional bodies as well as (sometimes competing) elites in member states. Viewed from this more anthropological perspective, UNESCO's principal function in the global and cultural arena, which it has been central in constructing, is to establish and perpetuate the technical and symbolic legitimacy of its ever-growing list of 'World Heritage' sites and, most recently, the so-called 'Representative List of the Intangible Cultural Heritage of Humanity', assembled in 2008. Simultaneously, these lists also act as status-conferring artefacts in the competition between nation states for global status and for their own internal purposes.

In this chapter I argue that one recent claim that the so-called 'Authorized Heritage Discourse' (for which UNESCO is the principal global-level purveyor) is

Figure 1.2 Cambodian soldiers patrolling at the Preah Vihear temple site as border tensions with Thailand escalate, July 2008 (Photo courtesy *The Nation*)

Eurocentric and crypto-imperialist is both redundant and a conceptual red herring: it misrecognises the real locus of power and exploitation in the global heritage game, which is the nation-state and not any dominant global institutional structure or discourse of heritage classification. My main point is that UNESCO's World Cultural Heritage program is as much, and probably more, a creature of its member states and their agendas as it is an instrument of UNESCO's specialists, intellectual apologists and affiliated professional bodies of conservation specialists. This state of affairs stems largely from the structure of the organisation and its treaty-style conventions, which mirror the parent UN body in making States Parties the key actors, thus leaving all key processes at a country level in the hands of national elites. That is not to say that the technical-normative and administrative systems presided over by UNESCO are not significant – they perform critical functions in allowing various actors to co-exist and maintain legitimacy through overseeing processes and authorising buzz words. However, they are not the key instrument that perpetuates marginalisation and dominance in the sphere of ideology and cultural symbolisation. I argue in this chapter that the World Heritage List (and other lists) has a simultaneous technical and normative function – that is, it both endorses technical processes of conservation, interpretation and management, and confers global recognition of sites. In the process UNESCO's professionals and consultants who work in this field reproduce their own status, identity and legitimacy in the technical order of conservation work. We might describe core administrators and their intellectual buttresses (following Turner 2002) as 'virtuous cosmopolitans' on the world stage who perpetuate the necessary myth that the world can be united by universal respect and amity through promoting heritage conservation – epitomised in the central legal-normative affirmation of the World Heritage Convention that there is a 'common heritage of mankind' requiring protection and promotion (Turtinen 2000: 10). On the level of normative values, the internationalist goals of key UNESCO personnel and affiliates to promote unity in diversity are indeed worthy, but the reality is messier and driven by parochialism and pragmatism at the level of member states.

UNESCO's member states use the nomination process and promotion of world heritage sites for their own domestic agendas of cultural hegemony and state nationalism (besides the well-recognised function of generating tourism income). It is this last mentioned process that exposes the most critical weakness in the global heritage system, highlighting the reality that nation-states have harnessed global systems more than been eclipsed by them. Certainly, many working in UNESCO's conservation programs are aware of the contradictions between cosmopolitan ideals and nation-state-driven realities. The relentless competition for global cultural and political capital between nations on the world stage is conspicuously expressed in competitions for the Nobel Prize and over venues for the Olympic Games (Lovell 2006). It is also revealed in the uses of UNESCO's World Heritage List and its new list of 'intangible heritage', where the thirst for the 'global accolade' among nation-states over the past decade has led to a veritable explosion of World Heritage listed sites (Smith 2002). This all suggests that Ulrich Beck's hope that his favoured 'new game' of interacting trans-national networks may supersede the 'old game' of competing nation-states is a vain expectation (Beck 2005: 3–4). I highlight in a number of examples in this chapter that world heritage sites have various uses for nation-states, and UNESCO's universalist project has been successfully appropriated for extremely pragmatic purposes. Despite this, the heritage system that is sustained by UNESCO persists because of the critical symbolic functions it serves for its key actors.

UNESCO and globalisation, the good and the bad

Perhaps one of the most remarkable characteristics of the rhetoric of UNESCO's key texts and pronouncements is the strategic use of the contrasting value-laden terms 'global' and 'globalisation', central binary tropes against and through which these texts establish the legitimate goals of the organisation's numerous programs. 'Globalisation' in popular usage is almost universally portrayed as a negative, invasive and destructive process, an accepted abbreviation for a demonic '[neo-liberal] globalisation' – the expansion of world capitalism at the expense of the weak nations of the South and their vulnerable peoples. Similarly, the use of the term in UNESCO's pronouncements summons the frightening prospects of a new world order (or disorder) where formerly distinctive ways of life – rhetorically condensed in the rights-laden term 'cultural diversity' – are no longer tenable. The texts of UNESCO's leadership and supporters, like those of its parent body, the United Nations, distinguish the benevolent global scope of the organisation and its allied 'international community' from the threatening processes of globalisation. Koïchiro Matsuura, UNESCO's Director-General, stated in the conclusion to a speech in France:

> In response to the globalisation of the economy, the international community must be resolute in promoting universality in the most profound sense of the word: a type of universality which both challenges all models and acknowledges and respects the contribution of all peoples to universal civilization. UNESCO sees globalisation as extending far beyond economic issues. It disrupts life styles and behaviour patterns, and overturns habits of decision-making and governance and forms of artistic expression. The challenge that it poses for UNESCO is that of perceiving all the complexity of its ramifications, so that in an inter-disciplinary and intercultural spirit we can devise strategies and policies to ensure that it works for the benefit of all, particularly those who are at present excluded from it.
>
> (Matsuura 2000: 404)

It is not surprising that country-based UNESCO commissions echoed the same view, which reflected in turn the rhetoric of the United Nations leadership: global effort was needed to contest bad forms of globalisation (see, e.g., UNESCO Task Force 1999; Boutros-Ghali 1995). In its expanding sphere of 'cultural' programs, UNESCO's stated role was now to act as a champion of 'diversity' *against* 'globalisation'. UNESCO's legitimacy in the contemporary world now became predicated on its role as a defender of the world's 'cultures' against globalisation as a destroyer of distinct identities. In affirming universal 'cultural rights', together with the codification, listing and management entailed by this imperative, a global span of organisation and management has been deemed essential to UNESCO's aims (UNESCO 2000: 81–82). This highlights a relatively new ideological rationale for UNESCO: it reflects the new salience of 'culture' which now surrounds a host of hotly debated issues in a post-Cold War world order, a period which has been marked by the disintegration of states, the rise of ethnic conflicts and religious fundamentalisms, the dissolution of borders, rapid population dispersal, and the apparent commodification and homogenisation of cultures symbolised by the spectre of 'McWorld'.

In the 1990s, 'peacemaking' and the promotion of global 'justice' became the leitmotifs of UNESCO under its director-general Federico Mayor, with 'culture' in a wide variety of modes being evoked as both a vehicle (a 'culture of peace') and an end (cultural rights and diversity) for creating a peaceful and tolerant world order (UNESCO 1995; Mayor and Tanguiane 1997: esp Ch. 1). The salvationist impera-tives connoted by the epithet 'global' represent a longer tradition of internationalism among intellectuals, and the 'global' prefix might be seen as simply an elaboration or re-badging of older terms that evoke the universal span of humanitarian effort in a spectrum of causes, from the abolition of slavery to the preservation of monuments (see, e.g., Iriye 2001; Lowenthal 1998). It is hardly surprising, then, that many staff in UNESCO's cultural heritage bureaucracy and specialists in ICOMOS see their organisation standing outside the homogenising globalisation process: this is essentially because they understand 'globalisation' to refer to capitalist market-driven homogenisation and cultural commodification (Askew and Logan 2002). In this they reflect the wider discursive environment of academic and intellectual debate where 'bad' globalisation is denounced and distinguished from beneficial and 'responsible' (good) forms of institutionally-guided globalisation, or seen to require resistance through 'global emancipatory politics' or 'globalisation from below' (see, e.g., Appadurai 2002: 1–21; Bourdieu 1998: 29–44; Holton 1998: 186–204; Woods 2002).

UNESCO, like its partner specialised agencies of the UN, is indisputably part of the multi-faceted phenomenon of globalisation – it is defined both by aims of universalism and operates its programs on a global scale. Some sociologists have gone so far as to propose that the UN and its principled declarations reflect an emergent 'world culture' – this is a sloppy use of the much over-used 'culture' word, used here to refer to a set of shared normative values (Drori 2005). UNESCO might be situated within global integration processes by means of Ulrich Beck's multi-dimensional view of 'globality', a term he coins to characterise the ways that 'we are living in a world society, in the sense that the notion of closed spaces has become illusory'. Beck argues that within this globality there are various logics of globalisation that should be recognised as relatively autonomous, including: ecology, culture, economics, politics and civil society. Such globality is irreversible because of a number of realities that include not only the global networking of finance operations, world trade and markets and the stream of images from the global culture industries, but also the universal demand for human rights and 'the emergence of a post national, polycentric framework of world politics, including transnational actors such as corporations, the United Nations and Non-government Organizations' (Beck 2000: 10–11). Beck, like others, locates the operations of organisations such as UNESCO within the overall condition of global interconnection, transnational governance and movements. In short, this organisation, together with many others, is viewed as part of an evolving world process where transnational organisation and governance through legal and regulatory mechanisms are both necessary and inevitable (Drori et al. 2006; Held 1991).

The prominent anthropologist Ulf Hannerz describes the profusion of international organisations making their presence felt in obscure local places throughout the developing world as 'a veritable carnival of acronyms', expressing a 'metaculture of modernity' layered across places in the world (Hannerz 1996: 53–54). Organisational and juridical/regulatory forms of globality situate the growing activities and claims to influence of the UN agencies in the world. But just as significant – as suggested by Hannerz's portrayal of their role in 'the global ecumene of modernity' – are the moral and symbolic dimensions of the UN's and particularly UNESCO's claims to 'speak for' the world, and their role in generating the iconic language and symbols that stand for universal normative values, or, as Hannerz describes them, 'metacultural commitments' (Hannerz 1996: 53–54). The question that follows this, of course, is: what are the implications and effects of UNESCO's undeniably global role, its status, and its programs for promoting, classifying and listing the world's 'heritage'?

Critiques and commentaries: UNESCO's 'globalisation' of heritage

UNESCO, its programs and procedures for 'World Heritage', together with the paradigms that these programs reflect, have come in for some scrutiny in recent years by conservation practitioners, academics and others. It is worth considering some of these commentaries and how they explore the relation between UNESCO, the constitution of 'heritage' and global power.

In an essay entitled 'Globalising Heritage', published in 2001, William S. Logan considers the extent to which UNESCO's role might be seen to mirror that of global organisations such as the post-World War Two Bretton Woods institutions, imposing global policies from the developed 'centre' of the world onto the developing 'periphery' societies. Closely affiliated with UNESCO's conservation work as a consultant, Logan takes seriously its global mission of preservation, but he is concerned nevertheless to consider whether UNESCO's global heritage system has imposed forms of homogeneous 'cultural globalisation' onto the non-Western world in terms of preservation practices and interpretation. Writing of UNESCO's key professional advisory groups on conservation, ICOMOS (International Council on Monuments and Sites) and ICCROM (International Centre for the Study of the Preservation and Restoration of Cultural Property), Logan notes that

> these organizations continue to play a powerful role on the global scene, laying down international standards for professional practice – 'world's best practice' – in the cultural heritage field as well as influencing thinking in those fields in less direct ways. In these respects UNESCO and its associated bodies may be said to be attempting to impose a common stamp on cultures across the world and their policies creating a logic of global cultural uniformity.
>
> (Logan 2001: 52)

He lists a number of specific ways that this organisational matrix has influenced conservation, including:

(1) Improving international practice.

>   For example,
>   establishing of codes of international best practice for cultural heritage professionals (such as the ICOMOS Venice Charter 1964);
>   imposing common conservation methodology and management plan requirements (for example: designation of World Heritage sites; provision of advice to museums on design, collections policy, interpretation techniques, etc.);

providing training programs and international seminars;

providing support groups for professionals and communities.

(2) Promoting particular sets of heritage values and conservation practices.

For example,

the development of international programs designed to encourage Member States to undertake selected conservation actions (e.g., annual Asia-Pacific Heritage Awards);

the provision of advisory input into national policies on cultural heritage places, museums, folklife protection, and education and training, including through the funding of foreign consultants.

(3) Establishing common management practices in World Heritage sites.

For example,

the funding of consultants to assist Developing Countries prepare World Heritage nominations according to the World Heritage Committee's 'Operational Guidelines';

assistance in the preparation of cultural heritage management plans for World Heritage sites (such as for Wat Phou in Laos);

the monitoring of those plans and policing of World Heritage sites using the World Heritage in Danger mechanism.

(Logan 2001: 52–53)

This would appear to be uniformity of a highly technical order, though these processes have clear substantive implications in matters such as classification and interpretation of sites. Yet Logan is ultimately unconvinced that these measures constitute a significant level of homogenisation imposed from 'the centre', largely because, as he demonstrates, UNESCO has progressively assimilated alternative approaches that have emerged from 'the periphery'. In particular he cites the advent of 'The Nara Document on Authenticity' in 1994, a document issued under the names of both UNESCO and ICOMOS, which affirmed that conservation practice needs to reflect the cultural values of particular societies. It affirmed that variant conservation practices were acceptable and indeed essential – they needed to reflect, for example, the values placed on symbolism in East Asia, which demanded continued reconstruction of religious monuments as opposed to purist preservation that was the norm in Europe. Logan also cites the progressive acceptance of 'intangible heritage' as a further example of the accommodation of alternative heritage forms into UNESCO's global lexicon.

In short, as Logan points out, 'it is no longer acceptable to provide a single, simple answer to the question of how do we identify and save heritage' (Logan 2001: 57). This, he highlights, is the result of the considerable accommodations made by UNESCO to demands to expand alternative modes of heritage. It is clear that Logan welcomes these trends, and in so doing he concludes that rather than imposing uniformity, UNESCO has actively accommodated change from 'the periphery'. In keeping with his commitment to UNESCO, Logan's principal concern remains technical – that is, how the proliferation of types of authorised 'heritage' around the world is challenging the capacity of organisations and professionals to effectively protect and manage this Pandora's Box. Logan briefly acknowledges the political uses of heritage listing among nation-states, but does not dwell on it, since, as mentioned, he is both committed to the necessity of UNESCO's global conservation management project, and pragmatic about how politics intrudes into all these processes. As for the proliferation of new forms of heritage that have emerged under UNESCO's stewardship over the past two decades, he is less ready to consider how they might reflect UNESCO's principal contemporary role as the distributor of symbolic prizes to competing nations in the global status game.

Logan's conclusion about UNESCO's progressive accommodation of heritage diversity implicitly responds to the somewhat out-of-date judgement made a few years earlier (1996) by J. Tunbridge and G. Ashworth that UNESCO and ICOMOS 'have not hitherto operated in a globally unbiased fashion appropriate to even-handed representation of the heritage of mankind' (Tunbridge and Ashworth 1996: 275). The concern of these scholars was to chart the emergence and multifarious applications of the epithet 'heritage' in the late twentieth century, and to discuss the dangerous consequences of this process in terms of economic exploitation (especially tourism and commodification), distortion and trivialisation, and ideological manipulation by political elites. Though succeeding in delineating and describing the many uses of heritage and its 'dissonance', Tunbridge and Ashworth are ambivalent and uncertain when they come to address the 'global' dimension. Identifying UNESCO and its affiliated professional associations as the principal actors in global heritage affairs, on a positive note they suggest that these agencies may facilitate 'international heritage reconciliation' involving restitution of property damaged or stolen in wars (hardly successful in Afghanistan or Iraq). On the other hand, with reference to the expansion of World Heritage Site listing into the Third World, they make the pessimistic point that 'there is a tendency for World Heritage Sites to be used as instruments of national aggrandisement by the more and less developed countries alike, potentially adding to international heritage tensions' (Tunbridge and Ashworth 1996:04: 276). This latter point is certainly prescient, and though their discussion of UNESCO and the global heritage bureaucracy is minimal, Tunbridge and Ashworth succeed in identifying the power of states in the production and manipulation of heritage as a major challenge to the ideal of fostering world amity through global heritage conservation programs.

Jan Turtinen, in common with Logan, has argued that UNESCO is a powerful actor in a global matrix of world organisations, reflecting the propositions of some scholars that a 'World Polity' or 'World Society' is a key feature of the contemporary era (Boli and Thomas 1999; Drori et al. 2006). Turtinen goes further, arguing that UNESCO not only operates as part of an organisational structure, but is 'a powerful producer of culture, and a highly influential actor, capable of defining and framing conditions, problems, and solutions, and thus framing the interests and desired actions of others, especially those of the world's nation-states'

(Turtinen 2000: 5). This argument rests on a number of assumptions, principal among which is the assumption that the procedures and technical criteria embedded in the official determinations of the 'World Heritage' status of various sites have a substantive role in producing uniformity in the meaning of 'heritage' across the globe. The other key assumption is that the bureaucratic units within UNESCO possess the power not simply to mobilise a wide range of groups (such as internationally-recognised specialists and national-level institutions) towards the technical objectives of material conservation and restoration, but that they also actively shape the meanings of particular historic sites through a representational process. Turtinen's model of this process is predicated on the view that UNESCO is both a power 'centre' and capable of producing a hegemonic model of cultural significance. He argues that, as a globalising project, 'World Heritage' involves global standardising and regulating processes and measures. The advent and application of the World Heritage category generated a paradoxical relation 'between the globally dispersed and diverse phenomena and the idea that they, in spite of all disparities, had something in common, and were constitutive parts of a distinct, universal and categorical entity, that is, "the World Heritage of humankind"' (Turtinen 2000: 6). Many would argue in response that 'World Heritage' is simply a pan-national category that recognises and celebrates remarkable human creations, helps mobilise resources for their protection, and then presents these phenomena to a wider world to celebrate and admire — nothing sinister, but well intentioned and benevolent. What, after all, should be problematic, exclusionary, or suppressive about the selection criteria that are applied by UNESCO's World Heritage Centre in evaluating cultural and natural sites? (See World Heritage: The Criteria for Selection at end of chapter).

Drawing on the arguments of a number of social theorists, Turtinen proposes that World Heritage is 'a cosmopolitan political project', one which aims to create a new political as well as imagined community (i.e. 'humankind'). It is a project which is idealistic and reformatory in aims, but also 'highly pragmatic, contradictory, and sometimes hypocritical in practice'. What does this mean? In concrete terms it means that globalisation forges new relationships between the local and the global spheres: that is to say, 'World Heritage' is a type of universalising grammar of rationalist modernity that changes local perceptions and realities. 'World Heritage', in summary, is a translocal and transnational project, and the categorisation and selection that is inherent to this discourse has the effect of mapping the world and selecting sites for conservation priorities in terms of immutable categories such as 'civilisation', 'culture', and 'tradition', which are indeed key paradigms reflected in UNESCO's pronouncements and conventions. It is certainly clear that essentialised concepts have been generated by UNESCO in association with the concept of 'universal value', but whether these universalising terms have really transformed perceptions at national and local levels is less evident. We should also recognise that professionals and academics have opposed the reifications and simplifications that UNESCO has produced, conspicuously in connection with the notion of 'culture' (Wright 1998; Arizpe 1998). There is no doubt, however, that the concept of 'universal value' has been critical in supporting the apparatus of World Heritage and its list-making project. Turtinen rightly identifies specialist groups – the 'righteous providers of scientific knowledge' – as the producers and authorising agents of this idea. The creation of the World Heritage system requires classification and standardisation, as embodied in the nomination process, which involves comparison between sites to rate their value on a hierarchy through the application of a 'global grammar' whereby dispersed local sites 'can be reinterpreted and reorganized as a heritage of humankind … allowing the sites to become local sites in a global framework and perspective, and to take on new meaning through that framework and perspective' (Turtinen 2000: 14). But is there anything seriously wrongheaded or insidious about this process, as is implied? That is: are local meanings leeched out or distorted in the process of being elevated to a global list? Does the list perpetuate an uneven hierarchy of importance among nations?

No-one could deny that the World Heritage list represents a view that not all sites are equally valuable. The concept of 'outstanding universal value' requires selection and evaluation on the basis that some things are more important than others. Yet the criteria for selection have in fact been subject to debate and change, and since the late 1980s UNESCO's heritage bureaucracy responded to pressures from UNESCO's assembly to widen the number of listed sites and make the list more representative of its member states. In 2005, Christina Cameron, a conservation professional with long involvement in UNESCO's World Heritage Committee, noted that there had been a change in the definition and application of the principle of 'outstanding universal value' from listing 'the best of the best' ('iconic' or unique sites) to listing 'representative of the best', the latter being a reflection of the necessity for comparison due to the surge in the number of nominated sites of similar character. As early as the 1980s, she notes, the World Heritage Committee was expressing concerns about the meaning of 'outstanding universal value', as nominations poured in from States Parties that had signed UNESCO's World Heritage Convention. In 1992 there were major concerns expressed among UNESCO's conservation specialists that a burgeoning number of new World Heritage sites were falling below the benchmark of 'outstanding universal value' (Cameron 2005: 2–3). Against the specialists' concerns to 'maintain standards' was a countervailing pressure to widen the geographic span of the list, and it was this pressure (combined with soul-searching among UNESCO's specialists) that led to the adoption in 1994 of a 'Global Strategy'. This mandated broad and 'dynamic' categories of universal application designed to accommodate diverse and complex sites, including cultural landscapes, industrial sites, modern architecture, and inhabited settlements. This Global Strategy, with its newly flexible frame of 'universal value', opened a Pandora's Box, expanding the range of acceptable sites, with their significance determined, in formal terms at least, by the principle of 'representivity' (Cameron 2005: 5).

It was in the 1990s that an increasing number of hybrid sites from Southeast Asia began to be listed, places marked by the impress of European colonialism as much as indigenous histories (for example Luang Prabang in Laos, listed in 1995; Vigan in the Philippines, 1999). Though the professionals continued to affirm the importance of rigour and selectivity, they were essentially fighting a rearguard battle in protecting the exclusiveness and professional sanctity of the list. The irony has been that the conservation purists of UNESCO have been cursed by the very success of the World Heritage program. Turtinen acknowledges the enthusiasm of nation-states in embracing World Heritage for their own purposes, but does not fully admit to the flexibility of UNESCO as an organisation. Though he is right in identifying the specialists and their bureaucratic processes as a source of power, he fails to acknowledge the limits to this power. There are two main reasons for this: 1) for the specialists the list is essentially viewed as a technical instrument that functions to ensure conservation and preservation (ideally, at least), and though they may classify the significance and meanings of sites on a scale of 'heritage values', they are not fully in control of the multiple meanings of sites at the national and sub-national level, and 2) UNESCO is not simply a bureaucratic agency: it is, through its assemblies and committees, a forum of states, and bureaucrats and specialists have to respond to them, and change accordingly. So, if we can view UNESCO as a 'centre', it is essentially a 'soft centre', and a malleable one at that (Askew 2003). One of Turtinen's points still remains valid, however: that 'World Heritage' has established a terrain, or field of competition among states, and UNESCO's lists have become indispensable to nations' global visibility and status.

Among critics of World Heritage and its global ramifications are those who might be dubbed advocates of 'insurgent heritage'; that is, they aim to critically deconstruct the whole notion of 'heritage' and critique its global authorising agents (UNESCO in particular) as purveyors of a power regime. Of these, Laurajane Smith is perhaps the most forceful, though she draws on the earlier arguments of Barbara Kirshenblatt-Gimblett, an anthropologist of folklore, museums and heritage tourism (Kirshenblatt-Gimblett 1995, 1998). The basic argument is that 'heritage' is not found, but made. Thus, Stonehenge or the Sydney Opera House are not *inherently* valuable: what makes them valuable are present-day cultural processes. The question of who has the power to define the meaning of the past and the selective construction of the past to support power regimes has been long discussed in the academy and by the burgeoning number of scholars in 'heritage studies', notably influenced by Eric Hobsbawm and his 'invention of tradition' thesis (Hobsbawm and Ranger 1983), and by David Lowenthal in his acclaimed book *The Past is a Foreign Country* (1985). Smith argues that 'the idea of heritage is used to construct, reconstruct and negotiate a range of identities and social and cultural values and meanings in the present' (Smith 2006: 3). Heritage is a 'discourse' that acts to make dynamic phenomena inert. The 'Authorized Heritage Discourse' (AHD) promotes the view that heritage is innately valuable, representing all that is good and valuable about the past. In common with other critics, Smith sets up a straw man by portraying this AHD as being based on a Western elitist idea of universal cultural values, one which marginalises alternative and 'subaltern' heritage, embedded in ideas that privilege monumentality and preservation for various purposes, including the construction of national identities (Smith 2006: 11–12). She identifies UNESCO and ICOMOS as the key global agents that have institutionalised this dominant heritage discourse and perpetuated it through technical and policy processes. In managing and interpreting heritage sites, these agents actively shape meanings, she argues, because dynamic meaning-making processes are defined out of sites, whose values are seen as immutable and materialised.

Smith is right in identifying UNESCO's fetish for classification, but I suggest that she exaggerates its effects, in particular by underestimating the persistence of nation-states' uses of heritage sites at the expense of UNESCO's universalising illusions. As with Turtinen, Smith's monolithic model of UNESCO's discursive power downplays the importance of its changing uses of significance criteria and the democratisation of the World Heritage List over the last two decades. She certainly acknowledges changes in the span and character of specialists' conservation declarations and principles, but this is not enough for her. This is because her ideological viewpoint is founded on her professional cultural advocacy work as an archaeologist with indigenous people in Australia, whose views of the past and of place are at variance with established modes of treating and 'managing' heritage. She is happy to essentialise the so-called AHD (which she alternatively names as the 'Western AHD'), but hardly seems conscious of her own reification of 'community'. In treating the Australia ICOMOS Burra Charter (1979) and its substantial revision in 1999 to accommodate people in the decision-making process and acknowledging their links to places, she complains that the charter fetishised 'place' while also reproducing the authority of expertise and paying only lip service to her preferred 'community values'. Allegedly, then, the revised Burra Charter re-affirmed the AHD without changing it.

Similarly, although Smith acknowledges the widening of UNESCO's heritage lexicon in the advent of 'intangible heritage' from the late 1990s, she argues that it did not go far enough, and served to reproduce the idea of hierarchy in selecting 'masterpieces'. She notes, as others have done, that there is a critical contradiction in UNESCO's proclamations to protect and preserve selected intangible heritage, since change is the essence of UNESCO's definition of intangible heritage as 'living culture'. Though she admits that UNESCO's recognition and institutionalisation of 'intangible heritage' marks a trend of change in the AHD, she claims that there has been no fundamental shift in the underlying power of the 'Western AHD', largely because UNESCO and ICOMOS are the principal controllers (Smith 2006: 106–14). Smith's uncompromising conclusion about the alleged persistence of the Authorised (Eurocentric) Heritage Discourse is based on a simplistic portrayal of transformations that have taken place – her postcolonial myth of European dominance is belied by the dominance of non-Western practices listed as intangible heritage, as well as the transformation of the World Heritage List itself and the influence of non-Westerners in key positions in its bureaucracy. I am not being an apologist for UNESCO here, simply affirming that substantive changes have occurred. The problems with UNESCO are its bureaucratic processes and its fetishism for list making, and all changes are channelled through these frames. All this being said, arguments by self-appointed representatives of the 'subaltern voice', such as Smith, misread the character and extent of UNESCO's power, since it is with the nation-states that the capacity for innovation and oppression ultimately lies. Notably, the rise of intangible heritage partnered UNESCO's proclamations about cultural rights and cultural diversity. Though UNESCO's global heritage apparatus has continually responded to the pressures of its critics, to the insurgents this is never enough to meet their ideals of a 'global cultural commons', presumably free of a rationalising and meddling bureaucracy and presumptuous conservation specialists. The radical solution that lurks beneath the complaints of insurgent heritage advocates is to do away with the heritage apparatus altogether, although this is surely impossible given its global embeddedness.

Barbara Kirshenblatt-Gimblett has rightly highlighted the centrality of the conservation 'List' as the essential artifact of the global heritage project (2004: 57). Contention over global heritage essentially converges on UNESCO's lists – how they are made, and who controls them. We may struggle against this product of the global bureaucracy's rationalist 'iron cage' all we like, but UNESCO and its lists have irreversibly established the terrain and stakes of the contests. The only alternative is to opt out of the global heritage game entirely, and not even heritage insurgents are prepared to do this.

Localities, states and World Heritage sites: preserving the appearance of harmony

Despite the rapid proliferation of World Heritage sites, particularly over the last decade, few academic studies have explored the various processes, negotiations and conflicts surrounding their emergence, management and meaning. Jan Turtinen, as noted already, interprets UNESCO's World Heritage program as a significant project of globalisation, one that involves the mapping and categorisation of places on a world scale according to a 'global grammar' by means of which UNESCO and its professional affiliates objectify the past (Turtinen 2000: 4–6). Turtinen's interpretation is a potentially illuminating framework for understanding UNESCO as an organisation that generates cosmopolitan representations of 'World Heritage'. But the persuasiveness of this interpretation is limited by the lack of any detailed delineation of how this discursive construction is deployed, specifically at the level of particular World Heritage sites. His outline of the nomination and World Heritage listing of Sweden's port city of Karlskrona in 1998 demonstrates little of the alleged hegemonising force of UNESCO's 'cosmopolitan project'. Rather, it highlights how both localities and national governments enthusiastically use the World Heritage List to enhance national status and encourage tourism for the highly pragmatic purpose of generating income (Turtinen 2000: 1–2). In light of this point, it would appear that the ideological project of World Heritage – if UNESCO's programs can be justifiably described as such, which I doubt – is not driven by 'new and powerful actors' as claimed by Turtinen; rather the key actors are old agents with new agendas, namely particular national governments and local conservation lobbies. Indeed, his key example highlights how the World Heritage List has become a resource for Western governments, who aim to use conservation and place marketing to help resuscitate marginal urban and regional economies through tourism. In Karlskrona there seems to be little dissent among local residents about the 'objectification' of their city's past. The successful nomination by the UK of the City of Liverpool for World Heritage Site listing (inscribed in 2004) is a further example of heritage classifications being used as a status symbol for purposes of economic regeneration. Turtinen's provocative thesis is ultimately unsuccessful because he fails to show convincingly how the legitimising texts and procedures of UNESCO find any opposition – indeed the evident *lack* of opposition to World Heritage discourse is the question demanding inquiry! His own evidence in fact suggests that 'World Heritage' may simply be a re-badging of those monuments and sites already objectified and commodified at the national or sub-national level for very practical and opportunistic ends.

By contrast, James Hevia makes a compelling case for identifying UNESCO as a complicit agent in the cultural homogenisation process in China, *not* by an active process of management or imposition as such, but by virtue of the aestheticised and depoliticised criteria used to determine eligibility and 'World Heritage' significance under the terms of the 1972 World Heritage Convention. In his discussion of the World Heritage site in Chengde, Hevia shows how the Manchu Dynasty palace and temple complex – containing a miniature replica of the Potala of Lhasa (listed by UNESCO as a World Heritage Site in 1995) – has been utilised by the Chinese state as a symbol of the harmonious integration by the Han Chinese majority of the Tibetan minority peoples. He highlights the Chinese state's agenda regarding the representation of Tibetan culture as follows:

> State curatorship of museum representation serves to transform stubborn difference into colorful multiculturalism, idealizing and depoliticizing the collective expressions of 'minority' groups. The effect is to make any resistance based on material interests or territorial claims invisible within the terms of a discourse on culture, which, whether one is in Beijing, an American University, Disneyworld's Epcot Center, or UNESCO headquarters, seems easy to think of as distinct from social structure, law, and state institutions.
>
> (Hevia 2001: 221)

Hevia argues that the Chinese state's discourse on 'culture' in its domestic conservation programs helps defuse more hard-edged political dissent regarding Tibet's incorporation (surrounding, for example, the state's intervention in the choice of incarnate Tibetan Buddhist lamas). He goes on to demonstrate that the cultural universalism and depoliticised aestheticism embedded in UNESCO's World Heritage site criteria serve to allow the Chinese state not only to succeed in nominating problematic sites such as the Chengde palace complex, but also allow it to capitalise on the prestige conferred by the World Heritage List. Citing passages from the successful nomination document that stress the 'perfect harmony' of materials and symbols in the Chengde site, he argues persuasively that the international vocabulary of cultural and artistic essences authorised by UNESCO and its specialists have played into the hands of an oppressive state with its own representational agendas.

Sites such as the complex at Chengde 'place Tibet firmly within the borders of the PRC' (Hevia 2001: 224). UNESCO has, it appears, avoided any comment on this process of symbolic incorporation of minority groups in China.

In his critical account of the movement for the preservation of the medina (old city) of the Moroccan capital of Fez, Geoff Porter outlines how this preservation campaign drew its strength from an officially-endorsed nostalgia linked to a national narrative that excluded key groups in the population of the spaces of the old city. In 1980, the Moroccan Ministry of the Interior followed up an earlier petition (presented in 1976) to UNESCO for the World Heritage listing of the medina), stressing that its proposed conservation plan aimed not simply to protect and restore buildings, but to reinvigorate the site as 'an ensemble of the social, economic, cultural and religious life that made the particular genius of the medina' (Porter 2001: 124). The case presented was calculated to encompass those key objectives that UNESCO's officials and experts would interpret as a worthy objective of heritage conservation. On a technical level, the nomination was recognised as acceptable because it met three of the criteria stipulated under UNESCO's operational guidelines for implementing the World Heritage Convention: Criterion 3 for sites bearing exceptional testimony to a 'cultural tradition'; Criterion 5 for sites that are outstanding examples of human settlement or land-use; and Criterion 6 for sites that are associated with events or 'living traditions'. Notably, the conservation scheme was used by Moroccan authorities to justify the relocation of 50,000 inhabitants from the medina, a measure which Porter argues was linked directly to an effort to exclude rural immigrants who were deemed by the elite to compromise the urbane Arabic legacies of the old city (embodied particularly in the educational role of the medina's main mosque and student quarter). As Porter notes, the World Heritage Convention 'does not allow for the authentication of heritage not endorsed by the representatives of an internationally recognized state' (Porter 2001: 130). It is not surprising that national-level practices of physical and cultural exclusion enacted in Fez went unrecognised by UNESCO: this is because the states have authoritative voices in claiming the grounds of cultural significance, and the role of UNESCO and its technical affiliate ICOMOS is specifically to assess the nominations in terms of the formal taxonomies of significance framed in the Convention and its operational procedures. Porter argues that the relocation of residents of rural origin out of the medina was not simply an exercise in 'urban redevelopment' (as claimed by the Fez planning authorities) but a symbolic practice of denying the historical role of these rural residents in contributing to Fez's lifeways and history (Porter 2001: 131–32).

Perhaps the greatest irony in the process of determining and representing Fez's historic significance is revealed in the fact that the bibliography of studies submitted to support the World Heritage nomination was dominated by French colonial evaluations and orientalist scholarship. According to one prominent Moroccan intellectual, Abdallah Hammoudhi (echoing Edward Said's thesis), the effect of such colonial science has been to produce static and essentialist concepts, 'bringing to a standstill what has been a changing social landscape' (Porter 2001: 142). Appropriated by postcolonial nation-states, these colonialist categories help to justify projects of symbolic domination.

The case of Fez also shows how states, through conservation projects, can harness the support of UNESCO and UN-associated agencies such as the World Bank to generate development funding. Thus, the Moroccan government received US$27.6 million for restoring the medina of Fez. The prominent development anthropologist Robert Hackenberg has argued that cultural heritage sites should be utilised more fully as development projects, and should be funded in order to serve 'local community' needs, particularly in relation to employment and income generation. Interestingly, however, he pays no attention to the ways that heritage conservation projects can be employed by state authorities to symbolically exclude different groups, as noted in the case of Fez, which he actually cites as a successful example of 'development' (Hackenberg 2002).

One of the few studies that considers the dynamics of national-level conservation policy and its connection to the contemporary state's twin concerns with tourist-generated income and constructing national narratives is Maurizio Peleggi's account of state-sponsored conservation efforts in Thailand (Peleggi 2002). Like other students of the politics of heritage conservation in Thailand (Askew 1996), Peleggi links the expanding efforts of Thai state agencies to conserve and restore monuments and sites from the late 1970s to an ideological project of defining 'Thainess' through framing an authorised version of Thailand's national history. In addition, the packaging of Thailand's identity for tourism promotion has been a nationally important official objective, reinforcing the economic imperative for preservation. According to Peleggi, UNESCO's bestowal of World Heritage site status on the historical parks of the old cities of Sukhothai and Ayutthaya in 1991 was important to the Thai government largely because this enhanced tourist-oriented packaging of Thailand's culture and history. Through being validated as a place of world cultural significance by UNESCO, Thailand's image could be re-configured away from its dominant association with sex-tourism and towards respectability (Peleggi 2002: 61). But when viewed from the perspective of the politics of conservation in Thailand, UNESCO appears as just one of the actors authorising and shaping representations of the past, and a minor one at that. The major forces of resistance to a hegemonic rendering of Thailand's past (cohering around key intellectuals and maverick academics championing various communities) have rallied not against UNESCO, but against a number of key state agencies which they accuse of privileging elitist and static interpretations of history – such as the Department of Fine Arts and the Rattanakosin Conservation Committee, which has implemented a plan for the renovation of the old city centre (Askew 2002).

Another major theme highlighted in the few published studies on World Heritage sites is that of the dynamism surrounding religious sites. Thus, James Hevia has noted that the restoration of the Buddhist temples at Chengde has attracted pilgrims and re-activated some popular folk devotional practices, including offerings to deities, the planting of prayer flags, and the piling of inscribed stones as memorials to pilgrimage. Popular religious practices can reinvigorate and attach meanings to sites in ways that elude official prescriptions of meaning and interpretation (Hevia 2001: 235). This theme of the dynamism of religious sites and their multiple interpretations is also stressed by the anthropologist Sherry Errington (1993) in relation to the Javanese Mahayana Buddhist monument of Borobudur (classified as a World Heritage Site in 1991), but in this case she emphasises how Suharto's New Order Indonesian state attempted to limit people's ritual and imaginative 'framing' of the monument.

The theme of variant meanings is taken further by Bruce Owens in his study of the Buddhist sacred site of Swayambhu, in Nepal. The hilltop stupa of Swayambhu and its surrounding area is located in one of the designated preservation zones located within the Kathmandu Valley, and classified as a World Heritage Site by UNESCO in 1979. Owens' study is directed not to a direct evaluation of UNESCO's role, but to the dynamism of the site itself, as revealed in the building of a path and wall surrounding the stupa. What he shows is that different ethnic groups and their sponsoring organisations are constructing sections of the monumental path and wall in order to express devotion and identity. There is not one 'local' community involved in this process, but numerous groups, some of which are not locally resident. In the context of Nepal's political changes, he interprets this process as one of ethnic competition for symbolic status. He draws on the anthropologist Margaret Rodman's proposal that particular places need to be seen as 'multivocal': that is, interpreted variously by different social actors (Owens 2002: 281–82). He notes that the continuing status of Swayambhu as a World Heritage zone is important to the Nepalese government, but the role of UNESCO in managing the site is actually minimal. Despite the development of a Conservation Master Plan (in 1989), and the formal requirements for sponsors of building activity to gain the approval of the Nepal Archaeology Department before construction, the actual outcomes are considerably varied and depart from design submissions (ibid.).

Owens concludes that Swayambhu is 'increasingly becoming a place of many places'. An overseeing organisation, the Federation of Swayambhu Management and Conservation, comprises a variety of interested groups with different and sometimes competing goals. He notes:

> The many different parties interested in Swayambhu's fate, both within and outside the Federation, have differences of opinion about what is to be preserved and for whom. Some favour the traditionally innovative practice of transforming sacred monuments through devotional activity (now possible on a new scale and accessible to many), and others privilege the monuments themselves. Some resent governmental and international interference with local initiatives and standards, whereas others decry the effects of local practices on a heritage they view as belonging to the world.
>
> (Owens 2002: 301)

Owens' study outlines a complex drama being played out around Swayambhu. In this context UNESCO plays a symbolic role that is important to the government of

Nepal, but not particularly significant to the key groups that are re-shaping the site itself. Moreover, the conservation plans enacted under the rubric of UNESCO's World Heritage site requirements seem to be ineffective in the task of managing new constructions around the stupa, and the state agency charged with monitoring the site appears to be limited in its authority. One might ask here: should UNESCO celebrate this as expressing 'cultural diversity', or condemn it as bad conservation management? In this particular case, we can also note that there is no single 'community' acting as a constituency to interpret the meaning of the Swayambhu site; rather, there are many groups.

The magic list and the agendas of states

A number of conclusions can be drawn from the above discussion. First is that the existing studies of World Heritage sites show that at the ground level UNESCO's direct presence in local life is generally limited, and its management stipulations are mediated through national and regional bureaucracies. Second, UNESCO's authorisation of World Heritage status for particular sites is most often the end product of a longer history of conservation projects generated at national and regional levels, and these are animated by varied agendas, some of which clearly involve the physical and symbolic exclusion of certain groups. Third, it is clear that many of the conflicts over the meaning of the past occur outside the purview of UNESCO's World Heritage program, and thus a search for conflicts focusing only on World Heritage listed sites may not in fact capture the full range of confrontations taking place. For example, Michael Herzfeld has studied the complex negotiations over local and national meaning of monuments and artefacts in the Cretan town of Rethemnos. UNESCO appears to have played no effective part in this process of revaluing and representing the past (Herzfeld 1991). In Thailand, the establishment of the historic parks of Sukhothai and Ayutthaya has had little significant impact on the ways of life of local inhabitants, largely because these ancient cities are no longer key centres of population. It is rather in the old centre of Bangkok (Rattanakosin Island) where state conservation policies are having the greatest negative impact on communities.

These controversial internal issues and struggles do not enter the purview of UNESCO's deliberating and policy-making bodies, and in turn this helps reinforce the assumption in UNESCO's key legitimising texts that cultural heritage promotion is a benevolent and neutral process – that World Heritage sites are the uncontested icons of each country's individual 'culture' and 'tradition'. The critical organisational level at which heritage policies and discourses are framed is still the national level, and the practical and symbolic consequences are fought over between people and their own bureaucracies. It is a major irony that, while major world development agencies are incorporating bottom-up programs of community development and resources management (with UNESCO championing these efforts and affirming the role of 'culture' in just about everything), there is no genuinely bottom-up heritage identification process allowed for in the World Heritage listing process. 'Heritage' and the attribution of its meaning need authorisation by nation-states. Notably, the program for 'Masterpieces of the Oral and Intangible Heritage of Humanity', announced in 1998 as a significant broadening of the heritage concept towards including marginal groups (later consolidated in the 'Representative List of the Intangible Cultural Heritage of Humanity', 2008), was reliant upon approval from national authorities. UNESCO's program for highlighting these 'masterpieces' relied once more on adding another icon list to circulate among states for status competition. Clearly, no potentially subversive 'histories' will ever emerge through a state-centred nomination process, notwithstanding UNESCO's inclusive rhetoric that accompanied the publicity for this new alternative list. Note the following caveat after UNESCO's enthusiastic invitation to NGOs and local communities to 'take the lead in identifying, preserving and drawing attention to their oral and intangible heritage':

> The intangible heritage is vast in extent and concerns each individual, for everyone bears within him the heritage of his own community. The safeguarding of that heritage must be triggered by individual initiative and backed up by associations, by specialists and by institutions; only then will the national authorities take it into account. UNESCO is there to give assistance whenever requested to do so by the authorities of a Member State.
>
> (UNESCO Masterpieces 1998)

As long as UNESCO deems States Parties to be the only authorised representatives of their countries' 'heritage values', the internal political agendas of these states – and the many localised conflicts emerging between these states and their people over the meaning and preservation of places – will remain invisible in the triumphant UNESCO texts that celebrate humanity's creativity, as viewed from the top of the world and the lofty heights of 'The List'.

The following interlinked propositions set out the ways that UNESCO's magic list of world heritage functions to dispense capital and resources in the global arena:

1   The World Heritage List is both a technical and iconic status-conferring artefact of global importance that acts to simultaneously legitimise and serve the distinctive interests of UNESCO, its experts, and its member nations.
2   At the global level of representation, the World Heritage List enhances UNESCO's legitimacy by virtue of its apparently representative, universal and depoliticised characteristics, celebrating the diversity of human creativity and culture.
3   The List derives one potent level of legitimacy from its apparently scientific scheme of classification (criteria of significance) and by virtue of the technical procedures employed to designate significance, develop sites and instigate plans to ensure particular standards of preservation.
4   The function of maintaining and governing entry to the List endows the specialists (ICOMOS etc.) with important legitimacy, confirming their role and

identity as specialised and qualified guardians of an object categorised as 'heritage'.

5   The List has iconic significance for UNESCO States Parties because it represents a desired status symbol. That is, the World Heritage listing of sites – despite performing functions of an ostensibly technical (conservation) and educational (display) nature consistent with UNESCO's universal and 'neutral' role – acts as a powerful signifier of hierarchy among nations, and generates competition for entry to the List.

6   The List also has resource significance for member states because the achievement of World Heritage status for a site attracts income through tourism. In certain cases, the preparation process preceding and following site listing may attract development aid and resources.

7   The 'universal' meanings ascribed to sites in the List have little influence on the ways that World Heritage sites are deployed by member states for their own domestic ideological or exclusionary purposes.

Conclusion

As a global organisation UNESCO is a multi-dimensional entity that defines and legitimises itself through activities that encompass deliberation, declaration and official classification, activities that engage the interests of a range of key actors who include: UNESCO bureaucrats; the political elites of nation-states; and intellectuals and 'specialists' (largely among the associated non-government organisations) who play a key role in promoting and implementing key programs. Focusing on UNESCO's 'World Heritage' program as an element of the organisation's cultural programs, I have argued that the global influence of UNESCO is registered not in any monolithic organisational capacity as such, or even in its capacity to enforce protocols and conventions, which is ultimately weak (Atherton and Atherton 1995; Maswood 2000), or in a hegemonising ideological role. Rather its key role in the global arena is to act as a generator of iconic symbols that serve to elaborate and organise an arena of status competition that centres on the multiple symbolic significance of its World Heritage List. This list is multi-valent in its operation, and I refer to it as 'magic' in an anthropological sense as a potent signifier to various actors: the 'List' and the host of procedures surrounding its maintenance serves both as a technical/bureaucratic instrument and a validator of heritage specialists' expertise; listed sites are a symbol of national status for governments; they are a tangible mechanism for drawing development aid for governments and tourism for private and/or state enterprises; the compilation and continuing elaboration of the World Heritage List and others (now including 'Intangible Heritage') validates the continuing activities of UNESCO as an arbiter of cultural status and inclusion – it is a harmony that obscures the forms of suppression and manipulation of symbols by its member states which pursue their own ideological agendas by appropriating globally-endowed status. Despite the best intentions of its advocates, as the umpire and accomplice in the global status game of heritage listing, UNESCO is a complicit partner in nation-states' domestic projects of cultural reification and domination.

WORLD HERITAGE: The Criteria for Selection

To be included on the World Heritage List, sites must be of outstanding universal value and meet at least one out of ten selection criteria. These criteria are explained in the **Guidelines for the Implementation of the World Heritage Convention** which, besides the text of the Convention, is the main working tool on World Heritage. The criteria are regularly revised by the Committee to reflect the evolution of the World Heritage concept itself.

Until the end of 2004, World Heritage sites were selected on the basis of six cultural and four natural criteria. With the adoption of the revised Operational Guidelines for the Implementation of the World Heritage Convention, only one set of ten criteria exists.

	Cultural criteria	Natural criteria
Operational Guidelines 2002	(i) (ii) (iii) (iv) (v) (vi)	(i) (ii) (iii) (iv)
Operational Guidelines 2005	(i) (ii) (iii) (iv) (v) (vi)	(viii) (ix) (vii) (x)

Selection criteria:

  i to represent a masterpiece of human creative genius;

  ii to exhibit an important interchange of human values, over a span of time or within a cultural area of the world, on developments in architecture or technology, monumental arts, town-planning or landscape design;

  iii to bear a unique or at least exceptional testimony to a cultural tradition or to a civilization which is living or which has disappeared;

  iv to be an outstanding example of a type of building, architectural or technological ensemble or landscape which illustrates (a) significant stage(s) in human history;

  v to be an outstanding example of a traditional human settlement, land-use, or sea-use which is representative of a culture (or cultures), or human interaction with the environment especially when it has become vulnerable under the impact of irreversible change;

  vi to be directly or tangibly associated with events or living traditions, with ideas, or with beliefs, with artistic and literary works of outstanding universal significance. (The Committee considers that this criterion should preferably be used in conjunction with other criteria);

vii   to contain superlative natural phenomena or areas of exceptional natural beauty and aesthetic importance;

viii   to be outstanding examples representing major stages of earth's history, including the record of life, significant on-going geological processes in the development of landforms, or significant geomorphic or physiographic features;

ix   to be outstanding examples representing significant on-going ecological and biological processes in the evolution and development of terrestrial, fresh water, coastal and marine ecosystems and communities of plants and animals;

x   to contain the most important and significant natural habitats for in-situ conservation of biological diversity, including those containing threatened species of outstanding universal value from the point of view of science or conservation

The protection, management, authenticity and integrity of properties are also important considerations.

Since 1992 significant interactions between people and the natural environment have been recognized as cultural landscapes.

Creating the List: Criteria for Selection.
<http://whc.unesco.org/en/criteria/>

Bibliography

Appadurai, A. (2002) *Globalisation*, Durham, N.C.: Duke University Press.

Askew, M. (1996) 'The Rise of *Moradok* and the Decline of the *Yarn*: Heritage and Cultural Construction in Urban Thailand', *Sojourn*, 11: 183–210.

Askew, M. (2002) 'The Challenge of Co-existence: The Meaning of Urban Heritage in Contemporary Thailand', in W.S. Logan (ed.) *The Disappearing 'Asian' City*, Hong Kong: Oxford University Press.

Askew, M. (2003) 'A Soft Centre? UNESCO and the Uses of World Heritage'. Paper presented at the research workshop: 'UNESCO as an Agent of Cultural Globalisation', Cultural Heritage Centre for Asia and the Pacific, Deakin University, Melbourne, Australia, 20 June.

Askew, M. and Logan, W.S. (2002) Interviews with UNESCO and ICOMOS staff, Paris, September.

Atherton, T-A. and Atherton, T.C. (1995) 'The Power and the Glory, National Sovereignty and the World Heritage Convention', *The Australian Law Journal*, 69: 637–38.

Beck, U. (2000) *What is Globalisation?* London: Polity Press, New Ed.

Beck, U. (2005) *Power in the Global Age*, Cambridge: Polity Press.

Boli, J. and Thomas, G. (eds) (1999) *Constructing World Culture. International Nongovernmental Organizations since 1875*, Stanford: Stanford University Press.

Bourdieu, P. (1998) *Acts of Resistance: Against the New Myths of Our Time*, Cambridge: Polity Press.

Boutros-Ghali, B. (1995) *Confronting New Challenges*, New York: United Nations.

Cameron, C. (2005) 'Evolution of the application of "outstanding universal value" for Cultural and Natural Heritage', in, Keynote speech by Ms Christina Cameron and presentations by the World Heritage Centre and Advisory Bodies, World Heritage Committee, 29th session, Durban, South Africa, 10–17 July. WHC-05/29 COM/INF.9B.

Drori, G.S. (2005) 'United Nations' Dedications: A World Culture in the Making?' *International Sociology*, 20: 175–99.

Drori, G.S, Meyer, J.W. and Hwang, H. (eds) (2006) *Globalization and Organization: World Society and Organizational Change*, Oxford: Oxford University Press.

Errington, S. (1993) 'Making Progress on Borobudur: An Old Monument in New Order', *Visual Anthropology Review*, 9: 32–59.

Hackenberg, R.A. (2002) 'Closing the Gap between Anthropology and Public Policy: The Route through Cultural Heritage Development', *Human Organization*, 61: 288–98.

Hannerz, U. (1996) *Transnational Connections: Culture, People, Places*, London: Routledge.

Held, D. (1991) 'Democracy, the Nation-State, and the Global System', *Economy and Society*, 20: 138–72.

Herzfeld, M. (1991) *A Place in History: Social and Monumental Time in a Cretan Town*, Princeton: Princeton University Press.

Herzfeld, M. (2008) 'Mere Symbols', *Anthropologica*, 50: 146–55.

Hevia, J.L. (2001) 'World Heritage, National Culture and the Restoration of Chengde', *Positions: East Asia Cultures Critique*, 9: 219–43.

Hobsbawm, E. and Ranger, T. (eds) (1983) *The Invention of Tradition*, Cambridge: Cambridge University Press.

Holton, R.J. (1998) *Globalisation and the Nation-State*, London: St Martin's Press.

Iriye, A. (2001) *Cultural Internationalism and World Order*, Baltimore: Johns Hopkins University Press.

Kirshenblatt-Gimblett, B. (1995) 'Theorizing Heritage', *Ethnomusicology*, 39: 367–80.

Kirshenblatt-Gimblett, B. (1998) *Destination Culture: Tourism, Museums, and Heritage*, Berkeley: University of California Press.

Kirshenblatt-Gimblett, B. (2004) 'Intangible Heritage as Metacultural Production', *Museum International*, 56: 52–64.

Kirshenblatt-Gimblett, B. (2006) 'World Heritage and Cultural Economics', in Ivan Karp, Corinne A. Kratz, Lynn Szwaja and Tomas Ybara-Frausto (eds) *Museum Frictions: Public Cultures/Global Transformations*, Durham, N.C.: Duke University Press.

Logan, W.S. (2001) 'Globalising Heritage: World Heritage as a Manifestation of Modernism, and Challenges from the Periphery', in D. Jones (ed.) *Twentieth Century Heritage: Our Recent Cultural Legacy: Proceedings of the Australia ICOMOS National Conference 2001, 28 November – 1 December 2001, University of Adelaide, Adelaide, Australia*: University of Adelaide and Australia ICOMOS.

Lovell, J. (2006) *Politics Of Cultural Capital. China's Quest For A Nobel Prize In Literature*, Honolulu: University of Hawaii Press.

Lowenthal, D. (1985) *The Past is a Foreign Country*, Cambridge: Cambridge University Press.

Lowenthal, D. (1998) *The Heritage Crusade and the Spoils of History*, Cambridge: Cambridge University Press.

Maswood, S.J. (2000) 'Kakadu and the Politics of World Heritage Listing', *Australian Journal of International Affairs*, 54: 357–72.

Matsuura, K (2000) 'Is the globalisation of the economy creating values for a new civilization?', *Prospects*, 30: 399–404.

Mayor, F. and Tanguiane, S. (1997) *UNESCO – an Ideal in Action: The Continuing Relevance of a Visionary Text*, Paris: UNESCO.

Owens, B.M. (2002) 'Monumentality, Identity and the State: Local Practice, World Heritage, and Heterotopia at Swayambhu, Nepal', *Anthropological Quarterly*, 75: 269–316.

Peleggi, M. (2002) *The Politics of Ruins and the Business of Nostalgia*, Bangkok: White Lotus.

Porter, G.D. (2001) 'Unwitting Actors: The Preservation of Fez's Cultural Heritage', *Radical History Review*, 86: 123–48.

Smith, L. (2006) *Uses of Heritage*, Abingdon: Routledge.

Smith, M. (2002) 'A Critical Evaluation of the Global Accolade: the significance of World Heritage Site status for Maritime Greenwich', *International Journal of Heritage Studies*, 8: 137–51.

Tunbridge, J.E. and Ashworth, G.L. (1996) *Dissonant Heritage: The Management of the Past as a Resource in Conflict*, Chichester: John Wiley and Sons.

Turner, B. (2002) 'Cosmopolitan Virtue, Globalisation and Patriotism', *Theory, Culture and Society*, 19: 45–63.

Turtinen, J. (2000) 'Globalising Heritage – On UNESCO and the Transnational Construction of a World Heritage', *SCORE (Stockholm Center for Organizational Research) Rapportserie* No. 12.

UNESCO (1995) *UNESCO and a Culture of Peace*, Paris: UNESCO.

UNESCO (1998) 'Masterpieces of the Oral and Intangible Heritage of Humanity'. Online. HTTP: <http://www.org/culture/heritage/intangible/index.sht> (accessed 18 May 2003).

UNESCO (2000) *World Culture Report 2000. Cultural Diversity, Conflict and Pluralism*, Paris: UNESCO.

UNESCO Task Force (1999) 'Contribution of the French National Commission for UNESCO to the Work of the Task Force on UNESCO in the Twenty-First Century'. Online. HTTP: <http://www.unesco/taskforce21/ contributions/ france_eng.htm> (accessed 28 April 2003).

Woods, N. (2002) 'Global Governance and the Role of Institutions', in D. Held and A. McGrew (eds) *Governing Globalisation: Power, Authority and Global Governance*, Cambridge: Polity Press.

Wright, S. (1998) 'The Politicization of "Culture" ', *Anthropology Today*, 14: 7–15.

Chapter 2

Politics and Power

The Hiroshima Peace Memorial (Genbaku Dome) as World Heritage

Olwen Beazley

Although assumed to be a depoliticised process, the nomination of places to the World Heritage List is deeply politicised at both the global and the local level. While UNESCO's rhetoric is that the 1972 *Convention Concerning the Protection of the World Cultural and Natural Heritage* (the World Heritage Convention) seeks to protect the heritage of humanity, a global heritage, it is clear from the events that surrounded the inscription of the Hiroshima Peace Memorial (Genbaku Dome) that this heritage is not always uncontested nor is it benign. Differing State Party ideologies and memories can result in global heritage assuming multivalent meanings. In the previous chapter, Askew suggests that UNESCO's World Heritage List has global influence and is

> an arbiter of cultural status and inclusion ... [it] obscures the forms of suppression and manipulation of symbols by its member states which pursue their own ideological agendas by appropriating globally endowed status.
>
> (Askew, Chapter 1, this volume)

Using Askew's proposition, in this chapter I will look at how the Hiroshima Peace Memorial (Genbaku Dome) became inscribed on the World Heritage List in 1996. I will examine how, while all eyes were on the US trying to silence the Japanese nomination at the global level, no attention was paid to how the nomination at the local level served to silence the voices of not only the non-Japanese victims of the atomic blast but also of the survivors.

> The Hiroshima Peace Memorial, Genbaku Dome, stands as a permanent witness to the terrible disaster that occurred when the atomic bomb was used as a weapon for the first time in the history of mankind.
>
> (Japan Agency for Cultural Affairs 1995: 10)

Introduction

At 8.15 a.m. on 6 August 1945, the nuclear bomb *Little Boy* was dropped from the United States (US) aeroplane the *Enola Gay*. It obliterated the city of Hiroshima.

Figure 2.1 The Hiroshima Peace Memorial (Genbaku Dome) World Heritage Site, April
2003 (Photo by the author)

This event brought a conclusive end to World War II and initiated the nuclear arms race of the Cold War (1945–89/91). The purpose of this chapter, however, is to focus on the events that led up to the commemoration of this event at the global level through the inclusion of the Hiroshima Peace Memorial (Genbaku Dome) on the United Nations Educational, Scientific and Cultural Organization's (UNESCO) World Heritage List (List). In doing so, it will challenge the often held assumption that the List and its very formulation are both depoliticised and inclusive and will demonstrate how global international relations play a large part in the success or failure of individual nominations, particularly those with multivalent meanings at the global level. It will also demonstrate how in the process of constructing state-framed narratives and memories associated with the Hiroshima Peace Memorial (Genbaku Dome) for inclusion on the global list, those at the local level were both silenced and excluded.

In 1996 in Merida, Mexico, the World Heritage Committee considered if the Hiroshima Peace Memorial (Genbaku Dome), the pre-eminent symbol of the first use of nuclear weapons, should be included on the World Heritage List for its 'outstanding universal value'.

The consideration of the Hiroshima Peace Memorial (Genbaku Dome) (Dome) nomination by the World Heritage Committee was the culmination of events that witnessed a series of contested narratives and contested memories about the place. The name on the nomination document, Hiroshima Peace Memorial (Genbaku Dome), mirrors this contestation, and reflects the antithetical nature of the heritage legacy of the place. Hiroshima Peace Memorial articulates peace; Genbaku Dome – translated from the Japanese to mean Atom Bomb Dome – articulates war. The main protagonists, Japan and America, had different views of how this nomination should be framed for inclusion on the World Heritage List and the symbolic status that should be attributed to it.

The place

Hiroshima, April 2003; it is a hot spring day. I wander through an urban riverside park under a cloudless, blue, Japanese sky. Voices of men, women and children fill the air, laughing and talking as they picnic beneath trees festooned with candyfloss-pink cherry blossom. This, however, is no normal park. Fifty-eight years earlier the park did not exist. Early on that summer morning, 6 August 1945, the voices here, of people bustling through the streets on their way to work and to school, and of those unwillingly in Hiroshima as enforced labour from Korea, were silenced for-ever. The tranquil park, in the centre of this vibrant Japanese city, is the Hiroshima Peace Memorial Park. It is where the first atomic bomb was dropped as a weapon of mass destruction.

The Hiroshima Peace Memorial Park (The Peace Park) on the banks of the Motoyasu River was designed by Tange Kenzo in 1949 and was built between 1950 and 1964 (Japan Agency for Cultural Affairs 1995). It commemorates many of those who lost their lives in the Hiroshima bombing, but not all, and contains the Dome

Figure 2.2 The Hiroshima Peace Memorial Park, April 2003 (Photo by the author)

and the Cenotaph for the Atomic Bomb Victims, together with many other memorials. The focus of the park is the Dome; the renamed ruin of the former Hiroshima
Prefectural Industrial Promotions Hall (Promotions Hall), a building constructed in
1915 to promote industrial production in the Prefecture. It takes its name from the
five-storey rotunda that is topped by the iron frame of the architectural dome. This
building is a surviving testimony to the events that occurred early on that August
morning.

The Promotions Hall was located 150 metres northwest of the hypocentre of the
atomic blast. It survived because the atomic blast occurred directly above the
building (Japan Agency for Cultural Affairs 1995). Today, when visiting the site,
one is struck by the size for the ghostly building. If compared to the high-rise
buildings of the once again thriving city of Hiroshima that form a backdrop to the
Dome on its eastern side, the Dome appears diminutive. When viewed from the east
side, the city side, looking across the river to the west, the ruined building is sil-
houetted against the sky. This desolate image provides a haunting mnemonic for the
events that allowed this building's survival but caused the total destruction of an
entire city and the loss of 140,000 lives.

The area identified for inscription on the World Heritage List, to commemorate
such a shattering event, is very small. The Dome is set on a piece of grassy ground
that is surrounded by a black, iron-railing fence. This fence circumscribes the
boundary of both the plot on which the Dome stands and also the World Heritage
area itself. The Peace Park is not included in the World Heritage area because at the
time the Dome was nominated the Park was less than 50 years old. Under Japanese

Figure 2.3 The Hiroshima Peace Memorial (Genbaku Dome) on the banks of the Motoyasu River, April 2003 (Photo by the author)

legislation, this meant that it could not be designated as an historic site and consequently could not be considered as part of the World Heritage nomination (Inaba 2003).

Every year on the 6th August the Peace Park is the location of an annual Peace Festival. The first such festival, The Peace Restoration Festival, was on 6 August 1946, and unlike the exclusionary narratives that were to eventuate later, it honoured the survivors of the bomb who were central to the festival: 'amidst tears, the surviving citizens of the city prayed for the peace of the souls of the A-bomb victims and pledged themselves to the restoration of world peace' (Kosakai 1990: 20).

The first Peace Festivals were closely monitored by the occupying Allied powers in Tokyo (Kosakai 1990). Nevertheless, the Festivals endured and achieved the first steps in securing the social construction of Hiroshima as a 'Mecca of World Peace' (Kosakai 1990). The peace festivals also probably helped secure the eventual inscription of the Dome on the World Heritage List as a symbol of hope for lasting peace, not only for the people of Japan, but for the entire world.

The Peace Park is a paradox. The place commemorates the first use of the atomic bomb on a live target. It also commemorates the birth of the nuclear age and the Cold War 'peace'. For the Japanese people it is an icon of peace. It is also a memorial to thousands of people who lost their lives as a result of the bomb and it is a focus for anti-nuclear peace protests. It is not, however, a memorial to all of those who lost their lives on the 6th August 1945, nor does it recognise and pay homage to those who survived. It is a place that has been publicly constructed to articulate and promote a peace ideology and memories formed by the new post-war Japan. In the post-war period the promotion of peace became the main objective for the city of Hiroshima and conformed to the newly developing post-war ideology of Japan as a nation pursuing peace and democracy (Gluck 2003). In 1949, The Hiroshima Peace Memorial City Construction Law (Peace City Law), Article 1, stated that 'this law aims at the construction of Hiroshima as a Peace Memorial City, a symbol of the ideal of making lasting peace a reality' (quoted in Kosakai 1990: 23).

It was under the Peace City Law that the land for the Peace Park was designated and constructed. The US supported the idea of transforming Hiroshima into 'an international showcase that would link the atomic bomb with post war peace' (Yoneyama 2002: 1) on the basis that it would help create Hiroshima as a 'Mecca' of peace and commemorate the birth of the atomic age (Yoneyama 1999). This, in fact, never occurred and there are no new monuments that specifically commemorate the beginning of the atomic age – only those that commemorate the tragic loss of life at Hiroshima in 1945 at the end of World War II.

The rationale behind the US support for transforming Hiroshima into a symbol of peace was political. The US wanted to illustrate that, through the use of the atomic bomb, world peace – or at least the end of World War II – had been achieved, and that it could be maintained by ensuring US atomic superiority and particularly its superiority to the Soviets. The rationale ultimately accommodated the American build-up of nuclear arms in the name of peace (Yoneyama 2002).

Figure 2.4 Cenotaph for the A-Bomb Victims, The Hiroshima Peace Memorial Park, April 2003 (Photo by the author)

The official message of peace from Hiroshima did not end with the Peace Law of 1949. The mayors of both Hiroshima and Nagasaki played a continuing role in spreading the message of peace and anti-nuclear proliferation. In 1975, the municipal assemblies of both Hiroshima and Nagasaki signed up to the *Agreement on Hiroshima and Nagasaki Partnership for Peace Culture Cities*; this agreement stated the cities' commitment to world peace (Tachibana 1996). The peace declarations from the two bombed cities continued and, by 1993, the mayors of Hiroshima and Nagasaki had called for 'an international agreement for the complete abolition of nuclear weapons to be concluded' (Tachibana 1996: 183).

The World Heritage nomination

The stories relating to the nomination and inscription of the Dome to the World Heritage List began in 1993 and they are as varied as they are intriguing. In 1993 it is purported that the US had informally suggested that the Dome should be part of a joint nomination with the Trinity Site, New Mexico, the site where, on 16 July 1945 as part of the Manhattan Project, an atomic bomb was first tested (Domicelj 1994, 2002). Yet, at the time the Dome was nominated to the World Heritage List in 1995, there was no collaboration between Japan and the US over the nomination; in fact, quite the reverse.

My research has uncovered variant memories of how the Dome was nominated to, and became inscribed on, the World Heritage List. Whatever the veracity of these stories obtained through oral testimonies, they illustrate that the framing of how the place and memories pertaining to it were represented was central to both the process of the nomination and the inscription of the site. It also illustrates dissonance in the performance of memory control at the different scales at which heritage operates (Graham, Ashworth and Tunbridge 2000). In the case of the Dome, I record the dissonance between the national and the international scales that became apparent both in the proposed nomination and in final inscription on the World Heritage List. The narratives of how the Dome became included on the List uncover both how the mechanism of World Heritage inscription works, through 'in the corridors' informal discussions, and how the tensions of global responsibilities, and international and domestic politics are played out in the World Heritage arena. I also explore how dissonance at the local and global level is concealed through Japan 'appropriating globally endowed status' (Askew, Chapter 1, this volume) for the site.

Dissonant narratives

In the US, a new thematic approach to the development of its tentative list for World Heritage inscription had been developed; one of the themes it had identified was that of 'scientific and technological achievement'. Under this theme, the US had added the Trinity Site, New Mexico (Domicelj 1994). In 1993, under the auspices of this thematic approach it is reported that a proposal for a joint nomination of the Trinity Site and Hiroshima was made to Japan by the US (Domicelj 2002).

Ms Joan Domicelj, a member of the ICOMOS delegation to Japan in 1993, reported that, whilst in Japan as part of the delegation, the Japanese told her that they had recently received, from the State Department in Washington, a message (letter) suggesting the joint nomination of the Dome and the Trinity Site (Domicelj 1994, 2002; Cleere 2002; Inaba 2003). Subsequently, neither the Japanese nor the Americans have been able, or perhaps willing, to corroborate these events.

Whilst it is possible that discussions at non-governmental organisation (NGO) level may have taken place, a number of members of the former US Delegation to UNESCO's World Heritage Committee, interviewed on this subject, have refuted that any such discussions took place with Japan at a State Party level (Reynolds 2003; Charlton 2004). Robert Milne, former member of the US Delegation to the World Heritage Committee and former US State Department official, also firmly refuted that such a thing could have happened without referring it to the Department of the Interior (Milne 2003). A senior member of the Japanese Delegation in 1993 also stated that no discussions were held at the State Party level, but allows that there may have been NGO level, corridor discussion at the World Heritage Committee meeting in Santa Fe in 1992 (Beazley 2006: 214).

A conversation that reportedly took place between a member of the Japanese Delegation and Dr Henry Cleere, the then ICOMOS International World Heritage Convenor, however, corroborates Domicelj's information and demonstrates that there had been a proposal at some level from the US for joint nomination in 1993/4 (Cleere 2002a). The conversation focused on how the Japanese could progress the nomination of the Dome following the US's purported withdrawal from a joint nomination of the Dome and the Trinity Site, New Mexico.

> ... there was a discussion at one time going ahead between the Japanese and the Americans for a joint nomination ... they [the US and Japan] were considering, very early, preliminary stage of discussion, the possibility of a joint nomination of Hiroshima and the Trinity site in New Mexico ...
>
> ... And I remember I was having lunch with the Japanese at a Bureau [World Heritage Committee Bureau] meeting one day and we'd talked about this, and they said that they wanted to go ahead with this and they weren't sure what the Americans' position was. Well, it just happened that the American delegate [to the World Heritage Bureau Meeting] was sitting a couple of tables away and so I went over and said, tell me about this. He said 'it's dead, forget it, absolutely forget it, if they want to go ahead they go ahead on their own'. This I think must have been Bush period or something, Reagan, I don't know but it was after there had been a change of control on the Hill [the White House] in Washington, it was when all the trouble really started.[1] So I then went back to talk to the Japanese and they were rather saddened by this ... they hoped that this [the joint nomination] could be a statement on the part of the two countries. One of them developed it and the other had it dropped on and you know if they can reconcile themselves it would have been a quite ... well they didn't think Hiroshima would get on the [World Heritage] List otherwise ...
>
> So anyway, we discussed this a little bit further and I said well if you are going to nominate it on your own how are you going to do it ... they said well we are thinking about this and they ran past me ... this paradoxical concept of it being a symbol of peace, in other words the first atomic bomb, the first one led to a period, at that time, of fifty years of non nuclear war ... So I said, yes, it is about the only way you could do it I think. So that was that.
>
> (Interview 14 August 2002, Dr H. Cleere)

The dissonant memories of the State Party representatives over the potential joint nomination of the Dome in 1993 highlights the political nature of this particular nomination and of the World Heritage process in general.

Whatever the facts of the matter in 1995 the Japanese proceeded alone with the Dome nomination and nominated it under cultural criterion (vi):

> Be directly or tangibly associated with events or living traditions, with ideas or with beliefs, with artistic and literary works of outstanding universal significance (the Committee considers that this criterion should justify inclusion in the List only in exceptional circumstances or in conjunction with other criteria cultural or natural).
>
> (UNESCO 1994)

The justification for inscription in the nomination documentation followed the format outlined by Cleere in the reported discussions he had with the Japanese delegate in 1993/4 (Cleere 2002):

> Firstly the Hiroshima Peace Memorial, Genbaku Dome, stands as a permanent witness to the terrible disaster that occurred when the atomic bomb was used as a weapon for the first time in the history of mankind. Secondly, the Dome itself is the only building in existence that can convey directly a physical image of the tragic situation immediately after the bombing. Thirdly, the Dome has become a universal monument for all mankind, symbolizing the hope for perpetual peace and the ultimate elimination of all nuclear weapons on earth.
>
> (Japan Agency for Cultural Affairs 1995: 10).

Ironically, Japan's independent submission of the Dome nomination did not end US involvement. In fact, the US became very active in its attempts to control the way the Dome was presented to the world through the World Heritage nomination process.

Sites associated with war 'are not a priority for the Convention' (Charlton 2004). Whatever the history and origin of the proposed Hiroshima Peace Memorial nomination, this was the US position in relation to its nomination in 1996. As a result, in the lead up to the World Heritage Committee meeting in Merida, which was to consider the inscription of the Dome on the World Heritage List, the US spoke out against the inclusion of war sites on the List and petitioned against it occurring (Milne 2003; Reynolds 2003). This may, however, have been little more than an agenda to prevent the particular inscription of the Dome on the World Heritage List, although this was also the position the US took in relation to the inscription of Auschwitz-Birkenau, Poland in 1978 (Milne 2003). Unlike the case of Auschwitz-Birkenau, however, there was more to the US objection to the Dome inscription than pure heritage philosophy and the inclusion of war sites on the List.[2]

In addition to philosophical arguments being made, there was also considerable lobbying by the US against the inscription of the Dome. This was reported by more than one respondent, although the former head of the US World Heritage Delegation at that time, John Reynolds, says he was not aware of any such lobbying. He said that if it was carried out it would have been by the US Mission in Paris under political directives from the State Department, or by the representative of the State Department who was at that time, in Reynolds' words, 'doing most of the negotiation' (Reynolds 2003).[3]

When it became clear that representatives of the US State Department were not going to be able to prevent the Dome nomination proceeding, by trying to convince ICOMOS of the unsuitability of war-related sites for inclusion on the World Heritage List, the US began to consider other ways in which it might be able to influence the format of the Dome nomination. Ironically, these considerations in the US State Department once more raised the possibility of a joint nomination with a site in the US. Robert Milne, a former member of the US Delegation working for the

World Heritage Centre at the time of the nomination, indicated that there was a discussion surrounding the possibility of seeking a joint transnational nomination with Japan and the US for the site of Hiroshima paired with either the Ferne laboratory, University of Chicago, or White Sands, New Mexico. This was being mooted as a counter nomination to that of the Hiroshima nomination going forward alone. It was suggested that such a nomination could signify both the beginning and the end of the nuclear experiment: Alpha to Omega (Beazley 2006: 228).

This report was also confirmed through an interview with US delegate James Charlton:

> ... there was some discussion of trying to figure out whether or not it made any sense to propose it [a joint nomination] ... our internal view and conclusion was that it did not ... and we didn't think it would work. And we didn't see a way to configure it ... that it didn't potentially make the matter even more difficult ... we never got to ... the official level, in Interior Staff, as far as I know [and] ... the State [Department] had [not] got to the point of saying well, we will propose Pearl Harbor, for example ... the proposal offering ... Pearl Harbor, or potentially some of the other sites as a counter proposal ... ran the very real risk of alienating the Japanese ... with their potentially thinking that the mere suggestion was intended to be deliberately provocative ...
>
> (Interview 7 May 2004, Mr J. Charlton)

Realising there was little scope for manoeuvre on the question of the suitability of war sites, or on the possibility of a joint nomination, the US Delegation then raised concerns regarding the historical integrity of the Dome nomination document. The US suggested to ICOMOS that the nomination should be altered to reflect the context of the events that led to the bombing of Hiroshima, that is, as a response to the continuing Japanese aggression in the Pacific. The US had also made representations, informally, through US ICOMOS to make it clear that they thought that:

> ICOMOS as a learned society ... as the formal review body, was not upholding what we [US] considered to be appropriate canons of historical analysis and writing.
>
> (Interview 7 May 2004, Mr J. Charlton)

The US Administration was particularly concerned that if the nomination was going to proceed there should be an historical context for the inscription. Nevertheless, these efforts by the US did not achieve any change in the ICOMOS support of the Dome nomination or in its recommendations to the Committee. Neither were attempts by the US to influence the Japanese to change their approach in the nomination document, putting Hiroshima in historical context in relation to the events of the entire war, successful. Japan continued with its rationale for inscription linked to the fifty years of world peace following the dropping of the bomb in spite of high-level lobbying by the US State Department (Beazley 2006: 229).

The US Delegation members at the World Heritage Committee meeting in Merida in 1996 were, on heritage grounds, supportive of the nomination. For domestic political reasons, however, they were not able to openly support the Dome nomination. In fact in order to protect the position of the US Administration with its veterans and the American public, at the meeting in Merida the Delegation was required to make a statement against the nomination (Reynolds 2003).

US Delegation support for the nomination is substantiated by information from John Reynolds regarding a meeting in Washington DC, in 1996, between the State Department and the National Park Service, both of which represented the US at the World Heritage Committee meetings. The meeting was held in preparation for the World Heritage Committee meeting in order to discuss the way the consideration of the nomination of the Dome was to be tackled by them. Reynolds reported that:

> ... everybody was sitting around trying to decide what to do and we knew that the Administration was pretty worried about the reaction from the American public, particularly ... the Veterans of the Second World War because they had just gone through the *Enola Gay* controversy over here ... and everyone was looking dour because nobody in the meeting was really a representative of the Administration and everybody in the meeting ... thought that in one way or another, that Hiroshima ought to go on the list and ought to be recognised. I said ... before we figure out the politics of this thing, let's agree on what the right thing to do is, where do we want to get if we weren't limited. And so then we quickly agreed that it should be on the List ... Then we started to evolve a way in which we could represent ourselves as positively as possible without getting the Administration in trouble and you know to tell you the truth I don't have the slightest idea what we decided at that meeting except that we wanted to be able to represent ourselves as powerfully as possible given the political environment.
>
> (Interview 19 August 2003, Mr J. Reynolds)

After all these deliberations, the US delegate to UNESCO's 1996 World Heritage Committee meeting did not oppose the nomination at the time of its consideration by the Committee. After it was successfully inscribed, however, as a matter of record and for the benefit of the US Administration, the following statement was made:

> The United States is disassociating itself from today's decision to inscribe the Hiroshima Peace Memorial on the World Heritage List. The United States and Japan are close friends and allies. We cooperate on security, diplomatic, international and economic affairs around the world. Our two countries are tied by deep personal friendships between many Americans and Japanese. Even so, the United States cannot support its friend in this inscription.

The United States is concerned about the lack of historical perspective in the nomination of the Hiroshima Peace Memorial. The events antecedent to the United States' use of atomic weapons to end World War II are key to understanding the tragedy of Hiroshima. Any examination of the period leading up to 1945 should be placed in the appropriate historical context.

The United States believes the inscription of war sites [is] outside the scope of the Convention. We urge the Committee to address the question of the suitability of war sites for the World Heritage List.

(UNESCO 1996)

Historical context

Why was it that in 1996 the US Administration was at pains to appear opposed to the Dome's World Heritage inscription when in 1993 it was apparently seeking it? The answer lies in the way both nations have constructed Hiroshima in their national and communal histories and memories. It can be suggested that many in the US consider the dropping of the atom bombs on Hiroshima and Nagasaki as the defining acts in the ending of World War II (Hogan 1996). Accordingly, it is apparent that they will only consider Hiroshima synonymous with the end of World War II and the achievement of peace only in this context. A joint scientific nomination with White Sands (as proposed in 1993) may have been acceptable to the US population at large; a sole nomination by Japan of Hiroshima, the site of the first atomic bomb used against a human target, without a clear historical context for the act, was not.

The defeated Japanese, conversely, reconstructed themselves and their values in the early post-war years as a nation looking towards peace and reconstruction, both political and physical (Dower 1996). To them, the Dome could be the focus of this new ideology, leaving the politics of World War II behind them but at the same time paying homage to their dead. The fact that Japan did not propose a joint nomination of Hiroshima and Nagasaki illustrates that the object of the memorial was not a war-related nomination, but a commemoration of the dropping of the atomic bomb on Hiroshima and the subsequent peace movement that grew in Japan. The peace rationale was to be the main message of the Hiroshima Peace Memorial (Genbaku Dome) nomination.

The US Administration's apparent u-turn in relation to the inscription of the Dome can be explained by the events that took place surrounding the proposed *Enola Gay* exhibit at the National Air and Space Museum, Washington DC, in 1993, at the very time the proposed joint nomination was purportedly being discussed. At this time, museum officials had planned an exhibition entitled *'The Crossroads: the End of World War II, the Atomic Bomb, and the Origins of the Cold War'* and had met with Japanese officials and museum professionals to discuss their display proposals. The exhibition was to display the aeroplane the *Enola Gay* and to provide an historical context to the atomic bomb drops on Japan (Harwit 1995).

The exhibition of the *Enola Gay* was designed to commemorate the 50th anniversary of the end of World War II. Its approach to the display of the aircraft that dropped the atomic bomb on Hiroshima was seen by many Americans to be unpatriotic because it portrayed the event in an objective historical context. Amongst other aspects, the exhibition illustrated the terrible effects of the atomic explosion and its aftermath at ground zero. The proposed exhibition displayed exhibits such as the 'shadow pictures', images of silhouettes of human forms that were created on stonework where people were sitting or standing when they were vaporised in the blast. By 1994, the proposed exhibition had caused a huge domestic political uproar (Harwit 1995). In September 1994 resolutions were passed in the American Senate stating that:

> any exhibit displayed by the National Air and Space Museum with respect to the *Enola Gay* should reflect appropriate sensitivity toward the men and women who faithfully and selflessly served the United States during World War II and should avoid impugning the memory of those who gave their lives for freedom.
> (Senate Resolution United States of America 1994)

The proposed exhibition was interpreted by many, including veterans, as a revisionist history of the era and one that cast Americans as racist war criminals (Harwit 1995; Wallace 1995). According to Harwit, Director of the Museum, much of this criticism was the result of display texts being read by critics without the accompanying graphics, which would have provided balance in the exhibition's message (Harwit 1995).

One can only wonder, however, if there was more than one political agenda in play during this period as messages from the Administration appear at times to conflict. From an interview with John Reynolds it has become evident that the US Delegation had received instructions from the US Administration, via the State Department, that they must not appear to be openly supporting the Dome nomination but at this stage apparently they were to try and support it

> ... we had been instructed to go to the meeting to do all we could to get it put on the list but we would not be able to vote yes.
> (Interview 19 August 2003, Mr J. Reynolds)

Reynolds confirmed that although the US Administration was not against the nomination of the Dome it could not support it for fear of a domestic backlash, in relation to the veterans groups and the *Enola Gay* controversy, as had happened three years earlier (Reynolds 2003). With this approach to the nomination, the US was simply protecting political interests at home.

James Charlton (2004) explains that the US Administration, through its Delegation, made very concerted efforts in its consideration of the Dome nomination to avoid a diplomatic incident with the Japanese while at the same time appeasing the US veterans:

... if you looked at the grand calculus of international politics ... we certainly didn't want to alienate the Japanese and our State Department didn't want us to alienate the Japanese unnecessarily. At least ... on issues involving a co-operation ... on something that's as mundane, by and large, as World Heritage. So some of the intellectual contortions and so on that we were going through, and our efforts to come up with ways that wouldn't inflame the situation further, I think a lot of it has to be viewed in that light.

... We really wanted to find, to continue to find ways to cooperate, we didn't want to cause unnecessary irritation or by the actions we took inflame the situation. And I am convinced that if we had simply gone in there [the World Heritage Committee meeting] and voted no, it would have made the papers of the world.

(Interview 7 May 2004, Mr J. Charlton)

The whole process surrounding the nomination of the Dome by Japan, and the response to it by the US, clearly demonstrates that 'global heritage of humanity' has multivalent meanings. It also demonstrates the economic imperatives of states parties to the Convention to foster continued global trade and good international relations and how these imperatives influence the way the Convention is operated and decisions within its mandate made.

World Heritage inscription – legitimising exclusion at the local level?

In addition to the dissonance of the Dome nomination at an international level, there was also dissonance at a local level. As Askew has argued, some World Heritage nominations are 'animated by various agendas, some of which clearly involve the physical and symbolic exclusion of certain groups' (Askew, Chapter 1, this volume). This is clearly demonstrated in a number of World Heritage nominations, as discussed by Askew in the previous chapter, and is also evident in the nomination and subsequent inscription of the Dome. Tunbridge and Ashworth (1996) argue that there are often dissonant memories associated with heritage places, because as one or more memories are privileged, others are silenced. While this privileging may not be uncommon at both the local and state level, the clear sanctioning of it by a States Party for inclusion on an international heritage register demonstrates strong identity formation in play. It also demonstrates that the World Heritage Committee and its Advisory Bodies are not always able to detect and influence or prevent the promotion of selective and hegemonic narratives. This supports Askew's proposition that States Parties' 'representational agendas' are un-opposed by UNESCO in the 're-badging of those monuments and sites already objectified and commodified at the national and sub-national level' (Askew, Chapter 1, this volume).

A significant methodological hurdle to ensuring the World Heritage List includes the global heritage of plural cultures and cultural identities, as opposed to those of nations and national identities, exists in the representation protocols at UNESCO.

As membership of UNESCO extends only to governments, which are represented by individuals, the representation of minority cultures and ethnic minorities within nation-states can be undermined. The representation protocols reflect and encourage the view that the cultures of nation-states are homogeneous and cohesive, and propagate the myth of one nation one culture (Anderson 1991). Cultural identity and national identity, as Tomlinson illustrates, are not one and the same thing; in fact, often they are heavily contested terrains (Tomlinson 1991). The implication for the representation and protection of cultural diversity is that however plural the Committee attempts to make the List, it will still only represent and reflect the heritage deemed suitable by the States Parties and their representatives who participate in the UNESCO discourse to promote it.

> Pluralism is a necessary part of UNESCO's existence as an institution for the conduct of the global conversation, so pluralism cannot be contested within its rhetoric: it is a given of UNESCO discourse.
>
> (Tomlinson 1991: 71)

What Tomlinson asserts is clearly apparent, but pluralism and true cultural diversity can never be achieved if the minority voices of the world are never heard through the very institution set up to provide a forum for a discourse between cultures. In this light, the World Heritage List, therefore, can never aim to be fully representative or inclusive of the heritage of the world as its concept struggles against the unwitting, but inherently exclusive, paradigm that is UNESCO.

At Hiroshima the dissonant memories and multivalent interests have been masked and silenced by the state-framed nomination and subsequent inscription of the Dome. These memories are those associated with the non-Japanese dead, especially of Koreans taken to Japan as forced labour during the war, and also of the *hibakusha*, the survivors of the bomb. The memory of the commemorated event associated with these groups is not one that sits easily with the State-sanctioned one that articulates the ideologies of the new post-war Japan. These memories are silenced by the dominant rhetoric of the Japanese government and its exclusionary practices (Yoneyama 1992, 1999) and subsequently globally legitimised by inclusion on UNESCO's World Heritage List. Thus, as Graham et al. underline, 'heritage privileges and empowers an elitist narrative of place' and 'dominant ideologies create specific place identities which reinforce support for particular state structures and related political ideologies' (Graham, Ashworth and Tunbridge 2000:37).

At a local level, the dissonant commemoration of the dead at Hiroshima has been a long-running issue for the Korean community still resident in Hiroshima (Yoneyama 1992). A metaphor for this dissonance is the Korean memorial to the victims of Hiroshima. From 1970 until 1999 the memorial was located not in the Peace Park but on the far side of the river that marks its boundary (Kosakai 1990). The location of the memorial in what was a less than auspicious position, at the junction of numerous roads, had caused some outspoken Japanese and Koreans living in Japan to question the dominant global narrative of the city of Hiroshima as a city of world peace. The following extract of a letter from one such person illustrates the dissonance in commemoration of the dead of Hiroshima:

> The fact that ... discrimination and exclusion against Koreans are present in Hiroshima, the city which is a so-called mecca of peace and the anti-nuclear, means that the city is disgracing itself in the world's eyes; it also indicates the shameful nature of Japan and its people, that they cannot imagine any victims other then their own kind. While proclaiming on the one hand, 'Rest in peace, as we shall not repeat the evil', the city is on the other hand already committing an 'evil', an evil which is called ethnic discrimination ... How can Korean atom bomb victims rest in peace when treated in such an unjust manner?
>
> (Onishi Masayuki 1986 quoted in Yoneyama 1992: 173)

The dominant memory of Hiroshima as a site of solely Japanese loss is one that the World Heritage inscription unwittingly sanctions. Nowhere in the justification for inscription does it mention other nationalities that were killed by the bomb; it especially does not mention the deaths of the mobilised Korean labour in Hiroshima as a result of Japan's aggression in Asia. The significance of this omission, of the forgetting by Japan of its role as aggressor in the war, once again illustrates Connerton's (Connerton 1989) point about creating a 'barrier' between the real past and the imagined future. It also illustrates how the dominant state memory can

Figure 2.5 The Hiroshima Peace Memorial Park, Korean Memorial, April 2003 (Photo by the author)

overshadow those of minority groups within a society, and in so doing portray the memory at a national and global level as consonant:

> This kind of memory transforms the fragmented images of the past into see-mingly coherent and consistent knowledge, at once shaping and limiting the majority's view of the minority. Such memories, moreover, gain material and form and continue to invest the dominant ideology as they become inscribed in institutions and embedded in everyday practices.
>
> (Yoneyama 1992: 199)

The Japanese *hibakusha*, as a group of survivors of the bomb also hold memories that do not conform to the state sanctioned commodification of Hiroshima as a city of world peace, looking only to the future, not to the past (Yoneyama 1992). In the aggressive construction of its post-war ideology of peace and progress, the city of Hiroshima, and the State Party of Japan, have also marginalised the voices of the atomic bomb survivors. Many of these survivors tell stories of their experiences of the bomb, often to school groups, in order to convey the horror of their experiences and what living through 6 August 1945, and the days, weeks and months after it, was actually like (Yoneyama 1992). Their dark stories provide a stark contrast to the bright and clean city of today's Hiroshima. They also tell these stories to com-memorate the dead who, somehow, since the first commemorative ceremony in 1946, have become whitewashed in the shiny narrative of peace: 'these survivors deplore the fact that the memories of the dead are shared less and less over the years (Yoneyama 1992: 17). Thus it can be seen that the state-sanctioned memory and construction of Hiroshima as a Mecca for world peace masks multivalent memories and narratives associated with the place. The sanctification of the place by the World Heritage Committee contributes to this masking in the 'imagined commu-nity' (Anderson 1991) of the heritage world and justifies it as a 'project of symbolic domination' (Askew, Chapter 1, this volume).

Conclusion

By using the example of the Hiroshima Peace Memorial (Genbaku Dome), this chapter has demonstrated that although cultural heritage, as identified through the World Heritage List, is ostensibly depoliticised, in fact it is a deeply political and sometimes contested terrain both at the global and local levels. It has also demon-strated that, as Askew (Askew, Chapter 1, this volume) has suggested, Turtinen's (2000) claim that UNESCO is a globalising force and producer of uniformity of heritage value is unfounded. The Hiroshima Peace Memorial nomination was wholly constructed and manipulated by the States Parties and by ICOMOS to meet nationalistic and international diplomatic imperatives. The World Heritage Committee is not a 'power centre and forceful, hegemonising model of cultural significance' (Askew, Chapter 1, this volume); in fact, by the time the Dome nomination reached the Committee the cultural symbols, values and memories that comprised the nomination had long since been contested, created and utilised at the national and global level. Further, the erasure of the Korean experience in the bombing of Hiroshima supports Askew's (Askew, Chapter 1, this volume) point that World Heritage inscription can assist in the unwelcome homogenisation of cultural difference within the boundaries of nation-states. UNESCO's processes do not provide an opportunity to question or validate the veracity of the heritage it legitimises through World Heritage inscriptions, only to assess it against predetermined heritage criteria. Thus States Parties are able to manipulate heritage to meet their own ideologies and memory constructions while at the same time disempowering and subjugating the memories and heritages of minority groups.

Notes

1 Dr Cleere has stated that this discussion must have taken place in 1994. The change in Washington was January 1993 from Bush to Clinton, which is probably what Cleere refers to. Mr Milne and Mr Masuda were both present at the sitting of the Bureau meeting in Paris June 1993 but Mr Masuda was not present in 1994. It is probable therefore that the Japanese delegate was not Mr Masuda or that the discussions took place in 1993. Cleere was quite clear however that Mr Milne and Mr Masuda were the individuals involved.

2 The US did not think such places as Auschwitz-Birkenau should be included on the World Heritage List because they did not reflect the great achievements of man, which the US strongly believed, was the purpose of the List (Milne 2003).

3 Through an introduction from Reynolds, an interview was sought with the individual concerned but unfortunately this was not secured. There may have been other reasons why the US was opposed to the Dome inscription on the World Heritage List. These reasons could relate to the broader political motivations that were behind the bombing in 1945. Contemporary war-time accounts have revealed that the major motivation for dropping the bomb was to send a sign to Stalin and the Soviet Union by showing the US's atomic power. It was intended that this would prevent the Soviet Union's aspirations for gaining a power share in the division of post-war Eastern Europe and the Far East. President Truman wanted to 'roll back' the Potsdam Agreement that agreed to the Soviet Union holding a portion of post-war power if they entered the war against Japan. Truman used the US's atomic capability and the results of its use as a warning to the Soviet Union (Burchett 1993; Sherwin 1995). They were also probably to do with the politics of the Cold War and how these politics in the early to mid 1990s still heavily influenced the way the US thought about World War II as a 'just' and 'good war' and the way they wished it to be represented to the World (Sherwin 1995). It is probable that it is for these historical reasons that the US did not desire the Dome inscribed on the World Heritage List without its historical context. The US may have also feared that the inscription would provide an indelible anti-American focus on the historical use of the atomic bomb, the start of the Cold War and the broader proliferation of weapons of mass destruction. For an excellent and detailed exploration of this issue see Yoneyama, L. 1992. *Hiroshima Narratives and the Politics of Memory*, Stanford University.

References

Anderson, B. (1991) *Imagined Communities: Reflections on origin and spread of nationalism*, New York, Verso.

Beazley, O. (2006) Drawing a Line Around A Shadow? Including Associative, Intangible Cultural Heritage Values on the World Heritage List, unpublished PhD Thesis, Australian National University, Canberra, submitted July 2006.

Burchett, W. (1983) *Shadows of Hiroshima*, Norfolk: The Thetford Press.

Charlton, J. (2004) 'The inscription of the Hiroshima Peace Memorial on the World Heritage List', unpublished telephone interview transcript, 7 May.

Cleere, H. (2002) 'The inscription of the Hiroshima Peace Memorial and the World Heritage Committee's Global Strategy', unpublished interview transcript, Paris, France.

Cleere, H. (2003) 'The Hiroshima Peace Memorial', Email (23 July 2003).

Commonwealth of Australia Permanent Delegation to UNESCO Paris (1996) 'Inward Cablegram: UNESCO: World Heritage Bureau and Committee Meetings, Merida, Mexico 2–7 December 1996', unpublished Australian and World Heritage Group Department of Environment Sport and the Territories, Canberra, Australia.

Connerton, P. (1989) *How Societies Remember*, Cambridge: Cambridge University Press.

Domicelj, J. (1994) 'Diverse Cultural Values and Conservation Principles', in D. Marshall (ed.) *Diversity, Place and the Ethics of Conservation*, Canberra: Australian Heritage Commission.

—— (2002) 'The inscription of the Hiroshima Peace Memorial on the World Heritage List, Criterion (vi) and the Global Strategy', unpublished interview transcript, 27 July, Leura, Australia.

Dower, J. W. (1996) 'The Bombed: Hiroshimas and Nagasakis in Japanese Memory' in M. J. Hogan (ed.) *Hiroshima in History and Memory*, Cambridge: Cambridge University Press.

Graham, B. Ashworth, G.L. and Tunbridge, J.E. (2000) *A Geography of Heritage: Power Culture and Economy*, London: Arnold.

Harwit, M. (1995) 'Academic Freedom in the "Last Act"' *The Journal of American History*, 82 (3):1064–83.

Huyssen, A. (2003) *Present Pasts: Urban Palimpsests and the Politics of Memory*, Stanford, California: Stanford University Press.

ICOMOS (1996) 'Hiroshima Peace Memorial Genbaku Dome, Japan 775', unpublished Evaluation Report, Paris.

Inaba, N. (2003) 'The inscription of Hiroshima on the World Heritage List', unpublished interview transcript, 5 April, Kyoto, Japan.

Japan Agency for Cultural Affairs (1995) 'Hiroshima Peace Memorial Genbaku Dome World Heritage Nomination', unpublished World Heritage Nomination 775.

Kosakai, Y. (1990) *Hiroshima Peace Reader*, Twelfth edition, Hiroshima: Hiroshima Peace Culture Foundation.

Milne, R. (2003) 'Inscription of Auschwitz and Hiroshima on the World Heritage List', unpublished telephone interview transcript, 28 February.

Reynolds, J. (2003) 'Inscription of the Hiroshima Peace Memorial on the World Heritage List in 1996', unpublished telephone interview transcript, 19 August.

Sherwin, M. J. (1995) 'Hiroshima as politics and history', *The Journal of American History*, 82 (3):1085–93.

Tachibana, S. (1996) 'The Quest for Peace Culture: The A Bomb Survivors' Log Struggle and the New Movement for Redressing Foreign Victims of Japan's War' in M. J. Hogan (ed.) *Hiroshima in History and Memory*, Cambridge: Cambridge University Press.

Tunbridge J.E. and Ashworth, G.L. (1996) *Dissonant Heritage: The Management of the Past as a Resource in Conflict*, Chichester: John Wiley and Son.

Turtinen, J. (2000) 'Globalising Heritage – On UNESCO and the Transnational Construction of a World Heritage' in SCORE (Stockholm Centre for Organizational Research) Rapportserie No 12, 2000.

United States of America (1994) 'Senate Resolution 257 – Relating to the "Enola Gay" Exhibit (Senate-September 19, 1994)', *The Journal of American History*, 82 (3):1136.

UNESCO (1994) 'Operational Guidelines for the Implementation of the World Heritage Convention', Paris, Intergovernmental Committee for the Protection of the World Cultural and Natural Heritage (World Heritage Committee).

UNESCO (1996) 'Report of the Rapporteur on the Twentieth Session of the World Heritage Committee, Merida, Mexico, 2–7 December 1996', unpublished World Heritage Committee paper WHC-96/CONF.201/21 ANNEX V, Paris.

Wallace, M. (1995) 'The Battle for the Enola Gay', *Museum News* 6062. (July-Aug) 40–45.

Yoneyama, L. (1992) *Hiroshima Narratives and the politics of memory: A Study of Power Knowledge and Identities*, Ph. D. diss., Stansford University.

—— (1999) *Hiroshima Traces: Time, Space, and the Dialectics of Memory*, Berkeley: University of California Press.

—— (2002) 'Remembering and Imagining the Nuclear Annihilation in Hiroshima', *The Getty Conservation Institute Newsletter*.

Chapter 3

World Heritage, authenticity and post-authenticity

International and national perspectives

Sophia Labadi[1]

Authenticity has always been an essential qualifying criterion for the inclusion of sites on the World Heritage List. Nonetheless, it might arguably be considered as one of the most slippery concepts in heritage conservation. This is testified by the numerous debates on this concept and its changing definitions and guidelines adopted by the World Heritage Committee up until the 1990s. This is also reflected in the profuse academic research in the 1990s, triggered in particular by the 1994 Nara Conference on Authenticity. Since then, reflections on authenticity have faded away in the academic sphere and at the intergovernmental level of the World Heritage Committee. However, numerous fundamental questions related to this concept remain: How have States Parties understood the concept of authenticity, and explained and represented it in their nomination dossiers of sites submitted for inclusion on the World Heritage List? Can different definitions of authenticity be detected according to the geographical location of nominated sites? What happened from 1994 onward? Can changes be detected in the way in which States Parties defined authenticity? Did they integrate the Nara Document on Authenticity in their explanation and representation of authenticity in nomination dossiers? If so, how?

The aim of this chapter is to answer these questions. To do so, it first details the evolution of the definition of authenticity at the international level of the World Heritage Committee. Second, it analyses the ways in which States Parties have understood and interpreted this concept and how they have integrated it into their nomination dossiers. The last section of this chapter explains the postmodern and post-structuralist dimensions of authenticity in World Heritage and argues that we may have arrived at a concept that could be more accurately termed 'post-authenticity'. The conclusion of this chapter suggests the need for publications showing States Parties' relative understandings of post-authenticity; these would help to demonstrate the principles of diversity that are fundamental to the Nara Document.

Changing definitions at the international level

1977–94: four degrees of authenticity

Although the authenticity of a site is an essential criterion for its inscription on the World Heritage List, this concept is not mentioned in the text of the *Convention*

Concerning the Protection of the World Cultural and Natural Heritage (henceforth referred to as the World Heritage Convention). Nonetheless, it appears in the first and subsequent versions of the *Operational Guidelines for the Implementation of the World Heritage Convention* (henceforth Operational Guidelines). These Guidelines constitute the basis for all decisions regarding the implementation of the World Heritage Convention (Slatyer 1984: 6). They are flexible, can be revised at any time by the World Heritage Committee and have been modified fourteen times over the past thirty-five years. The Guidelines thus illustrate the principle of evolutionary interpretation, in line with Francioni's (2002: 3) point that the meaning of a treaty provision is not identified in the light of the original intent and circumstances existing at the time of its adoption, but in light of the legal and social context existing at present.

In 1977, the first version of the Operational Guidelines was drafted (UNESCO 20 October 1977). Paragraph 9 clearly indicates that a site nominated for inclusion on the World Heritage List should meet the test of authenticity 'in design, materials, workmanship and setting; authenticity does not limit consideration to original form and structure but includes all subsequent modifications and additions, over the course of time, which in themselves possess artistic or historical values' (ibid.). Therefore, to be inscribed on the World Heritage List, a site needs to meet this test of authenticity as well as one or more of the six cultural heritage criteria that clarify 'outstanding universal value', the core concept of the World Heritage Convention. Explanation of the degree of authenticity of a nominated site is requested to be detailed in the nomination dossier form, the key document for the inclusion of properties on the World Heritage List. The mention, in this 1977 version of authenticity, that all subsequent modifications to a building are valuable and should be conserved, refers back to the principles of Article 11 of the 1964 *International Charter for the Conservation and Restoration of Monuments and Sites* (the so-called Venice Charter).

Although paragraph 9 of the 1977 version of the Operational Guidelines is rather short, further information on authenticity can be found in paragraph 8, which indicates that information must be provided on the state of preservation of the property in nomination dossiers (UNESCO 20 October 1977). Paragraph 8 also indicates that the state of preservation of the property should be evaluated in comparison to the state of preservation of other similar properties. Furthermore, during the 1977 session of the World Heritage Committee some delegates insisted that changes of the original function of the property did not violate its authenticity. The Committee nonetheless recognised that the authenticity of a building should be considered as lost when this new function had necessitated irreversible changes to the original form and to the material used in the work (UNESCO 17 October 1977: 5).

In 1979, Michel Parent (1979: 19) provided further and, for that time, forward-looking reflections on authenticity. He stressed the difficulty of assessing a concept which 'is relative and depends on the nature of the property involved'. He explains that the four degrees of authenticity detailed in the Operational Guidelines have to be assessed according to the property, its history and the culture where it belongs: 'the nature of a material, its finishing, its structural use, and its expressive use, the very nature of the civilization which built the building ... are all different factors according to which the idea of authenticity can be understood differently' (Parent ibid.). He illustrates his argument with the case of a wooden temple in Kyoto (Japan) in which decayed parts of timber have been replaced but which remains nonetheless authentic. He thus introduces, fifteen years beforehand, some of the conceptions that were to animate the Nara conference. What is interesting here is that Parent seems to stress that the definition of the four degrees of authenticity introduced in the 1977 Operational Guidelines provides a flexible framework that can be applied to the diversity of the world's properties. However, as will be highlighted later on, these four degrees of authenticity have not really been defined, understood or used as a flexible and relative framework.

In the 1980 version of the Operational Guidelines, the criterion of authenticity was revised (UNESCO October 1980 paragraph 18[b]). The sentence referring to the importance of subsequent modifications and additions in the 1977 paragraph from the Operational Guidelines on authenticity was removed. It was replaced by another sentence on reconstruction: 'the Committee stressed that reconstruction is only acceptable if it is carried out on the basis of complete and detailed documentation on the original and to no extent on conjecture' (ibid.). This addition has remained part of the definition of authenticity until the 2005 revised version of the Operational Guidelines. Neither the report of the 1980 session of the World Heritage Committee nor that of its Bureau record the reasons for this added guideline on reconstruction (UNESCO 29 September 1980; UNESCO 28 May 1980). This guideline might have resulted from the inclusion of the Historic Centre of Warsaw on the World Heritage List in 1980 (Figure 3.1). The Old Market Place and adjacent buildings were entirely reconstructed after their total destruction during the Second World War. As indicated by Pressouyre (1996: 12), this property was included on the List as a unique example of the excellent and careful reconstruction of a group of buildings to its previous appearance. However, the Committee might have feared that an increased number of reconstructed properties would be nominated for inclusion on the List following this inscription. Its inclusion certainly expanded the boundaries of the notion of authenticity and, as a result, made this term difficult to define. Indeed, with the inscription of this property on the List, authenticity could also be defined as its antithesis: that is, what is false, reconstructed (Robert 1995: 8).

In 1983, Parent presented further reflections on the notion of authenticity to the seventh session of the Bureau of the World Heritage Committee. He stressed, in particular, that erroneous or fanciful restorations should be condemned. He also discussed changes and additions to buildings from different centuries. On the one hand, Article 11 of the Venice Charter recommends that all contributions from succeeding centuries should be retained. On the other hand, Parent argued that some restorations, including those by nineteenth-century architects such as Viollet-le-Duc, were not undertaken in a sympathetic and authentic manner. These architects attempted to restore sites to their so-called original state, sometimes in a fanciful manner, ignoring the contributions from preceding centuries. Parent (1983: 4)

Figure 3.1 Old Market Place of Warsaw, reconstructed to its pre-Second World War appearance (Photo courtesy D. Vallee)

asked whether these fanciful restorations of sites should be regarded as betrayals of or contributions to the past. Parent then explained that the World Heritage Committee and ICOMOS (International Council on Monuments and Sites) had not always been rigorous in their evaluation of nominated sites that had been restored in a fanciful manner (ibid.). Subsequently, Pressouyre (1996: 11–12) made the same observation. On the one hand, the addition of the Historic City of Carcassonne in France to the World Heritage List was deferred in 1985 because of the interventions by Viollet-le-Duc. He restored the city at the end of the 19th century and made some decisions based on his own assumptions and not on historical facts. On the other hand, the Medieval City of Rhodes, which was restored in a fanciful manner in the Fascist era, was nonetheless inscribed on the World Heritage List in 1988.

Management Guidelines for World Cultural Heritage Sites, an official publication written by Feilden and Jokilehto and edited by ICCROM (International Centre for the Study of the Preservation and Restoration of Cultural Property) and ICOMOS, the two official advisory bodies (for cultural heritage matters) named in the World Heritage Convention, in collaboration with the World Heritage Centre, provides one of the most detailed explanations of the four dimensions of authenticity (Feilden and Jokilehto 1993: 66–75). However, it offers a Eurocentric understanding of them. Indeed, according to this publication, any necessary treatment should respect the *original* materials, workmanship, design and setting of the property. When discussing treatments in relation to authenticity of materials, for instance, Feilden and Jokilehto (1993: 67) stress that the historic fabric must be maintained, 'avoiding replacement of even the oldest structures so far as these form the historical continuity of the area'. For them, such a treatment should 'respect historic material, to distinguish new material from historic so as not to fake or to mislead the observer (…)'. They insist that the replacement of original materials is only acceptable 'if it is vital for the survival of the remaining original structure' (Feilden and Jokilehto 1993: 69). They are thus clearly committed to the principles of 'minimum intervention' in the sense that restoration work should only be undertaken when absolutely necessary and any treatment used should obey the rule of reversibility. These statements and viewpoints are in conformity with the vision of the World Heritage Convention, which aims to preserve sites for the benefits of future generations. By adopting the 'minimum intervention' viewpoint, present generations can leave monuments and sites in the same state as they enjoyed them for future generations.

These understandings and explanations of the four degrees of authenticity, in particular those related to authenticity of materials, do not take into account non-European approaches that do not consider the authenticity of a property as lying essentially in its original materials. Hence the importance of the 1994 Nara Conference.

From the 1994 Nara Document on Authenticity to the recognition of integrity

The difficulties in defining authenticity, noted in the previous paragraphs, were voiced during the World Heritage Committee sessions in the 1980s and early 1990s (see for instance UNESCO 14 December 1992). According to von Droste and Bertilsson (1995: 5), these difficulties were reflected in the very succinct explanation of the authenticity of sites in nominations for inclusion on the World Heritage List. For this reason the World Heritage Committee called for a conference on authenticity at its sixteenth session in 1992 (UNESCO 14 December 1992: 8). This conference, organised by the Japanese government and held in Nara (Japan) in November 1994, had two aims: first to define better the concept of authenticity and second to give a new dynamic to the World Heritage Convention and make it more relevant to the diversity of world cultures (von Droste and Bertilsson 1995: 7). Its location in a non-European country symbolised a move away from the Western interpretation of authenticity from the Operational Guidelines. Forty-five experts from twenty-eight countries participated in this conference. During this meeting it was recognised that whilst the word authenticity did not necessarily exist in all languages, the concept itself – of being true or genuine – did (UNESCO 21 November 1994). It was also acknowledged that most historic buildings are altered by the actions of nature and their day-to-day use and that these changes are part of their historic stratification and contribute to their value. This is a very important statement and recognises, for instance, that even fanciful restorations such as those undertaken by nineteenth-century architects such as Viollet-le-Duc are important contributions to the history of the building. As highlighted previously, the nomination of 'The Historic City of Carcassonne' was deferred by the World Heritage Committee in 1985 because of the interventions by Viollet-le-Duc. This property was, however, re-nominated and subsequently included on the World Heritage List in 1997, since it was recognised that the restoration campaign by Viollet-le-Duc was an important contribution to its history.

The *Nara Document on Authenticity* (henceforth referred to as the *Nara Document*) was also adopted at this meeting. It recognises that the values for which sites are being conserved provide a basis for assessing all aspects of authenticity (UNESCO 21 November 1994: Article 9). These values can be understood from diverse sources of information, such as historical or architectural ones. Article 11 adds that authenticity is a relative criterion that can change from one culture to another, 'and even within the same culture'. Most importantly, the *Nara Document* recognises that the authenticity of a site is rooted in specific socio-cultural contexts, corresponds to specific values and can only be understood and judged within those specific contexts and according to these values (Articles 11 and 12). In Japan, for instance, the conservation of wooden buildings is traditionally based on complete dismantling and reconstruction using new wood (Sekino 1996: 18). As Pressouyre (1996: 12) states, the authenticity of Japanese wooden buildings is 'essentially attached to function, subsidiary to form, but by no means to material'. This authenticity also lies in the act of reconstruction which employs traditional skills. This is reflected in Article 13 of the *Nara Document*, which details that the assessment of the authenticity of a building is based on a multiplicity of aspects, including 'form and design, materials and substance, use and function, traditions and techniques, location and setting, and spirit and feeling, and other internal and external factors'. This article clearly demonstrates that the four degrees of authenticity provided up to 1994 in the Operational Guidelines were far too narrow to judge the wealth and diversity of the world's heritage (see UNESCO February 1995, for example). Article 13 also demonstrates that the definition of authenticity provided in the Operational Guidelines over-emphasises the protection of the material dimension of cultural heritage, resulting in the exclusion of many non-European ways of caring for heritage.

Despite the importance of the *Nara Document* and the key definition it provides of authenticity, the World Heritage Committee did not modify paragraph 24 (b)(i) of the Operational Guidelines (see UNESCO February 1996, for example) until its 2005 revision. This gap between the adoption of the *Nara Document* and its inclusion in the Operational Guidelines has never been clarified by the World Heritage Committee. This is all the more difficult to understand since a number of official meetings stressed that relevant articles of the *Nara Document* should be included in the Operational Guidelines, including the 'Authenticity and Integrity in an African context' meeting, held in Great Zimbabwe in May 2000 (UNESCO 9 October 2000). The 1998 second edition of *Management Guidelines for World Cultural Heritage Sites* reflects this omission of the *Nara Document* in official texts related to the implementation of the World Heritage Convention. Indeed, this publication only refers to authenticity in terms of material, workmanship, design and setting; it does not deal with other forms of authenticity referred to and detailed in the *Nara Document*.

The 2005 version of the Operational Guidelines introduced the notion of 'integrity' in relation to cultural heritage and related it to that of authenticity in the title of section II.E: 'Integrity and/or authenticity'. Paragraph 88 defines integrity as 'a measure of the wholeness and intactness of the natural and/or cultural heritage and its attributes. Examining the conditions of integrity therefore requires assessing the extent to which the property: a) includes all elements necessary to express its outstanding universal value; b) is of adequate size to ensure the complete representation of the features and processes which convey the property's significance; c) suffers from adverse effects of development and/or neglect' (UNESCO February 2005: Paragraph 88). Paragraph 89 insists that the physical fabric of cultural heritage properties should be in good condition and 'the impact of deterioration processes controlled. A significant proportion of the elements necessary to convey the totality of the value conveyed by the property should be included' (ibid. Paragraph 89). Understandably, these elements, which must be representative of the outstanding universal value of the site, also need to be authentic. Whilst the title of section II.E seems to include the possibility of a choice between the conditions of 'integrity' and 'authenticity', paragraph 79 clarifies that cultural heritage properties *must* fully meet the conditions of authenticity. Indeed, a site or monument can easily fulfil the conditions of integrity and possess all the elements necessary and in adequate size to express its outstanding universal value, at the same time as these elements can be totally false and fail to meet the criterion of authenticity.

The first section of this chapter has thus detailed the different and evolving definitions of authenticity at the international level and the enlargement of the boundaries of this concept to make it applicable to the world's diversity. How have States Parties understood, explained and represented this concept of authenticity in nomination dossiers of sites for inclusion on the World Heritage List? Can different definitions of authenticity be detected according to the geographical location of nominated sites? Can different definitions of authenticity be detected before and after 1994? Have States Parties integrated the *Nara Document on Authenticity* in their explanations and representations of authenticity? If so, how? The next sections of this chapter seek to answer these questions.

Methodology

This section analyses the way in which States Parties have understood the notion of authenticity over the past thirty years. It is based on in-depth analyses of 106 nomination dossiers for sites located in 18 countries (see Figure 3.2). To detect changes in the interpretation of authenticity over time and across geographical location, the selection of sites was based on non-probability sampling. Three categories of sites were selected to allow multiple comparisons and to make the identification of patterns easier. The first group consists of religious properties from Europe, the largest category of sites on the World Heritage List (ICOMOS 2003

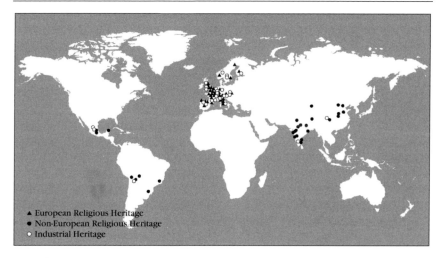

Figure 3.2 Location of sites which nomination dossiers were analysed (from Labadi 2007: 156)

and 2004). Because of the numerical importance of religious properties on the World Heritage List, it was decided to sample them further according to their geographical location. A second group of religious properties in non-European countries was thus formed; this group can still be considered as typical because of its substantial presence on the World Heritage List. In an attempt to contrast the results of the analyses, industrial heritage was chosen as a third and extreme group since it is a non-traditional category of cultural heritage, numerically under-represented on the World Heritage List. Because of the numerical importance of religious sites and to further reduce the variables, only religious heritage sites from the same States Parties that were already chosen for their industrial heritage sites were selected. The geographical location of sites selected was also an important factor to take into account since the definition of authenticity in the Operational Guidelines has been qualified as Eurocentric and as not being applicable to the reality of non-European countries. Analysing the representation of authenticity in non-European sites would highlight whether and how these 'Eurocentric' principles have been understood and adapted to these situations.

Using ATLAS/ti, a Computer Assisted Qualitative Data Analysis Software (CAQDAS), each sentence of each nomination dossier selected was coded. This computer programme was used since it facilitated the coding of texts and enabled it to be done more systematically, consistently and thoroughly than doing it manually. A complex system of codes and sub-codes was designed to analyse thoroughly the content of each nomination dossier (for more information on this coding system, see Labadi 2007: 155–57). The following sections focus on analysing the results of the systematic coding of the nomination dossiers selected with the term 'authenticity', 'restoration' and 'reconstruction'. In other words, the following sections detail results of analyses of sentences that mention directly or indirectly the term 'authenticity' or 'restoration' or describe the degree/state of authenticity and/or restoration. The coding of the sentences of nomination dossiers paid particular attention to the different explicit and implicit meanings that could have been given to these terms and their ambiguous uses. After having clarified how States Parties have understood authenticity in particular in relation to its changing definition at the international level, this chapter analyses whether practices of restoration and reconstruction confirm or refute these understandings of authenticity.

National interpretations of international definitions

Authenticity as 'original'

In most of the nomination dossiers analysed the authenticity of sites is related to their original state and form. In other words, the section on authenticity of nomination dossiers is used to claim that sites have remained in their original state and form since they were built. The definition of authenticity as 'original' also characterises sites nominated after 1994 and the adoption of the *Nara Document on Authenticity*. The definition of authenticity from this document does not seem to have trickled down to national and local level, as further detailed below. Thus, in the nomination dossiers analysed authenticity is most often understood by its etymological meaning, that is what is 'original as opposed to counterfeit' (Jokilehto 1999a: 296). The nomination dossier of the 'Völklingen Ironworks', a 'cathedral' to the nineteenth-century industrial age in Germany, is one such example. It indicates that 'the plant (...) is fully preserved in its original form, with the exception of minor modernizations' (Government of Germany 1993: 3). Another example is the 'Yungang Grottoes' representing Buddhist cave art in China in the fifth and sixth centuries CE. Its nomination dossier stresses that 'the principle of "keeping things in their original shapes" has been strictly observed, that is, utmost efforts have been made to maintain the authenticity of the cultural heritage' (Government of China 2000: 28).

This understanding of authenticity as 'original' and as 'having been frozen in time' is likely to have been a direct result of its definition in the Operational Guidelines as related to four degrees of authenticity: material, workmanship, design and setting. The worldwide and overwhelming use of this definition of authenticity from the Operational Guidelines also reflects its most common meaning as genuine and original, a meaning that makes sense for the majority of States Parties considered here. This understanding of authenticity as original might also reflect discourses constructed by States Parties to justify the outstanding universal value of sites. Elsewhere (see Labadi 2007) I have shown in detail that States Parties have provided descriptions of sites in their nomination dossiers that focus on continuity, uniformity and stability. It has been stressed that heritage properties have been used to construct the nation and national identities (Evans 1999: 2). Providing such images of heritage based on continuity, uniformity and stability helps to construct stable, solid and homogeneous nations and collective identities and to consolidate an 'imagined community' (Anderson 1991: 5). Insisting on the high degree of authenticity of the nominated property and on its preservation in its original form is a convenient way to confirm and strengthen this representation of the nation as stable.

Authenticity as a changing process

Only nine – a minority – of the 106 nomination dossiers analysed have interpreted authenticity as a dynamic process, reflecting the different changes that have affected sites over their history. Eight of these nomination dossiers were submitted after 1994 and might thus be a direct consequence of the debates and definition of authenticity from the Nara Conference and *Document*. Such a marginalisation of understanding authenticity can be justified, as previously stressed, in the exclusion of the *Nara Document* and its provisions from the Operational Guidelines until its 2005 revised version. Whilst the Nara Conference on Authenticity was organised, *inter alia*, to take better consideration of authenticity in non-European contexts, all these nomination dossiers that considered authenticity as a changing process concerned sites located in Europe.

Nominated in 1985, Durham Castle and Cathedral in England is the first nominated dossier from the sample where change is identified as an element of authenticity. This dossier introduces, before its time, some ideas that were to be voiced at the Nara Conference and written into the *Nara Document*. Indeed this dossier indicates that Durham Castle,

> founded soon after the Norman Conquest (…) has been rebuilt, extended and adapted to changing circumstances and uses over a period of 900 years: from being a key fortress in the defence of the border with Scotland, it was gradually transformed in more peaceful times into an imposing and comfortable palace for the Bishops of Durham; and since 1837, soon after the foundation of the University of Durham, it has served as a residential college for many generations of students and dons. As they stand today, the buildings reflect these changing functions and display a wide variety of architectural styles of different periods.
> (Government of the United Kingdom 1985)

This dossier is thus different from others written at that time which focused on demonstrating that the nominated site had stayed in its original and frozen state since its construction. On the contrary, the nomination dossier of Durham Castle and Cathedral details the changes that this monument has undergone over the centuries as a consequence of new functions, standards and fashions in both military and domestic architecture.

The nomination dossiers of Notre-Dame Cathedral in Tournai (Belgium, nominated for inscription on the World Heritage List in 1999) and New Lanark (United Kingdom, nominated in 2000) are two examples from the period after the adoption of the *Nara Document* that share and develop its conception of authenticity. Started in the twelfth century on already existing foundations, Notre-Dame Cathedral in

Tournai is of impressive dimensions and harmoniously combines Romanesque and Gothic styles. Its nomination dossier shifts away from the presentation of authenticity as the perfect protection of the site in its original form, frozen in time. Instead, this dossier stresses that the monument followed a similar history to most mediaeval churches of the region; that is, it was subject to gradual adaptations and additions due to new functions and fashions, followed by a campaign of restoration during the nineteenth century. This nomination dossier concludes that the authenticity of the monument should be evaluated in the light of the different campaigns of restoration and reconstruction. Another nomination dossier that associated authenticity with change is that of New Lanark, an eighteenth-century cotton mill village in Southern Scotland. This document explains that Mill 2 has been subject to widening over the centuries and stresses that 'the Venice Charter and Nara Document on Authenticity remind us that the widening of the mill is an essential part of the story of New Lanark' (Government of the United Kingdom 2000: 56).

These two examples illustrate Melucco Vaccaro's (1996: 203) view that buildings are hardly ever frozen in time and that they 'rarely come to light in the state in which they left the hands of their creators; they have usually been tampered with, altered, restored, re-used, and adapted' because of changes in use, fashion or ownership. These changes are nonetheless essential since they have also ensured the buildings' survival for future generations. Defining authenticity as a dynamic concept resulting from and reflecting the different historic changes of sites might therefore provide a better understanding of sites' actual history than describing them as static, original and frozen in time. Although the *Nara Document* corresponds better to the history of sites, the four degrees of authenticity relating to the 'original' – material, workmanship, design and setting of the site – have been used predominantly by States Parties in the nomination dossiers analysed because this was the official UNESCO definition provided in the Operational Guidelines. The tension between the Operational Guidelines' definition used by States Parties and the actual state of authenticity of sites, which in a number of cases does not fit these official guidelines, might explain the superficial explanation of authenticity found in the nomination dossiers analysed. The following section further highlights the problematic nature of authenticity through analyses of the references to 'restoration' and 'reconstruction' in nomination dossiers.

Authenticity, restoration and reconstruction

Analyses of the references to the concept of restoration and reconstruction in nomination dossiers help to reassess the representations of authenticity detailed in the previous section. As explained above, most of the analysed nomination dossiers define authenticity as the original state and form of the site, frozen in time. However, other sections of these same nomination dossiers, such as those on the history of conservation, report numerous restorations and reconstructions. This is particularly the case for most of the European religious sites, described in the nomination dossiers as having undergone restoration/repair during the nineteenth century. This is not surprising considering that 'many major monuments throughout Europe were in a state of disrepair at the beginning of the century (...) so there was scope for widespread reconstruction and restoration' (Pye 2001: 42–43). This is exemplified in the nomination dossier of the 'Vézelay Church and Hill' (Government of France 1979), a Benedictine abbey and important pilgrimage place on the Way of St James that is said to hold the relics of St Mary Magdalene. This dossier quotes the 1835 statement by Prosper Mérimée, French General Inspector of Historical Monuments, describing the Vézelay abbey as having walls cracked and leaning, rotted by humidity (ibid.). Pye (2001: 43) goes on to stress that, in the nineteenth century, 'buildings were repaired to maintain their function but often considerably altered or rebuilt to suit the restoring architect's concept of the style of the original, rather than by following the design and detail of the remaining structure'. This echoes the statement, quoted earlier, by Melucco Vacaro that sites are altered, restored and adapted to fit new functions or fashion and that they do not come to us in their original state. This is further made clear by the sections of nomination dossiers on restoration as removal of accretions.

According to Jokilehto (1998: 230), the principles of the Venice Charter have been recognised as the basic policy guidelines for the assessment of cultural heritage sites on UNESCO's World Heritage List. The Venice Charter (1964: Article 11) emphasises that 'the valid contributions of all periods to the building of a monument must be respected, since unity of style is not the aim of restoration. When a building includes the superimposed work of different periods, the revealing of the underlying state can only be justified in exceptional circumstances and when what is removed is of little interest. This respect for different periods was also stressed, as Brandi (1996: 235) points out, by the *Athens Charter for the Restoration of Historic Monuments*, adopted in 1931, which preceded the Venice Charter. Nine nomination dossiers of European religious sites and four of industrial heritage sites indicate that twentieth-century restorations have focused on removing later accretions to return the building to its original appearance. In some cases this seems to be justified and appears to be in conformity with the Venice Charter approach. In the 1996 nomination dossier of the 'San Millán Yuso and Suso Monasteries' located in Spain, for instance, it is explained that restoration works have attempted to recover the thirteenth-century appearance of the Suso Monastery. Whilst this dossier does not contextualise this restoration, the ICOMOS evaluation of its outstanding universal value explains it. This evaluation indeed stresses that 'a study of photographs from the pre-restoration period shows the later additions to have been of low cultural quality and disfiguring; their impact on the core structure was also superficial' (ICOMOS 1997).

In other instances, the justification for the removal of later accretions is more difficult to understand. This is the case, for instance, with New Lanark, the industrial village in Southern Scotland mentioned earlier. Its nomination dossier clearly indicates that most of the village was restored to its appearance in Robert Owen's time in the nineteenth century (Government of the United Kingdom 2000). Owen was manager and part owner of the mills. Above all, he is famous for his philanthropic and socialist visions and actions. Taking this point of reference is thus understandable since he is the most important character linked to the site. However, Jokilehto (1999b: 8) condemns this type of 'period restoration' that relies on choosing 'an earlier period as a guideline for the choice of what to keep, what to remove, and what to reconstruct. At the end of the restoration, the historic building tends to have lost its authenticity and to have become a modern interpretation'. Conversely, the ICOMOS (September 2001) evaluation of New Lanark stresses that its authenticity is 'relatively high' because the restoration and rehabilitation of the buildings were based on careful research, and graphic and written archives. Nonetheless, as detailed in the previous section on authenticity, the nomination dossier of New Lanark also stresses that Mill 2 has been subject to changes and widening over the centuries, changes that have been kept whilst most of the rest of the village has been restored to its nineteenth-century appearance. Hence the contemporary New Lanark is not a faithful image of its nineteenth-century appearance but seems more to be a modern interpretation with a combination of old and new buildings. Its nomination dossier does not explain why the later additions to some buildings have been kept whilst others have been removed. Therefore Jokilehto's comment that period restoration destroys the authenticity of the site by being a modern interpretation could be seen to apply to New Lanark. This perhaps justifies some comparisons of New Lanark to a theme park (McIntosh and Prentice 1999: 608) that mixes different epochs, but which 'never really exists in the form in which it is presented' (Bryman 1995: 128; see also Sorensen 1989: 65). According to Choay (2001: 145), these 'arbitrary destructions and restorations' are common. As examples she provides the centres of Old Quebec (Canada) and Provins (France) which are both World Heritage sites. According to Choay, these restorations aim to enhance sites and make them more appealing to the public (ibid.: 144). The example of New Lanark illustrates the disparate views that are held on authenticity, some people considering New Lanark an authentic site and others inauthentic.

World Heritage and post-autheniticity

Whilst authenticity has been defined in the Operational Guidelines up until their 2005 revised version as a scientific and precise notion with degrees related to design, materials, workmanship and setting, this chapter has demonstrated the postmodern and post-structuralist dimension of the concept. Hence the provocative reference to post-authenticity in the title. Indeed, analyses of the understandings of authenticity at the international level reveal 'the incredulity toward metanarratives' (Lyotard 1984), that is, scepticism toward this grand totalising master narrative, supposed to be applied and valid universally. This scepticism is reflected in the organisation of the Nara Conference and adoption of the *Nara Document on Authenticity*. This document recognises that the authenticity of a site is rooted in specific socio-cultural contexts, corresponds to specific values and can only be understood and judged within those specific contexts and according to these values. Despite the importance of the *Nara Document*, its provisions were not included in the Operational Guidelines until their 2005 revision. This delay might in turn be due to incredulity and fear towards the 'implosion of meaning' and the 'de-centring' of the definition of authenticity fostered by the *Nara Document*. The rational and universal four degrees of authenticity seemed indeed, from the outset, easier to explain for States Parties in nomination dossiers and to assess for the advisory bodies than authenticity as defined by the *Nara Document*.

Understandings of this notion at the level of States Parties and based on analyses of 106 nomination dossiers epitomise the concept of 'simulacrum' as defined and used by Baudrillard (1988). Baudrillard quotes *Ecclesiastes* to clarify his understanding of this term: 'simulacrum is never that which conceals the truth – it is the truth which conceals that there is none. The simulacrum is true.' As indicated by the analyses of references to the terms 'restoration' and 'reconstruction' in nomination dossiers, most sites are hardly ever frozen in time, because of changes in use, fashion, ownership as well as political and socio-economic contexts. However, in most nomination dossiers analysed, the section on authenticity presents sites as having remained in their original state and form. The analyses presented in this chapter highlight some existing contradictions in nomination dossiers of sites for inclusion on the World Heritage List.

Whilst some parts of these documents stress that the authenticity of the site is very high and has been preserved in its original and frozen form, others highlight that the site underwent restoration or reconstruction work. In some cases, these restoration works aim to remove accretions and to bring the site back to its original state and form. However, not all of the accretions are removed and sites tend thus to become modern interpretations, combining a mix of modern and old buildings. This situation illustrates the definition provided above of the simulacrum. Indeed, it can be argued that these contradictions between different sections of nomination dossiers are a direct result of the grand and universalising definition of authenticity in the Operational Guidelines, which suggests that it can be measured according to four precise and reasoned degrees. These contradictions reflect the efforts by States Parties to respect the four degrees of authenticity in the Operational Guidelines. For the past thirty years these representations of authenticity in nomination dossiers were considered to represent the truth and the reality since they refer back to the official meta-narratives of the World Heritage Committee system, which was the reality and truth of that time. These representations mask the absence of a basic reality of the four degrees of authenticity, which do not relate in any case to the actual state of authenticity of sites. These contradictory and unrealistic presentations of authenticity in nomination dossiers conceal the fact that the Operational Guidelines bear no relation to the reality of this concept until its 2005 revision. These representations of authenticity in nominations are thus simulacra in the sense that they do not conceal the truth. They are the truth themselves because they follow and reproduce a definition from the Operational Guidelines which is supposed to be the truth but in fact conceals that there is none. These nomination dossiers can also be qualified as representing a state of hyperreality, that is, the impossibility of distinguishing between a real phenomenon and a fake one because of the blurring of boundaries. Nomination dossiers are hyperreal because they trick the reader into believing that they represent the reality, since they reflect sanctioned definitions by the World Heritage Committee. However, they do not represent the reality because their points of reference, these sanctioned definitions, do not relate in any case to the actual state of authenticity of sites.

Furthermore, these representations of authenticity are not innocent and are even subject to manipulations. Indeed, as previously stressed, understanding of authenticity as 'original' might also reflect discourses constructed by States Parties to provide an image of the site, and, by extension, of the nation as stable, solid and homogeneous. These representations of authenticity might, hence, not only be due to the definition in the Operational Guidelines but also to the political uses of the past by governments that use a particular version of authenticity to justify the 'ownership of land claimed to have been held "since time immemorial"' (Kohl and Fawcett 1995: 5; Fowler 1987: 230; Lowenthal 1998: 235). Stressing the original condition of the site is also important to consolidate the unity and cohesion of the nation. The need to project an image of the nation as stable and coherent through heritage properties might reflect changes in the nature and function of States Parties, the results of supra-national processes of regional and global integration. Regional and local sub-national movements, including resurgences of cultural traditions and dialects, have also been developing as a way of counteracting the centralising power of the state. States Parties might therefore fear that a unique and coherent nation has been challenged by these supranational and sub-national movements and might therefore want to use nomination dossiers as a tool to reaffirm the coherence, stability and unity of the nation and its constituents.

Conclusion

Whilst authenticity has been defined in the Operational Guidelines up until their 2005 revised version as a scientific and precise notion with degrees related to design, materials, workmanship and setting, this chapter has demonstrated the postmodern and post-structuralist dimension of the concept. For this reason this chapter argues for the use of the term 'post-authenticity'. Indeed, the organisation of the Nara Conference and adoption of the *Nara Document on Authenticity* reflect the scepticism towards the grand totalising master narrative of the four degrees of authenticity, supposed to be applied and valid universally. Furthermore, analyses of 106 nomination dossiers of sites for inclusion on the World Heritage List demonstrate their representations of authenticity as simulacra. These representations are simulacra because they follow and reproduce the four degrees of authenticity from the Operational Guidelines which are supposed to represent the truth, but in fact conceal that there is none. As this chapter demonstrates, these four degrees of authenticity do not reflect the actual state of authenticity of sites. These nomination dossiers also represent a state of hyperreality, which is the impossibility of distinguishing between a real phenomenon and a fake one because of the blurring of boundaries between the actual state of authenticity of sites and their fake presentation following official guidelines.

What should be done in face of this situation? Now that the *Nara Document* has been fully integrated within the Operational Guidelines and thus the World Heritage system, publications on the diversity of the forms of post-authenticity could be released, as illustrations of the principles of this *Document*. These would help to break away from the quasi-monolithic understanding of authenticity as applied to World Heritage that has prevailed for the past 30 years and help to guide States Parties in providing more realistic representations of this concept in nomination dossiers.

Note

1 The author is responsible for the choice and the presentation of the facts contained in this chapter and for the opinions expressed therein, which are not necessarily those of UNESCO and do not commit the Organisation.

References

Anderson, B. (1991) *Imagined Communities: reflections on the origin and spread of nationalism*, London: Verso.

Athens Charter for the Restoration of Historic Monuments (1931) Online. Available HTTP: <http://www.icomos.org/docs/athens_charter.html> (accessed 25/03/2009).

Baudrillard, J. (1988) 'Simulacra and Simulations', in M. Poster (ed.) *Jean Baudrillard, Selected Writings*, Stanford: Stanford University Press: 166–84.

Brandi, C. (1996) 'Theory of Restoration, I', in N. Stanley-Price, M. Kirby Talley Jr. and A. Melucco Vaccaro (eds), *Historical and Philosophical Issues in the Conservation of Cultural Heritage*, Los Angeles: The Getty Conservation Institute: 230–35.

Bryman, A. (1995) *Disney and His Worlds*, London: Routledge.

Choay, F. (2001) *The Invention of the Historic Monument*, Cambridge: Cambridge University Press.

Evans, J. (1999) 'Introduction: Nation and Representation', in D. Boswell and J. Evans; (eds) *Representing the Nation: a Reader: Histories, Heritage and Museums*, London: Routledge: 1–8.

Feilden, B. and Jokilehto, J. (1993) *Management Guidelines for World Cultural Heritage Sites*, Rome: ICCROM (in collaboration with UNESCO and ICOMOS).

Feilden, B. and Jokilehto, J. (1998) *Management Guidelines for World Cultural Heritage Sites*, second edition, Rome: ICCROM (in collaboration with UNESCO and ICOMOS).

Fowler, D. (1987) 'Uses of the Past: Archaeology in the Service of the State', *American Antiquity*, 52(2): 229–48.

Francioni, F. (2002) 'The international framework of legal instruments', in UNESCO, *Workshop Abstracts: The legal tools for World Heritage Conservation – Sienna 11–12 November.* Unpublished UNESCO document, Paris: 1–4.

Government of Belgium (1999) *Nomination of Notre-Dame Cathedral in Tournai for inclusion on the World Heritage List*, Brussels.

Government of China (2000) *Nomination of Yungang Grottoes for inclusion on the World Heritage List*, Beijing.

Government of France (1979) *Nomination of Vézelay Church and Hill for inclusion on the World Heritage List*, Paris.

Government of Germany (1993) *Nomination of Völklingen Ironworks for inclusion on the World Heritage List*, Berlin.

Government of the United Kingdom of Great Britain and Northern Ireland (1985) *Nomination of Durham Castle and Cathedral for inclusion on the World Heritage List*, London.

Government of the United Kingdom of Great Britain and Northern Ireland (2000) *Nomination of New Lanark for inclusion on the World Heritage List*, London.

Holtorf, C. and Schadla-Hall, T. (1999) 'Age as Artefact: on archaeological authenticity', *European Journal of Archaeology* 2(2): 229–47.

ICOMOS, September (1997) *ICOMOS Evaluation of the Nomination of San Millán Yuso and Suso Monasteries for Inclusion on the World Heritage List*, ICOMOS, Paris. Online. Available HTTP, <http://whc.unesco.org/archive/advisory_body_evaluation/805.pdf>, (accessed 15/06/2004).

ICOMOS, September (2001) *ICOMOS Evaluation of the Nomination of New Lanark for Inclusion on the World Heritage List*, Paris: ICOMOS.

ICOMOS (2003) *Analysis of the World Heritage List and Tentative Lists: Cultural and Mixed Properties*, Paris: ICOMOS, unpublished document.

ICOMOS (2004) *The World Heritage List: Filling the Gap – An Action Plan for the Future*, Paris: ICOMOS.

International Charter for the Conservation and Restoration of Monuments and Sites (The Venice Charter) (1964) Online. Available HTTP <http://www.icomos.org/venice_charter.html>, (accessed on 24/03/2009).

Jokilehto, J. (1998) 'The context of the Venice Charter (1964)', *Conservation and Management of Archaeological Sites*, 2(4): 229–33.

Jokilehto, J. (1999a) *A History of Architectural Conservation*, Oxford: Butterworth-Heinemann.

Jokilehto, J. (1999b) *Conservation and Creative Approach*. Online. Available HTTP <http://personal.inet.fi/koti/marc99/jjokilehto.htm> (accessed 30/12/2002).

Kohl, P. and Fawcett, C. (1995) 'Archaeology in the service of the state: theoretical considerations', in P. Kohl and C. Fawcett (eds) *Nationalism, Politics, and the Practice of Archaeology*, Cambridge: Cambridge University Press, 3–18.

Labadi, S. (2007) 'Representations of the nation and cultural diversity in discourses on World Heritage' *Journal of Social Archaeology*. Vol 7(2): 147–70.

Lowenthal, D. (1998), *The Heritage Crusade and the Spoils of History*, Cambridge: Cambridge University Press.

Lyotard, J-F. (1984) *The Postmodern Condition: A Report on Knowledge*, trans. Geoff Bennington and Brian Massumi, Minneapolis: University of Minnesota Press.

McIntosh, A. and Prentice, R. (1999) 'Affirming Authenticity: Consuming Cultural Heritage', *Annals of Tourism Research* 26(3): 589–612.

Melucco Vaccaro, A. (1996) 'Introduction to Part III', in N. Stanley-Price, M. Kirby Talley Jr. and A. Melucco Vaccaro (eds) *Historical and Philosophical Issues in the Conservation of Cultural Heritage*, Los Angeles: The Getty Conservation Institute: 202–11.

Parent, M. (1979) *Item 6 of the Provisional Agenda. Comparative Study of Nominations and Criteria for World Cultural Heritage*, third session of the World Heritage Committee (23–27 October), CC-79/CONF.003/11 Paris: UNESCO. Online. Available HTTP, <http://whc.unesco.org/archive/1979/cc-79-conf003–11e.pdf> (accessed 24/03/2009).

Parent, M. (1983) *Speech by Mr. Michel Parent, chairman of ICOMOS, during the Seventh Session of the Bureau of the World Heritage Committee* (Paris, 27–30 June 1983). SC/83/CONF.009/INF.2. Paris: UNESCO. Online. Available HTTP <http://whc.unesco.org/archive/1983/sc-83-conf009-inf2e.pdf> (accessed 23/04/2009).

Pressouyre, L. (1996) *The World Heritage Convention, Twenty Years Later*, Paris: UNESCO.

Pye, E. (2001) *Caring for the Past*, London: James and James.

Robert, Y. (1995) 'L'authenticité: un concept inopérant pour la conservation du patrimoine? Une reflexion de Françoise Choay', *Les Nouvelles du Patrimoine*, 61, Mai: 7–8.

Sekino, M. (1996) 'The Preservation and Restoration of Wooden Monuments in Japan', in ICOMOS National Committee, Japan, *Monuments and Sites, Japan*. Paris: ICOMOS : 15–36.

Slatyer, R. (1984) 'The origin and development of the World Heritage Convention', *Monumentum* [Special Issue]: 3–16.

Sorensen, C. (1989) 'Theme Parks and Time Machines', in P. Vergo (ed.) *The New Museology*, London: Reaktion: 60–73.

Stovel, H. (1995) 'Working towards the Nara Document', in K. Larsen (ed.), *Nara Conference on Authenticity in Relation to the World Heritage Convention, Nara, Japan, 1–6 November 1994: Proceedings*, Paris: UNESCO (in collaboration with ICCROM and ICOMOS): xxxiii–xxxvi.

UNESCO (17 October 1977) *Report of the Rapporteur – Convention Concerning the Protection of the World Cultural and Natural Heritage – World Heritage Committee – First Session (27 June–1 July 1977)*. CC-77/CONF.001/9. Paris: UNESCO. Online. Available HTTP. <http://whc.unesco.org/archive/repcom77.htm> (accessed 23/03/2009).

UNESCO (20 October 1977) *Operational Guidelines for the Implementation of the World Heritage Convention*, Intergovernmental Committee for the Protection of the World Cultural and Natural Heritage CC-77/CONF.001/8 Rev. Paris: UNESCO. Online. Available HTTP <http://whc.unesco.org/archive/out/opgu77.htm> (accessed 23/03/2009).

UNESCO (28 May 1980) *Report of the Rapporteur – Convention concerning the Protection of the World Cultural and Natural Heritage – World Heritage Bureau – Fourth Session (19–22 May)*. CC-80/CONF. 017/4 Paris: UNESCO. Online. Available HTTP <http://whc.unesco.org/archive/repbur80.htm> (accessed 23/03/2009).

UNESCO (29 September 1980) *Report of the Rapporteur – Convention Concerning the Protection of the World Cultural and Natural Heritage – World Heritage Committee – Fourth Session (1–5 September 1980)*. CC-80/CONF.016/10. Paris: UNESCO. Online. Available HTTP <http://whc.unesco.org/archive/repcom80.htm> (accessed 23/03/2009).

UNESCO (October 1980) *Operational Guidelines for the Implementation of the World Heritage Convention*, Intergovernmental Committee for the Protection of the World Cultural and Natural Heritage WHC/2. Paris: UNESCO. Online. Available HTTP <http://whc.unesco.org/archive/repcom80.htm> (accessed 23/03/2009).

UNESCO (14 December 1992) *Annex II (Strategic Orientations). Report of the Rapporteur – Convention concerning the Protection of the World Cultural and Natural Heritage – World Heritage Committee – Sixteenth Session (December, 7–14 1992)*, WHC-92/CONF.002/12, Paris: UNESCO. Online. Available HTTP <http://whc.unesco.org/archive/repcom92.htm#annex2> (accessed 23/03/2009).

UNESCO (21 November 1994) *Information Note: Nara Document on Authenticity. Experts meeting, (1–6 November)* World Heritage Committee – Eighteenth Session, (12–17 December 1994). WHC-94/CONF.003/INF.008. Paris: UNESCO. Online. Available HTTP <http://whc.unesco.org/archive/nara94.htm> (accessed 23/03/2009).

UNESCO (February 1995) *Operational Guidelines for the Implementation of the World Heritage Convention*, Intergovernmental Committee for the Protection of the World Cultural and Natural Heritage WHC/2/Rev. Paris: UNESCO. Online. Available HTTP: <http://whc.unesco.org/archive/out/guide95.htm> (accessed 23/03/2009).

UNESCO (February 1996) *Operational Guidelines for the Implementation of the World Heritage Convention*, Intergovernmental Committee for the Protection of the World Cultural and Natural Heritage WHC/2/Rev. Paris: UNESCO. Online. Available HTTP <http://whc.unesco.org/archive/out/guide96.htm> (accessed 23/03/2009).

UNESCO (9 October 2000) *Synthetic Report of the Meeting on Authenticity and Integrity in an African context, Great Zimbabwe National Monument, Zimbabwe, 26–29 May 2000*, World Heritage Committee, Twenty-fourth session, Cairns, Australia 27 November – 2 December 2000. WHC-2000/CONF.204/INF.11, Paris: UNESCO. Online. Available HTTP: <http://whc.unesco.org/archive/2000/whc-00-conf204-inf11e.pdf> (accessed 23/03/2009).

UNESCO (28 May 2002) *Item 18 of the provisional agenda: Revision of the Operational Guidelines for Implementation of the World Heritage Convention: 3rd Draft annotated revised Operational Guidelines prepared by the March 2002 Drafting Group*, Convention Concerning the Protection of the World Cultural and Natural Heritage – World Heritage Committee, Twenty-Sixth session, (24–29 June 2002), WHC-02/CONF.202/14B, Paris: UNESCO. Online. Available HTTP. <http://whc.unesco.org/archive/2002/whc-02-conf202-14be.pdf > (accessed 23/03/2009).

UNESCO (February 2005) *Operational Guidelines for the Implementation of the World Heritage Convention*, Intergovernmental Committee for the Protection of the World Cultural and Natural Heritage WHC-05/2. UNESCO, Paris.

von Droste, B. and Bertilsson, U. (1995) 'Authenticity and World Heritage' in K. Larsen (ed.) *Nara Conference on Authenticity in Relation to the World Heritage Convention, Nara, Japan, 1–6 November 1994: Proceedings*, Paris: UNESCO (in collaboration with ICCROM and ICOMOS): 3–16.

Chapter 4

An ivory bull's head from Afghanistan

Legal and ethical dilemmas in national and globalised heritage

Juliette van Krieken-Pieters

> The motives which induced me to carry out this operation in Greece proceeded entirely from the wish to secure for Great Britain, and hence for Europe as a whole, the best possible knowledge, and the means of improving it, through the most outstanding works.
>
> (Lord Elgin, British diplomat (1766–1841), (care)taker of the Elgin or Parthenon Marbles)

> ... Until legalization, however, ethics are contrasted with law. Thus an action may be described as legal but unethical or, less frequently, ethical but illegal. In either case, the law is presumed to be in the wrong. Ethics has a higher moral status than law.
>
> (Merryman 1988: 21)

Introduction

It was January 2008 and I was again facing the small ivory bull's head from Afghanistan, included in the beautiful exhibition *Hidden Afghanistan* in the Nieuwe Kerk, in Amsterdam.[1] The exhibition consisted of artifacts mainly deriving from a collection that was hidden for about 15 years in the vaults of the Central Bank in the Presidential Palace in Kabul. In 1989 the collection, much of which had been on exhibit in the National Museum of Kabul, was secretly packed and stored in the vaults of the Central Bank. It was feared that otherwise its survival could not be guaranteed. This fear became reality when, during a bloody civil war following the retreat of the Soviet Union in 1989, the museum was heavily damaged and looted. The bull's head, which was not taken into protective custody, ended up, by the mid-1990s, at the Pakistani border town of Peshawar. It came to the *Hidden Afghanistan* exhibition via convoluted routes.

During many years of terrible fighting the hiding place with the stored items was kept secret. After years of insecurity and despite (or perhaps thanks to) rumours of the collection's demise, it was announced in August 2003 that the trunks and safes in the Presidential Palace were still intact. In 2004 it was revealed that the most

Figure 4.1 Bull head, Begram, Afghanistan, 1st century AD, ivory, 2.8 × 5.5 × 3.2 cm, National Museum of Afghanistan (part of travelling exhibition; photo courtesy SPACH)

precious items, the Bactrian Gold, consisting of 20,000 gold objects, were all present and in good condition.

As soon as the news about the recovery of the trunks with their precious contents – probably the most important objects in Afghanistan – was spread, the Afghan collection attained the status of globalised heritage. The National Geographic Society, in particular, was very keen on playing a major role in the revelation of this archaeological gem,[2] sometimes called 'the archaeological find of the 20th century'. The Society assisted with making an inventory and was given the right to publish a feature on the treasure in its magazine in December 2004. From that moment onwards many prestigious museums and institutes around the world were eager to host an Afghanistan exhibition. Initially the Afghans were very reluctant to let the collection leave the country. They felt they had lost so much already. They wanted to keep their treasure, their pride, their 'heart', inside the country.

It was, therefore, something of a surprise that the collection actually arrived in France in 2006. The French organisers themselves were not certain that the Afghans would let go of this treasure, even temporarily, until they saw the plane landing in France. In Paris' Musée Guimet a large part of the collection was properly exhibited for the first time. In Afghanistan the Bactrian Gold objects had been on display only for a day or at most a few days, for a select group of people. It is a strange feeling to be able to admire the objects in Europe, realising that most Afghans have never been able to enjoy them themselves.[3]

A legal and ethical dilemma

Let us return to the small ivory bull's head mentioned above. This piece was not lucky enough to be packed by the museum staff in 1989. It remained in the museum in Kabul. It is not known exactly when – probably in 1993 – but it was stolen from the museum (which was at that time seriously damaged and had been systematically plundered) and became part of the illicit trade in cultural property, a trade that still exists in both Afghanistan and Pakistan, especially Peshawar and Islamabad. From these places objects find their way to the rest of the world.

In 1993, in the middle of the civil war, a small group of knowledgeable and concerned people in Afghanistan and Pakistan started to discuss what to do to try to rescue as much as possible of the collections of the Kabul Museum, which was in a deplorable state after the fighting and plundering. As a result the Society for the Preservation of Afghanistan's Cultural Heritage (SPACH) was founded in 1994, in Islamabad, Pakistan. Forming part of this group as the first Secretary, I found it a sad but at the same time fascinating experience to be at the heart of the discussions. Several decisions were easy to make, others gave rise to long debate. The most difficult question was the following: Should SPACH buy pieces stolen from the National Museum in Kabul and keep them secretly, to be able to return them as soon as the situation was stable again? After long discussions with Board Members (including Afghanistan experts, Ambassadors and high UN officials) it was decided to buy only pieces that came without doubt from the National Museum and to do this very discreetly. This was a very difficult decision and gave me, as a lawyer who specialised in the international protection of cultural heritage, an insight into how far theory and practice can diverge. Of course legally this decision was entirely questionable: by buying stolen items one could be accused of the crime of receiving and could be fined. At the same time it was practically wrong in the sense that by buying stolen items one could be stimulating the region's illicit trade, not only encouraging theft, but also illicit excavations. Of course the illicit trade was already very much alive at that time: as soon as a country or a region falls victim to war or disaster, a heightened general focus is often accompanied by increased interest – not always benign – in its cultural property. A lack or destruction of facilities and decline in security can, combined with growth in poverty, theft, and illicit excavations, produce a flourishing illicit trade in art and antiquities.

The bull's head was one of the pieces SPACH acquired in the mid-1990s. This was quite exceptional. Many items were too expensive to buy and with great regret SPACH saw those artifacts disappear into the Western and Japanese art markets, maybe never to return to the museum in Kabul.

As could be predicted, SPACH has been criticised for its policy by UNESCO, ICOM (the International Council of Museums) and several archaeologists. But knowing the desperation of the situation at that time and not knowing for sure that the most beautiful pieces were safe,[4] it was a carefully considered decision made by people who shared a well-meant concern for the Afghan Cultural Heritage and who wanted to preserve as many pieces as possible for the Afghan people.

After the disasters of 2001, including the blowing up of the Bamiyan Buddhas and the destruction of numerous objects in the National Museum of Kabul, many of the critics acknowledged that with hindsight SPACH's action to acquire these very specific objects may have been correct. UNESCO even appointed SPACH as one of the so-called 'safe havens' for Afghan art. The website text of UNESCO's culture sector in Afghanistan read as follows:

The safekeeping and return of Afghan cultural property:
UNESCO's policy on the protective safekeeping of cultural property is straightforward. Where there is a serious danger to the survival of heritage, and at the request of the recognized government of the country concerned, UNESCO will arrange with NGOs the safe custody of objects donated to it and their return to that country when the situation allows.

UNESCO supports non-profit organizations working to take cultural objects into safe custody. It will not itself purchase objects that are being illicitly trafficked.

In the case of Afghanistan, and consequent to the destruction of heritage by the Taliban, UNESCO has created a special programme to assist in the rescue of cultural heritage of Afghan origin.

UNESCO, in partnership with the Foundation for Cultural Heritage in Japan, the Society for the Preservation of Afghanistan's Cultural Heritage (SPACH) based in Islamabad, Pakistan, and the Swiss Afghanistan Museum in Bubendorf, is currently taking Afghan cultural property found on the international art market into protective custody, particularly objects stolen from museums or discovered during illicit excavations.

These objects, once found and categorized, will be returned to Afghanistan when peace has returned to the country.[5]

One of the most interesting provisions is: '*It will not itself purchase objects that are being illicitly trafficked*'. Might this statement be vague enough not to forbid these 'safe havens' to purchase objects themselves? It seems that UNESCO tried to adjust the legal provisions to the practical demands of that moment in time.

In any case, the 'safe haven' concept appears to have been largely successful in the case of Afghanistan, both inside and outside the country. The first and best example of the strategy is the fact that the collection that was packed and stored in Kabul remained safe and is now travelling to several places of the Western world – which could be called a 'safe haven' per se. The second example are the pieces secretly acquired by SPACH that were handed over to the Musée Guimet in Paris to be kept safely until time would permit their return, and which form part of the same travelling exhibition.

The third example is the Afghanistan Museum-in-Exile in Bubendorf, Switzerland. It was established by Paul Bucherer in 1999 after a joint request to Switzerland from the Taliban and the Northern Alliance, two of the major fighting forces, to provide

Figure 4.2 Lion head, Begram, Afghanistan, 1st century AD, ivory, 4.0 × 5.5 × 2.0 cm, National Museum of Afghanistan (part of travelling exhibition; photo courtesy SPACH)

a 'safe deposit' to protect the remaining national treasures. However, getting the objects out of Afghanistan turned out to be extremely difficult. Nonetheless 1,423 artifacts were handed over to the 'safe haven' in Switzerland. After several years of safe custody, the entire collection of the Swiss Afghanistan Museum-in-Exile was handed over to the Kabul Museum in Afghanistan in March 2007.[6]

Nevertheless, Sir Colin Renfrew, archaeologist and one of the foremost authorities on cultural heritage protection, insists that the 'safe haven' concept is not without risks and potential problems: 'The real risk in accepting the "Safe Haven" principle, whereby approval would be implied that in some circumstances antiquities could be appropriately conserved outside their country of origin, is that either private collectors or museums might misuse it in order to extend their collections'.[7] In fact the validity of this concern was borne out in Afghanistan, especially during the time of the Taliban (1996–2001). The Norwegian collector, Schoyen, justified his illicit collecting of Afghan Buddhist manuscripts from the Bamiyan Valley in the 1990s as a case of 'rescuing' endangered heritage. The difference between this and the safe haven concept is that Schoyen's motivations clearly extended beyond preservation, as demonstrated by his attempt to sell his collection after the fall of the Taliban in 2001, at an astronomical profit.

The tension between art and antiquities as national property or international property is, of course, of very long standing. The example of the Elgin (or

Parthenon) marbles is probably the best known and most illustrative case in the field.[8] As it is so well known I will not elaborate on it, but will only mention that the British claim to be 'protecting' the marbles is somewhat undermined now that there is a fully equipped museum next to the Parthenon to host them. The question 'who has a right to the marbles?' is a question that ultimately boils down to competing claims, one based on legal rights and the other on moral rights.

Legal ramifications

What are the ramifications of all of this for existing ways of thinking about cultural property protection? Initially there were two main approaches: the nationalist view (cultural nationalism) as opposed to the internationalist view (cultural internationalism). The nationalist view stresses the relationship between cultural objects and national heritage and seeks to maintain objects inside their country of origin or to ask for their return or restitution if they have been removed at some point in the past. According to the internationalist view cultural heritage is of international interest and a free flow of objects should prevail. In these views it is primarily the ownership of the items that is at stake. However, more recently a third way of thinking has emerged: archaeologists and ethnographers argued that it should not be ownership but knowledge that prevails; that is, an object's meaning is best understood in its cultural context.

The first two views are reflected in the various international conventions concerning cultural property or cultural heritage. We can trace in the evolution of these conventions the development of these views over time.

The Convention for the Protection of Cultural Property in the Event of Armed Conflict (1954)

The Convention for the Protection of Cultural Property in the Event of Armed Conflict (1954), which came about as a reaction to the destruction of cultural property in the Second World War, reflected, to some extent, the *cultural internationalism* perspective. It was considered important to set out clear measures for the protection of cultural property, and for the first time the Common Heritage of Mankind principle was proclaimed in the Preamble of the Convention: ' ... *Being convinced that damage to cultural property belonging to any people whatsoever means damage to the cultural heritage of all mankind, since each people makes its contribution to the culture of the world* ...' In other words, the concept of a kind of cultural heritage belonging to the whole world that had become the responsibility of all contracting parties came into existence.

The Protocol to the 1954 Convention is applicable especially to movable heritage in the event of armed conflict and may be joined separately from the 1954 Convention. It states specifically that cultural property shall never be retained as war reparation, and requires each State Party, among other things, to: (a) prevent the exportation of cultural property from a territory occupied by it during an armed conflict; (b) take into its custody cultural property imported into its territory either directly or indirectly from any occupied territory; (c) return, at the close of hostilities to the competent authorities of the territory previously occupied, such cultural property which is in its territory, and pay an indemnity to the holders in good faith of such property.

The 'safe haven' concept used for Afghanistan is an interesting example of the provisions of the Protocol and the concept of 'Common Heritage of Mankind'. As Mr Feroozi, the chief researcher at the Ministry of Information and Culture of Afghanistan, proudly proclaimed during the closing ceremony of the exhibition, in April 2008 in Amsterdam: the Afghan objects had become the common shared heritage of the world.

The Convention on the Means of Prohibiting and Preventing the Illicit Import, Export and Transfer of Cultural Property (1970)

In the 1960s, during the decolonisation process, former colonies became aware of the extent of losses of their cultural property. This insight contributed to the drafting of the Convention on the Means of Prohibiting and Preventing the Illicit Import, Export and Transfer of Cultural Property (1970). This Convention reflected the *cultural nationalism* perspective: cultural objects belong to their countries of origin. As a result, many countries started to halt the export of cultural property and to claim back property that had been taken earlier. Several former colonial countries responded by acknowledging the rights of their former colonies to these objects by acceding to the Convention and/or restitution of objects.

The UNIDROIT Convention on Stolen or Illegally Exported Cultural Objects (1995)

Despite some success of the 1970 Convention on the Means of Prohibiting and Preventing the Illicit Import, Export and Transfer of Cultural Property, it turned out that the Convention did not have the anticipated results. Accordingly, the International Institute for Unification of Private Law (UNIDROIT), based in Rome, was asked to draft a new private international law Convention to complement the UNESCO 1970 Convention. As a result the UNIDROIT Convention on Stolen or Illegally Exported Cultural Objects was introduced in 1995. The provisions in this convention are much stricter and rigorous than in the 1970 Convention and the rights of the person or institution that has suffered loss of cultural property are much better protected. For example, unlike the 1970 Convention there is a uniform treatment for restitution of stolen or return of illegally exported cultural objects; all stolen and/or illicitly exported cultural objects are covered, not just inventoried objects; cultural objects that have been unlawfully excavated are to be considered stolen and protected (i.e. restituted) as such if this is consistent with the law of the State where the excavation took place. The 1995 UNIDROIT Convention also adds a moral dimension to the trade of cultural objects by only giving the right to compensation on condition of having exercised *due* (or reasonable) *diligence* at the time of acquisition (article 4 (1)). This diligence test may include a review of the character of the parties, the price paid, and whether accessible registers of stolen cultural objects and other relevant documentation were consulted (article 4 (4)). So the purchaser has to prove that he or she has acted with *'due diligence'* during acquisition of the object to have the right to *just compensation*.

As a consequence of these strict rules far fewer States decided to accede to the 1995 UNIDROIT Convention (29 States Parties)[9] than to the 1970 UNESCO Convention (117 States Parties).[10]

In 1972 the UNESCO Convention on the Protection of the World Cultural and Natural Heritage came into force. Although its primary purpose is not concerned with the prevention of theft of cultural objects it requires mention here to complete the list of relevant UNESCO Conventions. Other Conventions with some relevance agreed since the beginning of the new millennium include: the Convention on the Protection of the Underwater Cultural Heritage (2001), the Convention for the Safeguarding of the Intangible Cultural Heritage (2003) and the Convention on the Protection and Promotion of the Diversity of Cultural Expressions (2005).

These Conventions provide an interesting reflection of the developments in thinking about what exactly was in need of protection. In the 1954 and 1970 Conventions it is 'cultural property'. This shifted to 'cultural heritage' and even 'cultural expressions' in the Conventions of the twenty-first century. In addition, the distinction between tangible and intangible was emphasised at the turn of the millennium to fulfil a growing demand for the safeguarding of threatened living cultures.

Keeping in mind the goals and context of the most recent UNESCO Conventions it would appear that today the more nationalistic perspective seems to be prevailing over the internationalist one. This is probably because of the intergovernmental nature of UNESCO. It may also be a reaction to the globalisation process whose spreading tentacles are reaching now almost every corner of the globe, and which, it is widely perceived, threatens cultural diversity and integrity.

Indeed, the above-mentioned protective nationalist approach is most probably a response to what has been actually happening around the world. The illicit trade in art and antiquities is flourishing.[11] The reasons for this appear, at first, paradoxical: there has been an increase in both wealth and poverty. The number of wealthy people is growing fast, not only in the traditionally wealthy parts of the world, but also in places like China. This creates a demand for special and unique items. Recently flower bulbs became *en vogue* again, as they were in the Netherlands in the seventeenth century when they constituted an overheated speculative market. The demand for exotic, genuine art and antiquities is growing. Many art dealers and collectors specialise in art objects from countries that restrict their art trade, claiming that in that way they help to protect the items from deterioration and neglect. Another argument used is that the trade provides the countries of origin with financial resources. Often, so-called 'source countries', countries where the supply of objects exceeds the demand, are developing countries with high levels of poverty. If such countries fall victim to civil or military strife the risk of illicit trade by theft or excavation is greatly exacerbated. In such circumstances it is difficult to blame poor individuals for trying to earn a little income by illicit excavation. Alternative sources of income and education about the harm caused by their activities are needed, although it is acknowledged that this is much easier said than done in most cases.

Art dealers and collectors also make the argument that in purchasing these objects knowledge about a country and its culture is being spread. In fact, this argument is viewed with sympathy in some quarters. Recall the Norwegian collector, Schoyen, who purchased many antique manuscripts from all over the world. He digitised them and made them available on the internet to enable experts and others to study these hitherto often unknown pieces. The Afghan pieces were analysed, translated and published, undoubtedly adding to the reservoir of knowledge about the country. However, was Schoyen only motivated by scholarly generosity or also other goals? After the digitisation he offered his collection for sale in 2001. Several interesting facts should be mentioned. The price he asked was far more substantial than the prices he had paid for these pieces: it should be noted that the value in general, and price in particular, of objects rises by making them known to the world. The Afghan manuscripts were looted from the Bamiyan Valley during the 1990s, in the middle of the war, and smuggled out of Afghanistan to London, where Schoyen bought them from the Dickensianly-named London art dealer Sam Fogg. The 1995 UNIDROIT Convention on Stolen or Illegally Exported Cultural Objects was signed by Norway in 2001 and entered into force in that country in March 2002. Showing remarkable timing, Schoyen offered his collection for sale just before this date, aware, perhaps, that the Convention cannot be applied retroactively.

According to Norwegian law Schoyen's actions were legally right; from an ethical perspective they appear somewhat more dubious. Perhaps in response to years of debate among scholors,[12] politicians and journalists, Schoyen decided to return 65 Buddhist manuscripts to the National Museum of Kabul, including several pieces that had been looted from the same Museum during the same period as the ivory bull's head.[13]

In this context it should be mentioned that several archaeological journals, such as *American Antiquity*, now prohibit the publication of materials that are 'recovered in such a manner as to cause the unscientific destruction of sites or monuments; or that have been exported in violation of the national laws of their country of origin' (SAA 2003). Researching and publishing this material could help in authenticating and providing provenance for the objects, thus increasing the value and marketability of a private collection, with the possible effect of stimulating more looting and illicit trade (Prott 1995: 60).

Publication of details of art collections held in countries vulnerable to theft and illicit excavation is potentially dangerous. Before this can take place a basic system of protection should be established, including inventories, awareness raising among museum professionals, guards, custom agents and border police, besides ratification of the most important Conventions.

In resolving the tension between cultural nationalism and cultural inter-nationalism (in other words should heritage be seen as national or global heritage?), countries should, fundamentally, be able to decide for themselves. But as most countries prefer to maintain control over their cultural property, its trade needs to be regulated. However, caution needs to be exercised in determining the extent of any such regulation. Declaring all export of art illicit trade can be one of the major pitfalls of a national law seeking to prevent illicit trade, because by not providing regulations for *legal* trade the conditions for the establishment of a black market are created. The law could, in fact, be counterproductive.

Conclusion

Globalisation proceeds at a rapid speed. One response to it has been a nationalisation process in cultural heritage conventions. This runs counter to global trends, because the demand for art objects continues to rise. Formerly little-known regions now take centre stage but are unprotected and unprepared for the challenges posed by their new status. Measures are quickly needed if they want to retain their national heritage, and avoid the fate of the beautiful Afghan collection.

And what is going to happen to the Afghan collection after its *tour du monde*? When will it return to Afghanistan? It is to be hoped that some form of peace and security

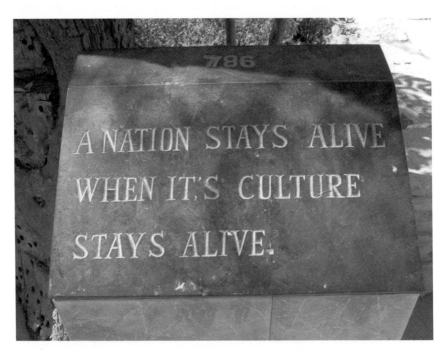

Figure 4.3 Inscription outside the National Museum in Kabul. (Photo courtesy J. van Krieken-Pieters)

will finally return to that troubled country so that these valuable works can be exhibited in the National Museum of Kabul. It would enable Afghans to enjoy their own heritage and to pay tribute to the maxim '*a nation stays alive when its culture stays alive*'. The bull's head is ready to go home after all these years of exile.

Notes

1 The collection was on display from December 2006 to September 2009 in France, Italy, the Netherlands and the U.S. (Washington D.C., San Francisco, Houston, New York).

2 In 2004 I had the honour and the pleasure to go with Mr. Massoudi, the Director of the National Museum in Kabul, to the first meeting in the National Geographic Society Building in Washington D.C. to talk about the publication of the Bactrian Hoard. With hindsight I realise what a special moment that was in the course of the preservation of Afghanistan's Cultural Heritage. From that moment onwards Afghanistan's treasures became more and more a globalised heritage. It was in those days nearly impossible to imagine that the precious objects would be part of a travelling exhibition to the Western World.

3 A different issue but appropriate in this context: The exhibition, *Benin: Kings and Ritual Court Arts from Nigeria*, went to the Art Institute of Chicago (A.I.C.) from 10 July to 21 September 2008 as the final station of this travelling exhibition. The exhibition, which started in Vienna and went to Paris and Berlin, generated considerable debate about restitution of stolen art. It is to be noted that the exhibition, which is the biggest ever held on Benin art, will not be seen in Nigeria.

4 SPACH was at one time given the right to inspect boxes with a record of what was packed, but turned the offer down to keep the boxes safely stored.

5 http: <http://portal.unesco.org/es/ev.php-URL_ID=3712&URL_DO = DO_TOPIC&URL_SECTION = 201.html> (accessed 5 December 2005).

6 See *International Herald Tribune*, 8 March, 2007.

7 Professor Renfrew, personal correspondence, December 2005.

8 The so-called Elgin Marbles are the marble figurative sculptures of the Acropolis in Athens that were taken 200 years ago from Athens to London by the British Lord Elgin, the then envoy of the English crown, to the Ottoman Sultan in Constantinople. At that time Athens formed part of the Ottoman Empire. Lord Elgin removed the sculptures with the permission of the Ottoman government. The Elgin Marbles were purchased in 1816 by the British government for a low price, after a parliamentary commission had pronounced that the works of art were of such exceptional cultural value that they should be owned by the state. That is how they ultimately ended up in the British Museum. The Elgin Marbles have been the subject of dispute between the British and Greek governments for several decades. The Greeks would like them back in their own country to give them a place in the brand-new Acropolis Museum. The British claim legal ownership.

9 On 15 May 2009.

10 On 15 May 2009.

11 Although the financial crisis might change this.

12 The indefatigable efforts by Atle Omland should be mentioned in this context. For more information see: http://folk.uio.no/atleom/manuscripts.htm.

13 The official website of the Afghan Ministry of Foreign Affairs reported:

The Schoyen Collection offered 65 historical manuscripts to Afghanistan National Museum. These manuscripts that are related to Buddhism traced back to almost two thousand years ago.

The Schoyen Collection is one of the largest private collections in the world and the owner of 13,000 valuable historical monuments. Mr. Martin Schoyen, the owner of this collection, gifted seven manuscripts in October 2007 and 58 manuscripts on 5 February 2008 to National Museum through the Afghanistan Embassy to Norway and the Ministry of Foreign Affairs.

Mr Schoyen had bought these manuscripts from smugglers and exhibited them at the Schoyen Collection. ... They were transferred to European markets by smugglers until Mr Schoyen got them. Then, the manuscripts were analysed, translated and published in three large volumes by Japanese and Norwegian archeologists.

'Sixty-five historical monuments are to go back home', announcement on the official website of Afghan Ministry of Foreign Affairs, posted on: Mar 08, 2008, (http://www.mfa.gov.af/detail.asp?Lang=e&Cat=1&ContID = 592).

Bibliography

Cambon, P. (2007) *Hidden Afghanistan* (catalogue), Amsterdam: Stichting Nieuwe Kerk.

Krieken, van, J. (2006) *Art and Archaeology of Afghanistan. Its Fall and Survival. A Multi-disciplinary Approach*, Leiden: Brill Academic Publishers.

Merryman, J.H. (1998) 'Cultural Property Ethics', *International Journal of Cultural Property*, 7: 21–31.

Prott, L.V. (1995) 'National and international laws on the protection of the cultural heritage', in K. Walker Tubb (ed.) *Antiquities. Trade or Betrayed. Legal, Ethical and Conservation Issues*, London: Archetype Publications: 57–66.

SAA (2003) *Editorial Policy, Information for Authors & Style Guide*, Society for American Archaeology, Washington D.C.

On the Schoyen Collection: http://folk.uio.no/atleom/manuscripts.htm

Chapter 5

Globalising intangible cultural heritage?

Between international arenas and local appropriations

Chiara Bortolotto

The United Nations Educational, Scientific and Cultural Organization (UNESCO) shares the widespread contemporary popular and academic concern about globalisation and responds by making the protection of 'cultural diversity' the pivot of its overall cultural policy. In particular, the 'threat of globalisation' is assumed to be especially dangerous for the most recent UNESCO heritage domain, Intangible Cultural Heritage (ICH). The Convention for the Safeguarding of the Intangible Cultural Heritage refers to the issue of globalisation in the preamble, recognising that:

> the processes of globalisation and social transformation, alongside the conditions they create for renewed dialogue among communities, also give rise, as does the phenomenon of intolerance, to grave threats of deterioration, disappearance and destruction of the intangible cultural heritage, in particular owing to a lack of resources for safeguarding such heritage.
>
> (UNESCO 2003)

The issue of the relationship between ICH and globalisation has been especially addressed by an International Conference, *Globalisation and Intangible Cultural Heritage*, held by UNESCO and the United Nations University in Tokyo in 2004. Globalisation is here assumed to be a threat to a 'fragile heritage' like ICH, which is considered the mainspring of cultural diversity (UNESCO and UNU 2004). If the set of global processes which threaten the 'richness' of world 'cultural diversity' is assumed as 'bad' globalisation by UNESCO, the discourse of the organisation set apart the 'globalisation with a human face'. As it is recalled by UNESCO Director General this kind of globalisation would create 'conditions for renewed dialogue among communities' and 'opportunities for interaction and dialogue, thereby contributing to the spread of knowledge about other cultures and heightening people's awareness of their own cultures' (Matsuura 2004: 13). UNESCO is therefore not only committed to addressing the issue of globalisation but takes it as a complex, multifaceted issue.

Nonetheless, from the standpoint of external observers, UNESCO is also a major globalising actor in that it is founded on the ideals of universalism, it is operated by a global bureaucratic apparatus and it advocates common cultural, educational and scientific policies on a global scale. In particular, UNESCO World Heritage (WH) interventions are considered by the observers of their impact at the ground level as introducing (or imposing) external values (cultural, economic, social) which would undermine local ways of coping with the past, memory and transmission of culture (McCoy Owens 2002; Shepherd 2006; Scholze 2008; Berliner forthcoming).

William Logan identifies several globalising features of UNESCO WH programs: improving international practice; promoting particular sets of heritage values and conservation practices; establishing common management practices in World Heritage sites. To these he adds effects of UNESCO intervention that have unintended consequences and involve social and economic change: gentrification and attraction of commercial services for international tourism (Logan 2002: 52–53). According to Jan Turtinen (2000), moreover, a universalist aim and a complex, highly structured praxis, based on uniform criteria descending from global to local contexts, gives World Heritage not just a global but also a globalising program.

The heritage paradigm underpinning WH differs in many regards from that of ICH. A gap of 30 years separates the establishment of the institutional domain of ICH from that of WH and this new heritage definition undoubtedly attempts to adapt to new social and cultural contexts as well as to more recent academic perspectives. In particular ICH is the outcome of a cultural relativist perspective influenced by post-modernist trends (Logan 2002). ICH attempts thus to shift from the universalism underpinning WH and the overall UNESCO early modernist perspective. The more inclusive and relativist idea of 'representativeness' replaces that of 'outstanding universal value'. More concretely, ICH involves a reflexive approach to heritage, as the potential of an element to be turned into something called 'heritage' is assumed to be established by its 'bearers'. In other words, rather than tailoring the heritage *interest* of an element to pre- and externally defined criteria, as was the case of WH, ICH would depend on the different subjective heritage *values* of different communities. This resonates with collaborative approaches to heritage, as suggested for example in north American anthropology and museology (Phillips 2003; Karp et al. 1997; Kurin 2007; Early and Seitel 2002) and adopted in the European Union's most recent approach to heritage (Council of Europe 2005), as well as with the idea of 'grassroots globalisation' put forward by Arjun Appadurai (2000).

Yet, relying on standard-setting instruments like international conventions or declarations undermines the principle of cultural relativism in that it involves the establishment of a uniform framework. Furthermore, the concrete empowerment of grassroots communities, as put forward by the bottom-up ICH approach, is considerably weakened by the national validation process necessary for heritage authorisation in the UNESCO system.

Despite the good intentions animating its advocates and the undeniable theoretical advances represented by the ICH paradigm, it would be difficult to argue that global ICH policies, and in particular the international Lists introduced by the 2003 Convention, do not have globalising outcomes. In this chapter I argue that globalising effects are a structural implication of actions driven by international fora and

I compare the case of the 1873 Vienna Universal Exhibition with UNESCO and the international negotiations leading to the 2003 Convention. This comparative analysis will also demonstrate that in the case of ICH 'globalisation' does not equate to 'Westernisation'.

In the perspective adopted in the presentation of this issue, international cultural policies or global heritage programs are not considered (only) as unbiased actions aimed at diffusing knowledge and education or concerted efforts made by nations to protect what is assumed to be a 'common heritage', but (also) as a means for international players to export cultural models via the global transposition of the founding principles of their national heritage protection systems. As we will see, international relations and diplomatic strategies play a major role in this process. This process involves exporting expertise and has therefore economic consequences. It involves also, more comprehensively, the export of cultural models. This means that the cultural background underlying such heritage treatments is exported to other cultures, which are called to deal and compromise with it. As this process basically transposes local models on a global scale it can be considered as falling into the realm of globalisation. The processes and the outcomes of national interpretations of this global paradigm have to do with the flow, circulation, transmission and appropriation of culture and are therefore a major, and unexplored, anthropological research field.

I will question the issue of globalisation and heritage policies through a comparative analysis of institutional acculturations to exogenous heritage domains and paradigms both in the Eastern (past) and Western (contemporary) worlds. I will consider the role played by international arenas and international diplomatic relations in these cases and I will focus on the impact of the Japanese paradigm of ICH on Western (Italian) heritage categories at the ground level. My case study considers in particular the actual possibilities of the understanding of the UNESCO definition of ICH with regards to the criterion of authenticity.

Vienna, Universal Exhibition, 1873

Four pages of the *Officieller General-Catalog* of the Vienna 1873 Universal Exhibition testify to the development of the Japanese industrial and cultural production at that time. Considerably less than the 84 pages for France or the 65 for Italy or the 17 for England or Romania or the USA, they are nonetheless evidence of the efforts of Meiji economic policy makers to promote the international trade of Japanese traditional handicrafts and of the strong support provided by the Japanese government for the participation of the handicraft industries in International Exhibitions (Conant 1991). After having successfully attended the 1867 Paris International Exhibition, the Japanese government carefully planned and sponsored an extensive exhibit in Vienna. The 1873 exhibition was a tremendous success and strengthened the popularity of Japanese traditional handicrafts in the West (Kikuchi 2004). This participation has in fact usually been associated with the spread of Japonism in European *fin-de-siècle* art and was undoubtedly a key event in the diffusion of the Japanese aesthetic (Pantzer 1990).

At the same time, this experience has been a founding event in domestic Japanese cultural history. Historians of Japanese designs and aesthetics emphasise the fact that in the catalogue listing the objects to be displayed at the 1873 Universal Exhibition of Vienna a new term appears, associating Japanese objects with the Western notions that informed the structure of the exhibition and the experience of the visitors: '*bijutsu*' was coined to translate the European notion of 'fine arts' into Japanese (Marra 2001; Kikuchi 2004; Guth 1996). Nonetheless, according to a historian of Japanese art and design, *bijutsu* applies to objects previously referred to as *gigei* (technical art), which embraced both concepts of 'fine art' and 'craft' (Kikuchi 2004). Translating at the same time '*Kunst*' (fine arts), '*kunstgewerbe*' (arts and crafts) and '*bildende kunst*' (visual arts), the idea of *bijutsu* as it is used in the program of the exhibition seems to be still a rather fuzzy notion associating fine and applied arts (Yoshinori 2003).

The concrete transformation of this new word into an institutional domain came shortly after the Vienna Exhibition, with the establishment of cultural institutions meant to exhibit or teach *bijutsu*. *Bijutsu* museums, galleries, exhibitions and schools defined the concept's actual domain and consolidated its meaning more clearly (Kikuchi 2004; Yoshinori 2003). Nonetheless, the transposition of the notion of fine arts into the Japanese context was puzzling and confusing. As Michael Marra

Figure 5.1 The Japanese pavilion at the Vienna international exhibition, 1873 (Photo courtesy MAK)

explains, the use of different Japanese expressions to translate 'art' as it is employed in Western aesthetic treatises is evidence of the fact that 'as late as 1883–84 there was neither consensus nor clarity on the meaning of "art" and that a distinction between "practical skills" and "autonomous art" was not yet established' (Marra 2001: 6). At the end of the nineteenth century, the idea of 'art' as a cultural and institutional category was an alien domain in the Japanese aesthetic and institutional culture. The Japanese acculturation to the Western notion of 'art' that followed the Vienna exhibition proves how the involvement in international fora requires engagement with the taxonomies animating the international arena: new institutional and cultural domains are driven by classificatory requirements necessary to deal and engage in dialogue with global contexts.

Paris, UNESCO, 2003

In June 2003, after two weeks of diplomatic negotiations hosted in the Paris UNESCO headquarters, the Convention for the Safeguarding of Intangible Cultural Heritage was drafted. The text was approved by the General Conference in October, came into force in 2005 and is now ratified by 114 countries.

During the negotiations, and even after the adoption of the text by the General Conference, delegates of many countries were uncomfortable with the concept of intangibility. The baffling issue of intangibility was the source of most mocking questions: 'Are the puppets tangible or intangible?', 'do you really think that *beuf à la bourgignonne* is intangible?' and so on. In the same vein a satirical article published in the *Atlantic Monthly* in 2001 wondered 'what could be the intangible equivalent of Angkor Wat or the Acropolis, of Tikal or the Taj Mahal?' (Murphy 2001: 20, 21).

Figure 5.2 Room 1, Unesco Headquarters, Paris (Photo courtesy Tito Dupret/ 1001wonders.org)

These reactions are evidence of the lack of Western cultural and institutional background in this field.

A new heritage domain had come into being but lacked an institutional background in Western heritage systems. We may wonder whether the disorientation of Western heritage professionals facing what was perceived as a slippery concept is similar to that of Japanese Imperial administrators when they tried to comprehend the notion of 'fine art' and to translate '*bijutsu*' into an institutional concept.

In fact, just as '*bijutsu*' translates 'kunst' from the Vienna Exhibition program, ICH corresponds to 'mukei bunkazai' from the Japanese Law for the Protection of Cultural Properties. Enacted in 1950, this law established the concept of 'intangible cultural properties'. The law was modified in 1954, dividing the field of 'intangible properties' into 'intangible cultural properties' encompassing the skills employed in drama, music and applied arts; and 'folk-cultural properties' comprising everyday manners and customs (Cultural Properties Protection Department 1950, Cap. I Art. 2(2); 2(3)). In the Japanese law, Intangible Cultural Properties consist of skills embodied by individuals or groups of individuals who represent the highest mastery of the techniques concerned. As is the case with 'Tangible Cultural Properties', among intangible cultural properties a special designation is attributed to the holders of 'important intangible cultural properties', commonly known as 'Living Human Treasures'. This recognition, intended for the intangible practice rather than the practising person or the material product, implies safeguarding measures in order to allow the transmission of the skills (Cultural Properties Protection Department 1950, Cap. III-2, 56–3).

Just as the Japanese idea of '*bijutsu*' was imported from Europe, the actual global institution of ICH owes much to its Japanese model. Yet, when Japan opened to the West in the Meiji era, the idea of 'fine art', which had gradually spread since the Italian Renaissance, had already affected the non-Western world, shaping its cultural institutions and programs. On the other hand, at the beginning of the twenty-first century ICH was still an exotic institutional curiosity, which, outside UNESCO, was taken into account only by specialists of Japanese or Korean cultural policies (Moeran 1997; Thornbury 1994; Jongsung 2003) and was not yet transposed into Western cultural policies.

Before 2003, the set of cultural expressions formerly referred to as 'folklore' had actually been addressed by cultural policies in Western European countries. These heritage domains (for example *patrimoine ethnologique* in France or *beni demoetnoantropologici* in Italy) did not, however, enjoy the kind of legitimacy conferred by UNESCO's authority. Most importantly, these heritage models were substantially different from the paradigm of 'mukei bunkazai' which inspired the UNESCO programme. They were mostly concerned with the promotion of the visible and tangible incarnation of popular and 'traditional' cultural expressions in museums (*ecomusées* in France and *musei etnologici* in Italy). At the same time they were strongly involved in professional research activities of ethnographic documentation. ICH, as it is defined by UNESCO, takes into account these museum-based and research-based actions but aims to be first and foremost an effective tool for intervention. Its goal is not to have heritage professionals exposing or documenting ICH but rather to allow the 'bearers' of ICH themselves to transmit their practices and know-how.

International relations and the import/export of cultural categories

Both the Vienna International Exhibition and UNESCO as the international forum for the negotiation of the 2003 Convention may be considered, *mutatis mutandis*, major arenas, if not players, in the flow and exchange of cultural classifications and heritage policies. Both are evidence of the will to export specific cultural models and the know-how which comes with them. As Jan Turtinen puts it, 'just like world exhibitions have been, and still are, arenas for international competition and ranking, World Heritage provides an arena for the same purposes' (2000).

Turning local phenomena into global ones, international fora play a major role in globalisation processes. Yet, while in the nineteenth century observers of international relations tended to use benign terms to designate the modernising influence exerted by Western countries in such contexts as universal exhibitions, today social scientists tend to define the intervention of international organisations in more critical terms as 'homogenising'.

In *fin-de-siècle* Vienna as well as in the contemporary UN system, the capacity to exert an influence in these negotiations depends on the position of the players and involves power relations. Despite different historical and geopolitical settings, these negotiations of cultural models in international arenas are founded on diplomatic strategies. Two observers of Japanese cultural policies underline the role played by international relations in importing and, more recently, exporting cultural paradigms to and from Japan: Henry Dyer, a Scottish engineer, and, 90 years later, Marc Bourdier, a French architect.

Henry Dyer was appointed Principal of the Imperial College of Engineering, founded in Tokyo in 1873 to transfer Western industrial methods and technology for the development of Japanese communication and industry. He described his Japanese experience in *Dai Nippon: The Britain of the East, a study in national evolution*. In this report he mentions the Western (namely Italian) influence on the establishment of a School of Art:

> For a year or two after I went to Japan my time was so fully taken up with the Imperial College of Engineering and the industrial establishments connected with it, that the art side of Japanese life to a large extent escaped my attention. I was led to take an interest in it by a proposal on the part of the Government to start a School of Art, in European style, in connection with the College. All the more important foreign Powers were anxious to have a hand in what they were pleased to call 'civilizing' of Japan. The Americans were influential in general education, the British in the navy and public works, the French in the military service, and the Germans in medicine. The Engineering College represented the United Kingdom, as we had on our staff graduates of English,

Scottish, and Irish universities. The Italians thought that their special sphere was that of art, and they were anxious that there should be a School of Art in which they could impart the methods and ideals of European art. To please them the Government established such a school, which was, for convenience, connected with the Engineering College.

(Dyer 1904: 207)

Within the College, a Technical Art School (*Kobu Bijutsu Gakko*) was opened in 1876 to teach Western fine arts to Japanese students. Hirobumi Ito, Minister of Public Works, appointed three Italian teachers: Antonio Fontanesi, Vincenzo Lagusa and Giovanni Vincenzo Cappelletti, teaching respectively painting, sculpture and drawing. The choice to identify the paradigm of Western 'fine arts' with the Italian one may be considered (also) as an achievement of Italian diplomacy. Hirobumi Ito was in fact a member of the Japanese delegation (Iwakura Mission) sent on a two-year diplomatic mission to the USA and Europe to obtain information regarding foreign laws and regulations that might be applicable to Japan.

Upon their arrival in Florence the mission was welcomed by Alessandro Fè d'Ostiani who had been appointed minister plenipotentiary to Japan and China in 1870 and who was a key player in the relation between the two countries at the time. In 1873, the same year as the Vienna Exhibition, he returned to Italy specifically to accompany the Japanese delegation.

Silvana De Maio maintains in her assessment of the Italian stage of the Iwakura Mission: 'In reality, the itinerary of the visit to Italy had been arranged in order to visit the origins of European civilization, classical antiquity and the art of the Renaissance' (De Maio 1998: 154). The delegation was taken to the Uffizi gallery, to the Vatican Museums and to the Basilica of St Peter as well as to visit monuments of ancient Rome like the Colosseum and the Spa Baths of Caracalla. The southern itinerary also included Pompeii and Herculaneum. Before leaving for Vienna, the mission was taken to Venice, where it visited the Basilica of St Mark, and to Milan. It is noteworthy that in this artistic tour was included a glimpse of Italian craftsmanship: a visit to a porcelain factory near Florence (Ginori) and to a glass factory in Venice (De Maio 1998: 154): the Italian experience and the arguments advanced by Fè d'Ostiani turned out to be convincing and would have excellent outcomes over the following few years. The Italian fine-arts model was eventually exported together with Italian experts hired by the Japanese government.

More than one century after the diplomatic agreement between Alessandro Fè d'Ostiani and Hirobumi Ito, Yuri Kodera, the *Console Generale del Giappone a Milano*, saluted the conference '*Il Giappone a Brescia-Brescia in Giappone*', organised in 2002 in Brescia, hometown of Alessandro Fè d'Ostiani. In his speech, the Japanese consul underlined how important was the role played by his diplomatic intervention in the Japanese choice of cultural leading models:

We owe much to the ambassador Fè d'Ostiani, if we, the Japanese, get acquainted with western technology and art. Without his presence, Japan would have been very different from the existing one, because despite the distance and geographical position, our country considers itself more or less as a western country in Asia. This fact is maybe also due to a very distinctive tendency of Japanese mentality: the Japanese are very good in assimilating and absorbing other cultures in their own culture, as happened in the far years of its own history with China and Korea [author's own translation from Italian].

This West-East influence was to be eventually overturned. In 1993, just one year after Japan ratified the Convention Concerning the Protection of the World Cultural and Natural Heritage, Marc Bourdier, an architect and Japanese heritage expert, concluded his analysis on the Japanese model of heritage protection with a question:

> The debates on the future of world heritage within international organizations in charge of its conservation are going to be especially interesting to follow in the near future if the seats of the highest administrative functions are to be held by representatives of the Nippon archipelago.
>
> Are we shortly going to witness a tremendous overturned transfer of skills, which we would never have imagined to happen in a field so specific to every country as that of the protection of the traces of its past? Such is the question that we have the right to ask ourselves when, on the international arena, Japan doesn't aim anymore just to economic supremacy, but also to a recognition in other, more significant, fields.
>
> (Bourdier 1993: 108; author's own translation from French)

A few years later, Noriko Aikawa, at that time chief of the Intangible Cultural Heritage Section, acknowledged that 'thanks to the generous sponsorship of the Japanese Ministry of Foreign Affairs' UNESCO was able to organise an international conference to draw up new guidelines for the Intangible Cultural Heritage Program. This was indeed a momentous event, because the idea of ICH, at the time still almost unheard of in the UNESCO environment, was clearly introduced and tackled (UNESCO 1993). Noriko Aikawa also recalls that 'the UNESCO/Japan Funds-In-Trust for the Safeguarding and Promotion of the Intangible Cultural Heritage was established in the same year, providing a yearly financial contribution that has given a significant impetus to the program' (Aikawa 2001). Acknowledgements of Japanese financial support open many UNESCO reports on ICH-related activities in the last 10 years, and prove that, far from being part of diplomatic and formal thanks, Noriko Aikawa's statement reflects an actual Japanese commitment to supporting UNESCO projects in the field of ICH. Japanese interest in and influence on the establishment of the 2003 Convention for the Safeguarding of the Intangible Cultural Heritage is openly recognised and has been compared to those of the USA in relation to the 1972 Convention Concerning the Protection of the World Cultural and Natural Heritage (Kono 2004).

A Japanese reply: the issue of authenticity

The eventual recognition of non-Western heritage values in the international arena was not to be easy or rapid. Just like Fontanesi, Lagusa and Cappelletti exported the Italian fine arts paradigm to Japan at the end of the nineteenth century, the experts who, several decades later, would influence the founding criteria to be adopted for World Heritage were mostly European archaeologists, architects and art historians. This cultural background shaped the documents known as the Athens Charter and the Venice Charter (1964) which were to be very influential on the earliest and enduring UNESCO heritage paradigm, conveyed by the 1972 Convention Concerning the Protection of the World Cultural and Natural Heritage (UNESCO 1972). While the Athens Charter introduced the idea of shared global responsibility for heritage protection, the Venice Charter formulated a theory of restoration which inspired the establishment of a 'test of authenticity in design, materials, workmanship and setting' as a condition for inscription on the World Heritage List (WHL), as outlined, since 1977, by the Operational Guidelines for the Implementation of the World Heritage Convention (see Labadi, this volume). According to Françoise Choay (2002), with the exception of one American, all the 118 experts involved in the drafting of the Athens Charter were European and out of the 56 texts published in the conference proceedings 21 were written by Italian authors. There is therefore no surprise if the Athens Charter was later considered a Eurocentric document. According to Paolo Marconi and Claudio D'Amato (2006) the same can be said for the Venice conference, which was strongly influenced by what they call the 'lobby of Italian art historians' and especially by the authority of Cesare Brandi for whom authenticity was an obvious value and an essential condition for heritage authorisation. In this way authenticity, which was a local and historically defined value, albeit dominant at that time, and essential for Western (namely Italian) archaeologists and art historians, was transposed into a global scale, and turned into a universal value.

After the nineteenth-century episode of the export of Italian aesthetic and cultural models to Japan, other Western heritage criteria were to be proposed to the Nippon archipelago through what Jan Turtinen calls the 'UNESCO international heritage grammar' (Turtinen 2000). As the world geopolitical order changed and UNESCO membership opened up to newly independent countries eager to share the prestige of having sites on the WHL, this paradigm became a problem and was subsequently criticised as 'Eurocentric' and 'monumentalist', that is assuming that heritage consists in built elements made of imperishable materials. The new world geopolitical order also had an impact on the secretariat of UNESCO. An African Director General was in charge from 1974 to 1987 and, 12 years later, a Japanese Director General took the lead for ten years (1999–2009). In this atmosphere of renewal, non-Western heritage models were taken into account. In 1994 UNESCO launched a program, the Global Strategy for a Balanced, Representative and Credible World Heritage List, with the objective of rebalancing the WHL (Labadi 2005). The critics of the idea of 'authenticity' as it is defined in the Operational Guidelines for the

Implementation of the World Heritage Convention assume that the imbalance of the WHL was (and still is) a consequence of the establishment of such a criterion. An obvious value for most Western monuments, the idea of 'authenticity' was in fact less pertinent to non-European properties. In particular, the authenticity of materials was hard to prove for African and other non-Western examples of ephemeral wooden architecture built of perishable materials (Saouma-Forero 2001).

The fact that Japan ratified the 1972 *Convention Concerning the Protection of the World Cultural and Natural Heritage* only in 1992 is evidence of the deep conceptual gap separating the Japanese heritage paradigm from the one adopted by UNESCO. The difficult inscription of the Japanese Shinto shrines on the WHL is considered by heritage experts as emblematic of the 'provincial' perspective of WH. These buildings have been ritually renovated every 20 years since 690. For that reason Japanese heritage experts claimed that the authenticity of these sites, rather than lying in the materials, as expected by UNESCO criteria, was to be found in the intangible dimension of the transmission over the generations of techniques and skills of specialised craftspeople (Bourdier 1993; Takashina 1997; Inaba 1995). Therefore, the heritage value of the shrine is not assumed to be embodied in the building itself but in the dynamics of its reconstruction by means of traditional skills transmitted from generation to generation and in its continuing use.

Japan was the main UNESCO contributor of extra-budgetary funds since the withdrawal of the USA in 1984 and particularly uncomfortable with UNESCO heritage criteria. For these reasons this country played an important role in this reconsideration of the whole UNESCO heritage paradigm. In 1994, just one year after its ratification of the 1972 convention, Japan organised a conference in order to reassess authenticity as a founding criterion for inscription on the WH List. The debate raised by the Japanese claims underlined the ethnocentrism of the concept of authenticity as formulated in the Venice Charter and adopted by the Operational Guidelines. Authenticity was criticised as a Western model exported through specialist terminology in the field of architectural restoration. The Nara Document on Authenticity eventually recognised authenticity as a social construct and acknowledged its cultural relativity (Larsen 1995).

Ten years later, in 2004, in the new era of intangible heritage, another conference was organised by Japan in Nara to mark the 40th anniversary of the Venice Charter and the 10th anniversary of the Nara Document. Once more 'authenticity' was the order of the day: the experts convened in Nara asserted that 'considering that intangible cultural heritage is constantly recreated, the term "authenticity" as applied to tangible cultural heritage is not relevant when identifying and safeguarding intangible cultural heritage' (UNESCO 2004).

Authenticity and heritage authorisation of Matera

Did UNESCO finally get rid of the slippery and contested criterion of authenticity? Valdimar Hafstein (2004) argued that the rejection of the term does not involve the rejection of the idea, which would still be operative in the UNESCO discourse on

ICH. Nonetheless the official abolition of authenticity as a criterion for inscription on the UNESCO list of intangible cultural heritage is definitely one of the most interesting innovations that has arisen from the establishment of 'intangible heritage' proposed by UNESCO. The complexity and range of this process stand as UNESCO's most daringly innovative and most problematic propositions in this area. The reconsideration of the value of authenticity reflects UNESCO's process of realignment with regard to the definition of the concept of culture. Over the last two decades, UNESCO has in fact absorbed some contemporary anthropological theories, and aims today to see culture as a dynamic process of contingent social construction that plays itself out on local, national, and global scales. Such a definition would replace the idea of culture as a system of values profoundly rooted in the past and in land, and shared by homogenous groups, an idea that is still common currency, especially in the rhetoric of identity politics.

The abolition of the criterion of authenticity is called for by non-Western countries (among whom Japan is particularly active), is accepted in the international arena, is supported by international policies, and matches with contemporary anthropological theories. Yet, how is this innovation going to be absorbed into the practice of local Western (for example, Italian) heritage politics, founded on a longstanding 'fine arts' and monumental paradigm which finds its raison d'être in the idea of authenticity? As Sophia Labadi demonstrated with regards to World Heritage, the interpretations of the notion of 'authenticity' given by States Parties are extremely disparate and often incongruous with UNESCO's perspective. How is its complete abolition to be interpreted at the different national levels?

As is argued in other chapters in this volume (see Beazley's Labadi's and Askew's chapters), actual national interpretations of instruments, programs and ideas negotiated within UNESCO may be substantially different to their original reference and can be used or abused for local political ends. Yet, local transpositions of the UNESCO heritage paradigm have interesting consequences also for the concrete treatment of heritage and affect therefore local heritage criteria and representations. This very practical question raises a key anthropological issue: that of acculturation. Do cultural and heritage stakeholders acculturate to new heritage categories and criteria? And, if so, how?

My argument shall take as its inspiration a field-study conducted in Matera, a town of 60,000 inhabitants in Southern Italy, in the spring of 2006. The historic neighbourhood of Matera, the 'Sassi', was inscribed on the WHL in 1993. Icons of the city of Matera, the Sassi Barisano and Caveoso, are a stratified and settled system of inhabitable caves carved into the limestone slopes of a deep canyon drained from a stream. These are organised as a complex of cisterns, terraces and stairways constructed according to principles whose ecological sustainability is emphasised in the heritage discourse. One-room houses hosting humans and animals, these dwellings became, in the late 1940s, the national symbol of the backwardness and underdevelopment of the south of Italy. The question of 'what to do with the Sassi' became the subject of much preoccupation, and a special law was passed in 1952, which would eventually lead to the evacuation of the grotto dwellings. 'Frozen' in the 1950s, the site did not undergo the transformations of recent years. The authenticity of the materials and design of the Sassi is therefore considered irreproachable, in the evaluation of the ICOMOS experts, who explain that thanks to its complete evacuation in the 1950s the site has not been compromised, as is often found to be the case in similar sites elsewhere (ICOMOS 1993: 14).

During my fieldwork I focused on the local strategies for promoting local clay whistles (*cucù*), a form of 'traditional' craftsmanship matching the UNESCO definition of ICH. Some 10 cm high, they have the shape of a standing bird or cock. Horizontal polychromous stripes cross the body of the bird-whistle, previously covered with white lime, and connect the head and the tail of the bird, where the whistle pipe is placed. According to scientific references, the pottery tradition in the whole area of the Apulian Murge plateau is indeed induced by the nature of the soil, rich in clay. The abundance of this resource led to the development of economic activities such as the production of kitchen clayware and brick furnaces in the twentieth century. Beside these main activities, craftsmen and kiln workers would cook the small presepio figurines and whistles as a side job (Piangerelli and Sgró 1995). Following ethnologists' interpretations, these objects used to have a para-liturgical function: they were in fact sold until the 1960s at the fair held every May at the sanctuary of the Madonna di Picciano, 12 km from Matera. Until the renovation of the sanctuary in the late 1960s and the consequent demolition of the stands surrounding the church where these objects were sold, pilgrims would prove the accomplishment of their pilgrimages by buying a whistle in Picciano (Sgró 1995). Today the objects experience a second life as identity symbols and are reproduced on signs and logos or turned into monuments (Bortolotto 2009).

These objects and the intangible practices and representations associated with them are neither inscribed on nor candidates for inscription on one of UNESCO's ICH Lists. Nonetheless they meet the definition of ICH put forward by the convention: they are an example of 'traditional craftsmanship', 'object, artefacts' underpinning 'practices, representations, expressions, knowledge, skills [...] that communities, groups and, in some cases, individuals recognize as part of their cultural heritage' (UNESCO 2003 art. 2.2 (e)). They are 'transmitted from generation to generation' and 'constantly recreated by communities and groups in response to their environment, their interaction with nature and their history', and 'provide them with a sense of identity and continuity' (UNESCO 2003 art. 2.1).

Local initiatives attempt to upgrade these objects into the realm of cultural heritage. As we saw, according to UNESCO, intangible heritage is not to be apprehended in terms of authenticity. Does this idea meet local systems of heritage authorisation and promotion?

New initiatives aimed at promoting 'traditional' and 'typical' products are being developed in order to underline their association with the 'traditional' values that provide the typical architectonic quality of the site, for which Matera is now famed throughout the world. The heritage identity of Matera is in fact based on the 'traditional' culture depicted as a 'mixture of craftsmanship and popular knowledge' (Laureano 1993: 12). The initiatives of local heritage stakeholders have therefore seized classic heritage values, conceived for tangible heritage, namely that of authenticity, and reproduced them on the field of the intangible. The establishment of a label of authenticity for 'artistic crafts' is the most explicit evidence of this movement.

Matera DOC

In 2003, the special Board of the Chamber of Commerce of Matera (CESP) launched a project called 'Promotion and appreciation of the DOC and "typical" labels: artistic craftsmanship' to promote the 'culture of typical products underlying their geographical, social and productive roots'. The creation of a collective label 'Matera DOC artistic craftsmanship', to be conferred upon artisan businesses in Matera and the province, has the aim of 'protecting and promoting the artistic vocation of the craftsmen of Matera and of their province, and of safeguarding traditional and cultural heritage'.[1]

The acronym DOC (Controlled Denomination of Origin) was introduced in the Italian regulation in 1963 in order to distinguish and protect the origins of certain products. Now entered in everyday language, DOC has become, by extension, synonymous with 'original' and 'authentic'. The creation of the 'Matera DOC' label, on the model of the better known label used for wine, provides the guarantee of the authenticity of the product, indicating its 'local origin'. On this point the discourse of the promoters of the label is clear: in the products of the label 'are narrated the events of a region, its territory, its customs, and its people'[2] and the skills of the artisans are considered tools that keep alive a tradition which is assumed to be inherent with a territory.

Guaranteed by the collective mark, the authenticity of these goods is produced by the results of the spatial component (geographic origin) and the temporal component (historic depth of the techniques of production). Rooted in the historical-geographic unity which founds the idea of 'territory', authenticity is the product of the crossover point between the natural dimension (in relation to the provenance of the primary materials) and the cultural dimension (continuation of know-how and skills).

The association of this project with the heritage authorisation of the Sassi is taken as a guarantee and, in order to render this connection even more explicit, the CESP has designed a route – La Via delle Botteghe – with the aim of integrating craftsmanship among the tourist attractions of the site.

This example demonstrates how local heritage stakeholders mobilise and exhibit numerous kinds of evidence in order to prove their conformity with tradition and the embeddedness of the local culture. In so doing they guarantee their authenticity and uniqueness. The case of Matera proves therefore that when 'culture' is not just an abstract concept but a concrete object which mobilises political, economic, and identity issues, authenticity is actually still considered as a founding value by local stakeholders for both tangible and intangible heritage.

Conclusion: lost and found in translation

The Nippon–Italian exchange of classifications of cultural expressions shows that despite the fact that heritage systems used to be considered among the most intimate national strategies, they can actually be exported and even turned into global paradigms. Yet, far from being universal, founding ideas of each heritage system, as with the interpretation given to authenticity, are negotiated in specific cultural and historic contexts. As with any acculturation process, this implies a creative appropriation that twists the original one in many respects. This process of creative translation is indeed evidence of what UNESCO would call 'cultural diversity'. From a more technical and operational perspective, the diversity of the institutional cultures called to implement UNESCO ICH international programs makes the consistent application of the convention a complex task to deal with for international heritage specialists.

Notes

1 Regulation for the concession and use of the label 'Matera DOC artigianato artistico' (Matera DOC artistic craftsmanship).
2 This quotation is drawn from the introductory text published in the leaflet distributed by the CESP.

Bibliography

Aikawa, N. (2001) 'The UNESCO Recommendation on the Safeguarding of Traditional Culture and Folklore (1989): Actions Undertaken by UNESCO for Its Implementation', in P. Seitel (ed.) *Safeguarding Traditional Cultures: A Global Assessment of the 1989 UNESCO Recommendation on the Safeguarding of Traditional Culture and Folklore*, Washington: Smithsonian Institution Press:13–19.

Appadurai, A. (2000) 'Grassroots Globalisation and the Research Imagination', *Public Culture*, 12(1): 1–19.

Athens Charter for the Restoration of Historic Monuments (1931). Online. Available HTTP: <http://www.icomos.org/docs/athens_charter.html> (accessed 25 March 2009).

Bortolotto, C. (2009) 'The giant cola cola in Gravina: intangible cultural heritage, property, and territory between UNESCO discourse and local heritage practice', *Ethnologia Europaea*.

Bourdier, M. (1993) 'Le mythe et l'industrie ou la protection du patrimoine culturel au Japon', *Genèses* (11): 82–110.

Choay, F. (ed.) (2002) *La Conférence d'Athènes sur la conservation artistique et historique des monuments (1931)*, Paris: Editions de l'Imprimeur.

Conant, E.P. (1991) 'Refractions of the Rising Sun. Japan's participation in international exhibitions 1862–1910', in: Sato Tomoko and Watanabe Toshio (eds) (1991) *Japan and Britain: an Aesthetic Dialogue 1850–1930*, London: Lund Humphries: 79–92.

Council of Europe (2005) *Framework Convention on the Value of Cultural Heritage for Society*, Faro, 27 October. Online. Available HTTP: <http://conventions.coe.int/Treaty/EN/Treaties/Html/199.htm> (Accessed 15 July 2009).

Cultural Properties Protection Department, Japan (1950) Law for the Protection of Cultural Properties. Online. Available HTTP: <www.wipo.int/tk/en//laws/pdf/japan_cultural.pdf> (Accessed 15 July 2009).

De Maio, S. (1998) 'Italy', in Ian Nish (ed.) (1998) *The Iwakura Mission in America & Europe. A New Assessment*, London: Curzon Press: 149–61.

Dyer, H. (1904) *Dai Nippon. The Britain of the East, a study in national evolution*, London: Blackie and Son.

Early, J. and Seitel, P. (2002) 'UNESCO Draft Convention For Safeguarding Intangible Cultural Heritage: "No Folklore Without the Folk"', *Talk Story*: 22:19.

Guth, C.M.E. (1996) 'Japan 1868–1945: Art, Architecture, and National Identity', *Art Journal*, 55(3): 16–20.

Hafstein, V. (2004) *The Making of Intangible Cultural Heritage: Tradition and Authenticity, Community and Humanity*, PhD Thesis, Berkeley: University of California.

ICOMOS (1993) *WHL Advisory board evaluation World Heritage List, Matera, N°670*, Online. Available HTTP: <http:/whc.unesco.org/archive/advisory_body_evaluation/670.pdf> (Accessed 12 August 2009).

Inaba, N. (1995) 'What Is the Test of Authenticity for Intangible Properties?' in Knut Einar Larsen (ed.) *Nara Conference on Authenticity*, Paris and Tokyo: UNESCO WHC and Agency for Cultural Affairs: 329–32.

International Charter for the Conservation and Restoration of Monuments and Sites (The Venice Charter) (1964) Online. Available HTTP: <http://www.icomos.org/venice_charter.html> (Accessed 24 March 2009).

Jongsung, Yang (2003) *Cultural Protection Policy in Korea: Intangible Cultural Properties and Living National Treasures*, Seoul: Jimoondang.

Karp, I., Mullen Kreamer, C. and Lavine, S.D. (eds) (1992) *Museums and Communities: the Politics of Public Culture*, Washington: Smithsonian Institution Press.

Kikuchi, Y. (2004) *Japanese Modernisation and Mingei Theory: Cultural Nationalism and Oriental Orientalism*, London–New York: RoutledgeCurzon.

Kodera, Yuri s.d. Saluto in occasione della conclusione del ciclo di conferenze 'Il Giappone a Brescia – Brescia in Giappone', 10 maggio 2002. Online. Available HTTP: <www.fujikai. it/public/ ... /20020510_conferenze_console.pdf> (Accessed 19 July 2009).

Kono, Toshiyuki (2004) 'The Basic Principles of the Convention for Safeguarding of Intangible Heritage: A Comparative Analysis with The Convention for Protection of World Natural and Cultural Heritage and Japanese Law', in Masako Yamamoto and Mari Fujimoto (eds) *Utaki in Okinawa and Sacred Spaces in Asia: Community Development and Cultural Heritage*, Tokyo: The Japan Foundation: 37–43.

Kurin, R. (2007) 'Safeguarding Intangible Cultural Heritage: Key Factors in Implementing the 2003 Convention', *International Journal of Intangible Heritage*, 2:10–20.

Labadi, S. (2005) 'A review of the Global Strategy for a balanced, representative and credible World Heritage List 1994–2004', *Conservation and Management of Archeological Sites*, 7 (2): 89–102.

Larsen, K.E. (ed.) (1995) *Nara Conference on Authenticity*, Paris and Tokyo: UNESCO WHC and Agency for Cultural Affairs.

Laureano, P. (1993) *Giardini di pietra. I Sassi di Matera e la civiltà mediterranea*, Torino: Bollati Boringhieri.

Logan, W.S. (2002) 'Globalising heritage: World Heritage as a manifestation of modernism, and challenges from the periphery', in D. Jones (ed.) *Twentieth Century Heritage: Our Recent Cultural Legacy. Proceedings of the Australia ICOMOS National Conference 2001*, Adelaide: University of Adelaide and Australia ICOMOS.

Marconi, P. and D'Amato, C. (2006) 'Premessa alla revisione della Carta di Venezia', in INTBAU Conference, *The Venice Charter Revisited: Modernism and Conservation in the Postwar*

World, Venice, Italy, 2–5 November 2006. Online. Available HTTP: <www.intbau.org/References/marconi.damato.vc.commenti.it.pdf> (Accessed 14 September 2009).

Marra, M.F. (2001) *History of Modern Japanese Aesthetics*, Honolulu: University of Hawaii Press.

Matsuura, Koïkiro (2004) 'Foreword', in International Conference, *Globalisation and Intangible Cultural Heritage*, Tokyo, Japan, 26–27August 2004, Paris: UNESCO/United Nations University. Online. Available HTTP: <http://unesdoc.unesco.org/images/0014/001400/140090e.pdf> (Accessed 12 August 2009).

McCoy Owens, B. (2002) 'Monumentality, identity, and the state: local practice, World Heritage, and heterotopia at Swayambhu, Nepal', *Anthropological Quarterly*, 75(2): 269–316.

Moeran, B. (1997) *Folk Art Potters of Japan. Beyond an Anthropology of Aesthetics*, Richmond, Surrey: Curzon Press.

Murphy, C. (2001) 'Immaterial civilization', *The Atlantic Monthly*, Sept. 288 (2): 20–21.

Pantzer, P. Wieninger J. (ed.) (1990) *Verborgene Impressionen: Japonismus in Wien 1870–1930 (Hidden Impressions: Japonisme in Vienna 1870–1930)*, Wien: Österreichisches Museum für Angewandte Kunst.

Phillips, R. (2003) 'Community collaboration in exhibitions: toward a dialogic paradigm. Introduction', in Laura Peers and Alison Brown (eds) (2003) *Museums and Source Communities: A Routledge Reader, New York: Routledge: 153–70*.

Piangerelli, P. and Sgró, F. (1995) 'Puglia', in Paola Piangerelli (ed.) *La terra il fuoco, l'acqua, il soffio. La collezione dei fischietti di terracotta del Museo Nazionale delle Arti e Tradizioni Popolari*, Roma: De Luca: 267–70.

Saouma-Forero, G. (ed.) (2001) *Authenticity and Integrity in an African Context*, Paris: UNESCO.

Scholze, M. (2008) 'Arrested heritage. The Politics of inscription into the UNESCO World Heritage List: The case of Agadez in Niger', *Journal of Material Culture*, 13(2): 215–32.

Sgró, F. (1995) 'Basilicata', in Paola Piangerelli (ed.) *La terra, il fuoco, l'acqua, il soffio. La collezione dei fischietti di terracotta del Museo Nazionale delle Arti e Tradizioni Popolari*, Roma: Edizioni De Luca: 301–3.

Shepherd, R. (2006) 'UNESCO and the politics of heritage in Tibet', *Journal of Contemporary Asia*, 36(2): 243–57.

Takashina, Suji (1997) 'Le patrimoine de la mémoire', *Cahiers du Japon*, 2: 56–64.

Thornbury, B.E. (1994) 'Cultural properties protection law and folk performing arts', *Asian Folklore Studies*, 53(2): 211–55.

Turtinen, J. (2000) *Globalising Heritage – On UNESCO and the Transnational Construction of a World Heritage*, SCORE Rapportserie (12) Stockholm: Stockholm Centre for Organizational Research. Online. Available HTTP: <www.score.su.se/pdfs/2000–2012.pdf> (Accessed 6 June 2008).

UNESCO (1972) *Convention Concerning the Protection of the World Cultural and Natural Heritage*, Paris, 16 November. Online. Available HTTP: <http:whc.unesco.org/archive/convention-en.pdf> (Accessed 13 July 2009).

UNESCO (1993) UNESCO *International Consultation on New Perspectives for UNESCO Programme: The Intangible Cultural Heritage*, June 1993, Online. Available HTTP: <http://unesdoc.unesco.org/images/0014/001432/143226eo.pdf> (Accessed 18 July 2009).

UNESCO (2003) *Convention for the Safeguarding of the Intangible Cultural Heritage*, Paris, 17 October 2003. Online. Available HTTP: <http://unesdoc.unesco.org/images/0013/001325/132540e.pdf> (Accessed 10 August 2009).

UNESCO (2004) *Yamato Declaration on Integrated Approaches for Safeguarding Tangible and Intangible Cultural Heritage*, Nara, Japan, 20–23 October. Online. Available HTTP: <http://portal.unesco.org/culture/en/files/23863/10988742599Yamato_Declaration.pdf/Yamato_ Declaration.pdf> (Accessed 18 July 2009).

UNESCO and UNU (2004) International conference, *Globalisation and Intangible Cultural Heritage,* Tokyo, Japan, 26–27August 2004, Paris: UNESCO/United Nations University. Online. Available HTTP: <http://unesdoc.unesco.org/images/0014/001400/140090e.pdf> (Accessed 12 August 2009).

Yoshinori, Amagai (2003) 'The Kobu Bijutsu Gakko and the Beginning of Design Education in Modern Japan', *Design Issues*, 19(2): 35–44.

Part II

Heritage, development and globalisation

Chapter 6

Heritage tourism
The dawn of a new era?

Tim Winter

For many years tourism has been one of the principal ways through which the relationship between heritage and globalisation is analytically articulated. Countless studies since the 1970s have considered the arrival of tourism as the precipitator of modernity, of modernisation and of widespread social transformation. There is little doubt this tradition of scholarship will continue to thrive and evolve. By way of a contribution to this research, this chapter sets out to illustrate why current debates in this field need to shift direction, and why frameworks which better reflect the realities of today's global tourism industry need to be developed, most notably ones which can better account for the ongoing rise of non-Western forms of tourism.

In recent years the limitations of accounts which conflate global tourism (read globalisation) with Westernisation (read the Western tourist) have become increasingly apparent. The rapid growth of domestic and intra-regional tourism in Asia, understood as an important manifestation of a 'rising Asia', is calling into question many of the conceptual frameworks and analytical models that have oriented the field of tourism studies to date. Indeed, as I have argued elsewhere, tourism studies is now faced with the challenge of overcoming its Anglo-Western biases if it is to adequately deal with the multi-polar complexities of global tourism in the future (Alneng 2002; Winter 2009; Winter, Teo and Chang 2009). In this chapter I will demonstrate why similar analytical shifts and reforms are required in 'Heritage Studies'. Too often heritage scholarship frames tourism in monolithic terms. In the vast majority of the heritage literature the very word itself – 'tourism' – has come to be a metaphor for destruction, erosion, or commodification. More infrequently, but increasingly so, it is read in less pejorative terms and seen as a source of revival, empowerment or grassroots development. But regardless of the author's persuasion, 'the tourist' is presented throughout such accounts as the embodied carrier of such forces and processes, challenges and opportunities. In an attempt to offer analytical clarification, the heritage field, both in academic and policy environments, often dissects this conceptual monolith into the sub-categories of 'eco-', 'cultural', 'mass' or 'quality' tourists.

However, these categories continue to be conceived and re-conceived with the underlying assumption that 'the tourist' – as modern subject – resides in the post-industrial, global north. Since the 1970s the vast majority of English language studies on tourism and heritage tourism have looked at 'Western' tourists and their impact on communities, places and environments (Winter et al. 2009). This does not mean, however, that 'non-Western' forms of travel have been ignored entirely, but the dominance of a Western-centric notion of tourism means such studies have been analytically subsumed within theories developed in the metropole (Connell 2007, 2009). English language scholarship on heritage rarely questions these prevailing Western-centric paradigms, meaning that accounts of heritage tourism and tourists conceived in the historical, cultural and social changes of Europe and North America are consistently invoked in universalist ways. In looking to address this situation this chapter is not concerned with deconstructing 'the tourist'. Instead my interest here is to illustrate how a form of non-Western tourism, in this case intra-regional Asian tourism, is emerging as a powerful force of social transformation for a series of heritage landscapes. In presenting such an analysis my intention is to highlight why ongoing shifts in today's globalisation mean those concerned with heritage need to look much more closely at non-Western forms of travel and the impact they are now having. In essence, the chapter argues that current analyses of tourism and heritage tourism, with their in-built geographic, national and ethnic biases, need to evolve so that they don't remain blind to important social, cultural and economic shifts now occurring.

Heritage development in Asia: a new era of regionalism

In October 2008 three Cambodian and two Thai soldiers were killed over the disputed temple complex of Preah Vihear. An outstanding example of Khmer architecture dating from the tenth and eleventh centuries, Preah Vihear has been a highly contentious marker of the boundary between Thailand and Cambodia for the past hundred years. On 7 July 2008 Cambodia was awarded its second World Heritage Site, with Preah Vihear being listed in controversial circumstances. While Cambodia's capital, Phnom Penh, erupted into celebrations, Thailand's foreign minister resigned over the issue just three days later. Indeed, the listing of the site became a pivotal issue in the domestic politics of both countries, with politicians on either side of the border using inflammatory rhetoric over the issue to legitimise their credentials in the lead up to their respective national elections. As tensions escalated in the weeks following Preah Vihear's listing, both Thailand and Cambodia moved hundreds of troops and heavy military equipment into the area. The standoff lasted several months, with insults being traded between the two governments and shots exchanged. On 14 October the two sides opened fire on each other again, resulting in the death of three Cambodians and the wounding of seven Thai soldiers. A week later one of the Thai soldiers died from his wounds, and one other was accidentally killed by his weapon.

These events mark the latest chapter in a long-running story of disputed ownership. In 1904 a joint commission made up of Siamese and French administrators, established for mapping the region, proposed a treaty which created a border largely following the watershed line of the Dangrek mountains (Cuasay 2001; Thongchai Winichakul 1994). Given that Preah Vihear surmounted a 525-metre-high spur, the treaty placed the temple within Siamese territory. However, as French cartographers submitted maps to Bangkok in 1908, demarcating the new boundaries between Siam and their protectorate, Cambodge, the border line was modified to give sovereignty over the temple to the French.[1] In the wake of France's diminishing control over the region during World War II, Thailand moved to regain control of territories it had previously ceded, including the Preah Vihear site and surrounding areas. In 1962 the International Court of Justice in The Hague upheld the 1908 boundary line, awarding ownership of the disputed site to Cambodia. Located high up on the very edge of Cambodian territory, Preah Vihear would subsequently become one of the last strongholds for soldiers loyal to the Khmer Rouge regime.

Clearly, then, reference to the political machinations surrounding the construction and subsequent negotiation of state boundaries over the course of colonial and postcolonial administrations helps us interpret the events of 2008. However, in addition to being a site of political significance, Preah Vihear has now become an important economic resource: one that is evidently worth fighting over. Both countries understand well that World Heritage guarantees attention and visibility in the highly lucrative international tourism industry. To date, the number of tourists to the site has been small compared to sites like Angkor, Sukhothai or Ayutthaya. Up until the early 2000s the area was inaccessible from the Cambodian side because of the ongoing fighting in the region and the presence of mines in the vicinity of the temple complex. Given its location high up on the cliff, access to the site is considerably easier from the Thai side, with a sealed road and parking facility enabling visitors to drive up close to the entrance. Not surprisingly then, up until this point the vast majority of tourists have reached Preah Vihear from this direction. In 2008 the Royal Government of Cambodia moved to secure greater control over the management of tourism at its newly listed World Heritage Site by constructing a sealed road that would snake its way up the side of the spur (see Figure 6.1). Indeed a significant component of the dispute concerning World Heritage listing centred on the surrounding zoning regions and their implications for site management, including the collection of entrance fees. With Cambodia now awarded full authority over the temple, the Royal Government will look to establish a new ticketing scheme, with foreign tourists likely to be charged somewhere in the order of US$20 per visit. In the longer term, the most substantial income for the government will come from land transactions and the development of hospitality infrastructure, including hotels, restaurants and entertainment facilities. Rumours have also been rife about the construction of a cable car system for transporting tourists up to the site.[2] However, in order for this localised tourist infrastructure to emerge, and for the Preah Vihear region to evolve as a major destination in its own right, Cambodia first needs to build a sealed, all weather road southwards to the Siem Reap–Angkor area. And, more crucially, it is only when we consider such a transformation – of what just a few years ago was considered to be a 'remote' location into a significant tourist destination – within its wider geographical context, that we begin to really

Figure 6.1 Road Construction, Preah Vihear (Photo by the author)

understand what is now unfolding around heritage tourism in Southeast Asia, and why we need to shift our analytical gaze accordingly.

On returning from a visit to China in October 2008, Cambodia's Prime Minister, Hun Sen, announced he had accepted a gift of US$290 million from the Chinese government to fund the construction of the road linking Preah Vihear to Angkor. Of course, and as Mauss (2002) reminds us, such 'gifts' are always motivated by a number of factors. In this case, however, two key issues can be identified. First, Asia's geopolitical landscape is rapidly shifting, as reflected in the intra-regional aid and investments, that have increased steadily since the end of the Cold War and associated tensions in Southeast Asia. China in particular has increased its presence in countries like Laos and Cambodia. In fact as Cambodia continues to recover from an era characterised by civil war, genocide and foreign occupation, Chinese interests in the country are now enabling the Royal Government to be less beholden to the demands made by aid agencies such as the World Bank or Asian Development Bank for monetary and budgetary discipline. From the Chinese government's perspective, becoming Cambodia's leading bi-lateral donor of aid has allowed it to secure influence at a moment when other countries from Northeast Asia are seeking to establish strategic alliances in Southeast Asia.

The second key factor here is the rapid growth of domestic and intra-regional tourism in Asia. From 2000 onwards Cambodia's inbound tourism industry has seen a major change in direction, with 'Western' tourists being supplanted by Asians as the country's key source markets. By 2007 more than 70 per cent of visitors to the country travelled from within the region. An annual growth rate of around 20 per cent in inbound tourism over several years has, in large part, been driven by the increase in tourists coming from China, Taiwan and, most notably, Korea. Accompanying this rapid growth in arrivals has been an extremely sharp increase in intra-regional tourism-related investment. Organisations like JICA (Japanese International Cooperation Agency) have long played a significant role in assisting with the construction of tourism-related infrastructure across Southeast Asia. In recent years, however, Japan has been joined by Korea and China in this area. Indeed, while China has a substantial record of aid to Cambodia, intra-regional tourism has provided a valuable context for mobilising new partnerships between the Chinese state and Cambodia's growing Chinese diaspora.[3] As I have documented elsewhere, Angkor's tourism industry has been profoundly transformed since 2000 by a private sector of Chinese, Korean and Taiwanese entrepreneurs operating businesses in the Siem Reap region (Winter 2007a). Such developments are in line with the analysis offered by Ong (2006) concerning the neoliberal directions states throughout Southeast Asia are now taking. Although she gives little attention to tourism, Ong identifies a new track of market-driven ideology within the region, a process that is re-articulating citizens and places. Indeed, today the expansion of Siem Reap's urban landscape continues apace, and while it is rarely acknowledged officially, it is widely understood within the town's communities that much of the financing for the construction of whole new 'quarters' is tied to investors from Northeast Asia (see Figure 6.2). In late 2008 the ground-breaking ceremony took place for a new road which would allow more traffic to by-pass the Angkor Archaeological Park. In recognition of the controversial nature of the project, one official from the local management authority,

Figure 6.2 New Urban Quarters of Siem Reap (Photo by the author)

APSARA,[4] confirmed the sealed road would be a joint venture between the Korean government and the Korean business community of Siem Reap.[5] The former would finance the foundations of the road, while private sector money would fund its surfacing.

Not surprisingly these Chinese- and Korean-funded initiatives for road construction linking provinces in the northwest of the country form part of much larger plans for heritage tourism-related infrastructure development. To date tourism in Cambodia has been overwhelmingly oriented to the Angkor site. Trips to the country's more 'outlying' or 'remote' temples have always been associated with adventure or risk, undertaken by a small number of travellers seeking to 'get off the well trodden path' of Southeast Asia tourism (Winter 2006, 2007b). The introduction of sealed roads will bring a number of significant temple sites within range of the mainstream tourism sector. Indeed, over the coming years it is highly likely that a ribbon of heritage tourism development will emerge connecting up a number of temples to the north of Angkor, including Beng Melea, Preah Khan, Koh Ker, and Preah Vihear, as well as Banteay Chmaar in the far northwest of the country.

Of course the Angkor–Siem Reap area will continue to be the central commercial hub within this larger development plan. In fact, growing intra-Asian tourism means that, over the coming years, tourism-related development in this area will accelerate rapidly. Discussions between the government and Korean investors have taken place concerning the construction of an 'urban resort', just south of the existing Siem Reap city. At the time of writing little information concerning this project has been released publicly. However, members of the Siem Reap community who have attended presentations of the project indicated the proposal – for what they described as a 'new town' – including hotel complexes, facilities for horse racing, a golf course and housing. In both Siem Reap and Phnom Penh precedents exist for such projects. In January 2009 Cambodia's Prime Minister, Hun Sen, opened Siem Reap's second golf course, part of a US$450 million project that included one hundred and sixty residential properties, spas, a hotel, restaurants and a race course, all of which have been financed by the Korean company KTC Investments. In Phnom Penh investments from Northeast Asia in real estate projects increased sharply in 2007–8. The Korean developer GS Engineering and Construction is currently overseeing the construction of a fifty-two-storey tower that will be home to a convention centre, residential apartments and an international school. Expected to be complete around 2012, the *International Finance Complex* will dramatically change the capital's skyline. However, the single biggest foreign direct investment to date is the proposed US$2 billion urban complex 'Phnom Penh New Town'. Positioned on the outskirts of the capital, the satellite city will include residential villas and condominiums, trade and financial centres, office buildings, shopping centres, hotels, schools and hospitals. A joint venture between a number of Korean and Cambodian companies, the 300-acre development is being managed by World City Co., part of Landmark Worldwide, a Korean development company, with South Korea's Shinhan Bank acting as the chief financier. Construction of the first phase, an area of residential properties, commenced in 2007.[6]

Cambodia is not alone in witnessing such developments. In late 2008 the *Vientiane Times* in Laos reported on a proposal to construct a US$2 billion, 3,000-hectare site near Luang Prabang, an historic town lying just over 200 kilometres to the north of the capital Vientiane. As a parallel to the ones in Siem Reap, the proposed development includes tourism, residential and recreational facilities. To be known as 'Diamond City', the project would be a joint venture between eleven Korean and four national investors. The newspaper confirmed that a memorandum of understanding between the companies had been signed and the proposal was now moving forward for government approval. Given the lack of infrastructure in the region, the project would also include the construction of a bridge crossing the Mekong, various roads, and utilities like electricity, water and telecommunications. Economic justification for the project centres upon a rapidly growing tourism industry, and the importance of Luang Prabang within it. Since becoming a World Heritage Site in 1995 the town has emerged as a key international tourist destination, both in its own right and as a base for eco-tourism trips in rural areas to the north. As with Cambodia, inbound tourism is now dominated by regional markets, with more than 70 per cent of tourists coming from neighbouring countries. To facilitate the ongoing development of the Luang Prabang region, plans have been progressing to upgrade the airport. While this project began as an Asian Development Bank initiative, a loan from the Chinese government has been put in place to fund the construction of an extended runway and larger facilities, both of which will facilitate the arrival of much larger, long-distance aircraft (see Figure 6.3).[7]

Figure 6.3 Luang Prabang Airstrip (Photo by the author)

In November 2007 a joint World Heritage Centre/ICOMOS mission undertook a Reactive Monitoring Mission for Luang Prabang. Its final report expressed strong concerns about both existing and proposed forms of development around the World Heritage property. Accordingly, its executive summary states:

> Around the perimeter of the Town of Luang Prabang, several proposed development projects, including a new airport and a new town on the right bank of the Mekong, would have an adverse impact on the World Heritage property, both in terms of visual integrity and noise pollution.
>
> (Boccardi and Logan 2008: 2)

At various points throughout the report, these concerns are documented in greater detail:

> Tourism infrastructure proposals already approved include a 900 ha tourist complex with golf course south of the historic core, under an MOU signed with a South Korean company. If constructed, such developments will eat into the agricultural areas and further disrupt drainage patterns in the area and may overwhelm the town's tourist-carrying capacity.
>
> (ibid.: 17)

In addition to extending the buffer zones of the World Heritage Site, the report also suggested the airport be relocated to a site further away from the historic town centre, rather than be expanded. By way of a conclusion the report indicates that current real estate development trends have to be reversed if Luang Prabang's World Heritage status is to be maintained:

> The Mission is convinced that the Town of Luang Prabang is at a crucial stage in its development and that decisions taken now will determine the safeguarding of the Town's OUV [outstanding universal value] or its complete loss. ... Unprecedented pressure from development is posing new strains on the site, in the face of which the competent authorities appear unable to cope. If the Lao traditional heritage in particular continues its steady decline, the Town of Luang Prabang is heading towards a situation that would justify World Heritage in Danger listing. There is an urgent need to prepare an up-to-date inventory and map to reveal the full extent of the changes that have occurred in the inscribed area ... The current negative trend needs to be immediately reversed by much more thorough enforcement of the heritage protection regulations.
>
> (ibid.: 27)

Elsewhere in Laos, plans for another 'satellite city' have been drawn up for Vientiane. On this occasion the foreign investment is coming from Vietnam. In December 2008 the Lao government signed an agreement with the Long Thanh

Golf Investment and Business Joint Stock Company, a developer based in southeast Vietnam. As with the proposal for Luang Prabang, this 557-hectare, US$1 billion project will be comprised of hotels, a golf course, offices, shops and residential properties.[8] Although Vientiane is not a World Heritage Site, as the capital city it naturally serves as a key tourism hub and destination. As Logan, Long and Hansen (2002) demonstrate at length, the city boasts an extensive cultural and natural heritage and remains an important focal point of Lao national identity. Indeed, with so much attention lavished on Luang Prabang the authors contend that the government has yet to fully recognise the cultural and historical significance of its capital city.[9]

Corridors of commerce

In addition to the upgrading of airports and urban infrastructure, development projects addressing the region's key transport corridors are now greatly improving the connections into these various Southeast Asian cities. With organisations like the Asian Development Bank, Association of Southeast Asian Nations (ASEAN) and the World Bank assisting governments to increase the economic integration of the Asian region, the construction and upgrading of sea and air ports, rail lines and roads remains a long-term commitment. The cases highlighted above all lie within the Greater Mekong Subregion (GMS), an area within which many infrastructure projects are currently being funded by the Asian Development Bank (see also Sofield 2008; Vatthana Pholsena and Banomyang 2007). The scale of the Bank's investment in the GMS, along with the role of intra-regional tourism in this, is apparent in the following excerpt from its 2008 publication, *Emerging Asian Regionalism; a Partnership for Shared Prosperity*:

> As of April 2008, more than 150 new investment projects related to transport corridors have been proposed. These include 31 high priority projects with an estimated cost of US$2.4 billion, including 20 road, 2 railway, 4 airport, and 5 water transport projects. Nine transport corridors have been identified to connect the north, central and south areas of the GMS into a single loop.
>
> The development of the transport network will enable Yunnan province of the People's Republic of China and northern Lao People's Democratic Republic to gain access to international seaports in Thailand and Viet Nam; provide a continuous land route between the South China sea and the Andaman sea; offer access to seaports in northeast Thailand and the central regions of Lao PDR; accelerate the westward flow of goods, eventually to India and ease the movement of goods and people, especially tourists, in the region.
>
> (Asian Development Bank 2008: 216)

Not surprisingly, Siem Reap, Luang Prabang, Phnom Penh and Vientiane are key nodes within this ever-expanding GMS network. Indeed the importance of connecting these cities as linked up 'destinations' is evident in the inclusion of tourism in the Bank's list of six regional indicators for advancing integration; the others are trade policy cooperation, foreign direct investment, equity markets, macroeconomic links and intra-regional trade (ibid.: 42–45).

Gambling on the future

One of the key drivers of the Asian tourism market today is the casino and gaming sector. Over the last decade or so publications like *BusinessWeek* and *Forbes* have periodically reported on the 'boom' in the casino industry across Asia.[10] With gambling historically being illegal in countries like China, Vietnam and Thailand, this sector has expanded in interesting ways. For example, in the border regions of Poipet-Aranyaprathet (Cambodia/Thailand) and Moc Bai-Bavet (Cambodia/Vietnam) more than a dozen large casinos have been built. Initially the client base for these businesses consisted of Thai and Vietnamese gamblers. More recently, expansion has come from the arrival of high-spending tourists from China, Taiwan and Korea. Cambodia has been particularly aggressive in targeting the gaming intra-regional tourism sector, with the country now hosting more than thirty legally registered casinos, most of which are grouped in clusters in the above border regions, the southern resort town of Sihanoukville, as well as in Phnom Penh and Siem Reap.[11] But it is in the current property developments in Macao and Singapore that we can really begin to see how significant this sector will be in the future, notwithstanding the global economic downturn beginning in late 2008. Following Macao's lead, Singapore has begun constructing a number of integrated resorts estimated to cost in the region of US$6 billion.[12] In Macao, the city's unprecedented scale and speed of casino development enabled it to overtake Las Vegas as the gaming capital of the world in 2007. This was achieved in large part through a vast US$10 billion investment by Las Vegas Sands, which included the centrepiece US$2.3 billion Venetian Macao.[13] Clearly for both Singapore and Macao the decision to roll the dice on such vast investments has been predicated on an anticipated long-term growth in intra-regional tourism. More specifically, for both cities financial success will be impossible unless they are able to attract millions of high-spending gamblers from mainland China every year.

Seen together the cases of Singapore and Macao illustrate the importance of gaming as an economic driver of development and urban planning, and the centrality of Asian tourism in that process. For Macao, the fast-changing urban landscape is having a significant impact on its urban heritage. Listed as a World Heritage Site in 2005, the *Historic Center of Macao* is under growing pressure from both rising pollution and congestion, and the construction of large buildings. One of the city's iconic sites, the Guia Lighthouse, is now being visually disconnected from the sea through the construction of office towers and casino-hotels. For Imon (2008), such construction, which began after the relaxation of height restrictions in 2002, is gradually denuding Macao of its historic meaning as a trading port. He suggests the desire for casino owners and architects to make bold architectural statements is undermining the integrity of the built environment around the historic centre. In addition to the challenges of big urban construction programs, a rapid rise in visitor arrivals – from 11.5 million in 2002 to 27 million in 2007 – is delivering major problems for those involved in the management of the city's most popular heritage attractions. As Imon demonstrates, much of Macao's growing popularity as a tourist destination now rests on the fact that it combines an internationally recognised cultural heritage with a highly sophisticated entertainment industry.

In light of the earlier discussion, I would thus suggest that over the coming years this combination of heritage and entertainment will be a defining feature of the World Heritage regions of Angkor and Luang Prabang, as well as the historic cities of Phnom Penh and Vientiane. And looking further afield, the legalisation of gambling on offshore islands in Taiwan in January 2009 is indicative of a wider shift in parliamentary attitudes towards casinos across the region. It is also crucial to note that World Heritage has become a very powerful brand in Asia. Governments throughout the region are now well aware that World Heritage not only offers substantial prestige on the international stage, but also guarantees for the state the wealth generation associated with tourism. With this in mind, it is likely that sites like Halong Bay in Vietnam, Gyeongju in South Korea, or Sukhothai in Thailand will be exposed to large-scale developmental initiatives over the longer term. Crucially, however, and as this chapter has set out to illustrate, 'the tourist' of such initiatives will not be white and Western, but will be domestic or regional.

Conclusion

Forty per cent of the world's population lives in Asia, a region that witnessed unprecedented socio-economic growth over the 1990s and 2000s. The global financial crisis that began in late 2008 sharply put the brakes on this upward curve of development. It is therefore difficult to assess when and how many of the proposed developments outlined here will be realised. What is for sure, however, is the longer-term trend of a rising middle class in Asia, an increasingly cosmopolitan group characterised by a desire to travel. With that long-term demand in place there is little doubt private investors and governments will look to build infrastructure oriented towards the Asian consumer.

In highlighting such future trajectories, I would suggest a number of significant heritage landscapes in Asia are now entering a new era, one that will be characterised by increasingly powerful forces of social and economic transformation. Southeast Asia in particular, including cities like Hong Kong and Macao, offers us important signposts to the future. If the historical development of tourism in Europe, which evolved and expanded geographically from its domestic and intra-regional beginnings, is any sort of guide, we can see that the early growth of Northern Europeans travelling south to the Mediterranean offers us a parallel to the tourists from Northeast Asia travelling south today. And, therefore, in the same way as European tourism expanded outwards to the rest of the world it is highly likely the same will happen with Asian tourists in the future. However, two defining characteristics of contemporary Asia, scale and speed, undoubtedly mean unfamiliar and unprecedented challenges will continue to unfold. To date the heritage industry has implicitly read international/global tourism vis-à-vis 'Western' tourism. In this chapter I have presented a series of examples, which, when seen together, vividly illustrate why the field of heritage needs to undertake a number of analytical shifts and reforms. If we are to address the shifting nature of globalisation in the twenty-first century, new ways of looking at, thinking about, interpreting and conceptualising the interface between heritage and tourism are required urgently.

Notes

1 For detailed discussion of events surrounding Preah Vihear in the early decades of the twentieth century see Cuasay 2001.
2 There are enough historical precedents of planned cable cars to suggest it is unlikely that UNESCO would allow such an intervention to proceed.
3 For an account of Chinese investments in Cambodia see: *China's growing influence in Cambodia*, http://www.atimes.com/atimes/Southeast_Asia/HJ06Ae01.html
4 Authority for the Protection and Safeguarding of the Angkor Region.
5 This was confirmed by a departmental director of APSARA at a Pacific Rim Council for Urban Development workshop held in Siem Reap, 26–29 October 2008.
6 For further details see http://worldcitycambodia.com and http://www.camkocity.net. Various videos offering a virtual tour of the city have also received much attention on sites such as YouTube. For example see http://www.youtube.com/watch?v=xG982cT9sCI
7 For an account of Chinese aid into Laos see: *Communist capital flows downstream: China's aid to Laos*, http://www.chinadevelopmentbrief.com/node/454
8 For further details see: *Giant investment project to Laos submitted to Government*, http://english.vietnamnet.vn/biz/2009/01/822656/
9 For an excellent account of post-war Laos see also Vatthana Pholsena (2006) *Post-War Laos: The Politics of Culture, History, and Identity*, Singapore: ISEAS.
10 See for example: *Asia's Casino Boom*, http://www.forbes.com/2006/06/08/casino-sands-singapore-cx_0609oxford.html and *A Crazy Casino Boom in Asia: Global entertainment players are doubling down on casino developments around the region*, http://images.businessweek.com/ss/07/03/0316_asia_casino/index_01.htm
11 For further details see http://www.gamingfloor.com/Asian_Casinos.html
12 For further details see: *Downturn raises odds at Singapore casinos*, http://www.atimes.com/atimes/Southeast_Asia/KA15Ae01.html
13 See http://www.venetianmacao.com/en/

Bibliography

Alneng, V. (2002) 'The Modern Does Not Cater For Natives: travel ethnography and the conventions of form', *Tourist Studies*, 2 (2): 119–42.

Asian Development Bank (2008) *Emerging Asian Regionalism: a Partnership for Shared Prosperity*, Mandaluyong, Philippines: Asian Development Bank.

Boccardi, G. and Logan, W. (2008) *Reactive Monitoring Mission to the Town of Luang Prabang World Heritage Property Lao People's Democratic Republic 22–28 November 2007, Mission Report*, Paris: UNESCO.

Connell, R. (2009) 'Peripheral visions – beyond the metropole', in J. Kenway and J. Fahey (eds). *Globalizing the Research Imagination*, London: Routledge: 54–72.

Connell, R. (2007) *Southern Theory: The Global Dynamics of Knowledge in Social Science*, Cambridge: Polity.

Cuasay, P. (2001) 'Borders on the fantastic: mimesis, violence, and landscape at the Temple of Preah Vihear', *Modern Asian Studies*, Vol.32 No. 4: 849–90.

Imon, S. (2008) 'Managing change in the historic city of Macao', *Historic Environment*, Vol.21 No.3: 16–21.

Logan, W. Long, C., and Hansen, R. (2002) 'Vientiane, Laos: Lane Xang's capital in the age of modernization and globalisation', in W. Logan (ed.), *The Disappearing City: Protecting Asia's Urban Heritage in a Globalizing World*, Hong Kong: Oxford University Press: 51–69.

Mauss, M. (2002) *The Gift*, London: Routledge.

Ong, A. (2006) *Neoliberalism as Exception: Mutations in Citizenship and Sovereignty*, Durham: Duke University Press.

Sofield, T. (2008) 'The Tourism in transition economies of the greater mekong subregion' in J. Cochrane, *Asian Tourism: Growth and Change*, Oxford: Elsevier: 39–54.

Thongchai Winichakul (1994) *Siam Mapped: a History of the Geo-Body of a Nation*, Honolulu: University of Hawaii Press.

Vatthana Pholsena (2006) *Post-War Laos: The Politics of Culture, History, and Identity*, Singapore: ISEAS.

Vatthana Pholsena and Banomyang, R. (2007) *Laos: From Buffer State to Crossroads?* Chiang Mai: Mekong Press.

Winter, T. (2006) 'When Ancient 'Glory' Meets Modern 'Tragedy': Angkor and the Khmer Rouge in contemporary tourism', in L. Ollier and T. Winter (eds) *Expressions of Cambodia: the politics of tradition, identity and change*, London: Routledge: 37–53.

——(2007a) 'Rethinking Tourism in Asia', *Annals of Tourism Research*, 34(1): 27–44.

——(2007b) *Post-Conflict Heritage, Postcolonial Tourism: Culture, Politics and Development at Angkor*, London: Routledge.

——(2009) 'Asian tourism and the retreat of Anglo-western centrism in tourism theory', *Current Issues in Tourism*, 12(1): 21–31.

Winter, T., Teo, P. & Chang, T.C. (2009) *Asia on Tour: Exploring the Rise of Asian Tourism*, New York: Routledge.

Chapter 7

The glocalisation of heritage through tourism

Balancing standardisation and differentiation

Noel B. Salazar

Heritage meets global tourism

Year after year, the tourism and travel industries proudly present global statistics showing steady increases in international tourist arrivals and receipts (UNWTO 2008), and a growing contribution to the world total GNP (WTTC 2008). Even if the collection of these figures is fraught with methodological problems, the numbers are illustrative of the trend: tourism, or travel-for-leisure, is on the rise across the globe (albeit unevenly). Given the pervasiveness and local particularity of heritage, it is not surprising that heritage tourism is among those niches growing most rapidly (Timothy and Boyd 2006). Such special interest tourism is being developed, both as a primary objective and as a by-product of other leisure activities, by a wide variety of stakeholders on local-to-global levels. While people have journeyed to witness historic places of cultural importance since ancient times, what is new is the ever-increasing speed, intensity and extent of travel and tourism. Private and public sectors worldwide, whether or not in collaboration, are converting cultural heritage resources into destinations and attractions, in a bid to obtain a piece of the lucrative global tourism pie.[1] The money visitors spend on admission fees, souvenirs, transport, and food and accommodation contributes billions every year to the global economy and employs millions of people directly and indirectly (Timothy and Boyd 2003).

Apart from economic incentives, heritage tourism serves important political purposes. On the domestic level, cultural heritage is commonly used to stimulate pride in the (imagined) national history or to highlight the virtues of particular ideologies. In the supranational sphere, heritage sites are marketed and sold as iconic markers of a local area, country, region or even continent, and the journey abroad as an opportunity to learn about the 'Other' – some go as far as promising a contribution to worldwide peace and understanding. At the same time, tourism is increasingly recognised and used as an agent of socio-cultural change. The mounting struggles over who controls heritage tourism reflect its growth and success (Salazar and Porter 2004; Porter and Salazar 2005). Cultural heritage tourism in particular has been advocated as an attractive alternative to mass tourism, providing sustainable livelihoods to small local operators, protecting and sustaining the cultural resources, and educating tourists and locals alike (NWHO 1999). Cultural heritage management is now commonly seen as a strategic tool to maximise the use of heritage within the global tourism market (Nuryanti 1997). This goes hand in hand with the overall trend to privatise goods and services, making heritage tourism more entrepreneurial and entertainment-oriented, and leading to new types of conflict over ownership and appropriation.

Some argue that the globalisation of heritage through tourism has led to a greater respect for (both material and living) culture than previously existed. However, the transformation of sites into destinations and cultural expressions into performances is seldom straightforward. Conservation and preservation along with developing and managing visitation are major issues facing the cultural heritage tourism sector (see Figure 7.1). The interface and relationship between heritage and global tourism is extremely complex. In a tourism setting, heritage can be (mis)used in a variety of ways for a variety of purposes by a variety of stakeholders. This chapter discusses some of the most pressing challenges that lie ahead in cultural heritage tourism and stresses the importance of heritage interpretation for its sustainable development. The case study of central Java, Indonesia, illustrates the general trends and shows the urgent need for more dialogue and collaboration between the fields of heritage management and tourism.

Figure 7.1 Learning to respect heritage through tourism? Locals at Borobudur, Indonesia (Photo by the author)

Global standards versus local distinctiveness

That tourism is a global phenomenon is not debated. Both constituted by and con-stitutive of globalisation processes, tourism includes huge movements of people (tourists as well as tourism workers), capital (investments and tourist dollars), tech-nologies of travel and the circulation of closely related tourism media and imagin-aries (Salazar in press). There is a striking complicity and circularity in the relationship between transnational tourism and (neoliberal) globalisation. They are inseparable from one another, as hybrid parts of the same set of processes. The set is 'hybrid because it is made up of an assemblage of technologies, texts, images, social practices and so on that *together* enable it to expand and to reproduce itself across the globe' (Urry 2002: 144). Cultural heritage management, too, is caught up in a complex web of global interconnections and dependencies between stakeholders at various levels. Tourism development in particular has been instrumental in globa-lising heritage, its management, interpretation and appropriation.

Engaging with global tourism inevitably necessitates a certain degree of world-wide integration and homogenisation, which are given tangible form via the stan-dardisation of training, service and hospitality benchmarks. Indeed, for the global system of travel and tourism to work efficiently, internationally agreed standards need to be imposed across the board. That is why regulatory mechanisms and instruments of standardisation and control, developed at the international level, are becoming increasingly pervasive. One readily understands that this makes sense for areas such as transport (e.g. the Universal Safety Oversight Audit Programme of the International Civil Aviation Organisation) and food (e.g. the International Organi-sation for Standardisation's Food Safety Management Systems Standard). Universal criteria for service and customer care, on the other hand, are contested. Although UNWTO and the International Organisation for Standardisation have been suc-cessful in creating international yardsticks in the area of tourism services (ISO 18513: 2003), sector-based interest groups see them as redundant and costly.[2] One major criticism is that the promotion of standardised services runs contrary to the tourists' desire for diversity in the travel experience, as well as negating cultural and geographical diversity in destinations – one of global tourism's driving forces.

The challenge of standardisation is extremely relevant in the context of cultural heritage management. Heritage destinations worldwide may be adapting themselves to the homogenising trends of global tourism, but, at the same time, they have to com-modify their local distinctiveness in order to compete with other destinations (cf. Chang 1999). After all, it is the local particularity of heritage (sometimes branded as 'national') that tourists are most interested in witnessing and experiencing. In other words,

> [T]he more globalisation, of which tourism is a main agent, homogenizes habits and landscapes all around the world, the more whatever is available of the past tends to be iconicized as a symbol for national identification and, in touristic terms, as a unique sight.
>
> (Peleggi 1996: 445)

Tourism marketers and imagineers around the globe capitalise on the following assumption: If all places on earth and their inhabitants have a culture, and if this culture is necessarily unique to a specific place and people, then its transformation into heritage – cultural assets in the form of the built environment, a living heritage expressed in distinctive local customs and song, dance, art and handicrafts, etc., and museums – should produce an exclusive product reflecting and promoting a distinctive place or group identity. Heritage is thus used to endow peoples and places with what in marketing terms is called a product's 'unique selling point'. Ironically, pioneering projects of originality and uniqueness have been successfully replicated to the point where they no longer express the sense of a locally distinctive identity that was the intention of their creators and promoters.

The global increase in tourism has exerted pressure on many heritage sites. The process of 'tourismification' of heritage confronts those stakeholders involved and communities affected with a whole set of complex issues, including authenticity, interpretation, heritage contestation, social exclusion, contested space, personal heritage, control and preservation (Timothy and Prideaux 2004; McKercher and Du Cros 2002). Glocalisation – the patterned conjunctions that shape peoples and places and by means of which they shape themselves – is a first approximation that suggests equal attention to globalisation and localisation (local differentiation) existing in a complex two-way traffic (Salazar 2005; Robertson 1995).[3] It is a fitting term to denote the intertwined processes whereby new boundaries are created between local-to-global orders, and all gain strength. As an analytical concept, glocalisation directs our attention to the institutions and power relations through which globalisation as well as localisation are made possible.

In this context, it is important to point out that there are significant economic, social, political, management, conservation and interpretation differences between developed and developing countries in terms of heritage tourism. Especially poor countries have a hard time achieving the international standards set by the tourism sector (Salazar in press). There are many issues in the less-developed world that create everyday obstacles to the sustainable development and management of heritage, including the role of local communities in decision making, sharing in the benefits of tourism development, empowerment and power, ownership of historic places and artefacts, lack of funding and skills and forced displacement to accommodate tourism growth (Hampton 2005). The promise of sustainable heritage tourism becomes all the more difficult to realise if we take account of the fact that low-income nations receive only a fraction of global tourism revenue (UNWTO 2008).

The expansive growth of tourism after World War II greatly helped to promote the cosmopolitan idea of a common heritage, to be valued, shared and enjoyed by the global ecumene. In fact, global tourism and world heritage recursively reinforce and enhance each other in an ever-growing and influential lobby. UNESCO's high-profile campaigns to safeguard Abu Simbel in Egypt (1966), Borobudur in Indonesia (1973) and Angkor Wat in Cambodia (1993) are salient examples of this. World Heritage Sites (WHS), such as the three examples above, are considered to be the centrepieces of global heritage tourism (Shackley 1998). The World Heritage List is a rapidly growing catalogue of the cultural and natural heritage that, according to the 1972 UNESCO Convention on the Protection of the World's Cultural and Natural Heritage, is of 'outstanding universal value from the point of view of history, art or science' (after having been nominated nationally and accredited internationally). The first twelve sites were inscribed in 1978. Thirty years later, the list includes 679 cultural, 174 natural, and 25 mixed sites in 145 countries (with European and Judaeo-Christian sites continuing to dominate).[4] The original purpose of WHS designation was to assist with management and preservation of the sites and to encourage the development of management plans.

The mere inscription on the WH list usually coincides with a boost in visitation rates (Pedersen 2002). UNESCO's list thus plays an instrumental role, not only in safeguarding heritage, but also in increasing international visitor numbers (and all the problems associated with this). Many WHS have quickly become major attractions. With millions of tourists visiting the 878 sites each year, tourism has not only been economically rewarding, it has also become a major management concern. By definition no two WHS are alike, but they all share common problems such as the need for a critical balance between visitation and conservation. Many sites lack trained personnel and policy makers sometimes lack the experience necessary to use tourism as a tool for sustainable development. In 1999, ICOMOS adopted its International Cultural Tourism Charter, a policy document detailing the importance of managing tourism at places of heritage significance.[5] The overriding importance of tourism to WHS, both as an opportunity and, if poorly managed, as a threat, was recognised by the World Heritage Committee when it authorised the World Heritage Centre, in 2001, to develop a Sustainable Tourism Programme.[6] This has resulted, among other things, in a practical manual on tourism management (Pedersen 2002).

Since 2004, National Geographic's Centre for Sustainable Destinations has asked hundreds of experts to rate tourism destinations on several criteria. The idea behind this yearly exercise is to improve stewardship and attract the most beneficial, least disruptive forms of tourism. In 2006, the panellists evaluated 94 WHS destinations. Among the highest-scoring cultural sites were the Alhambra (Spain), Vézelay (France), Guanajuato (Mexico), Córdoba (Spain), Bath (UK) and Évora (Portugal). At the bottom of the list were the Upper Middle Rain Valley (Germany), Kyoto (Japan), Assisi (Italy), Avignon (France), the Loire Valley (France) and the Banks of the Seine (Paris). These type of rankings, together with the biennial World Monuments Watch list of 100 most endangered cultural heritage sites and UNESCO's own list of World Heritage in Danger, provide opportunities to raise public awareness, foster local participation, advance innovation and collaboration, and demonstrate effective solutions.

Such actions are necessary because the tendency to adopt top-down heritage planning and management procedures has often resulted in the disenfranchisement of local people, giving greater prominence to expressions of national, 'official' culture and nationalism at the expense of local culture (Wall and Black 2004). This kind of approach has tended to freeze sites and displace human activities, effectively excluding local people from their own heritage. With tourist awareness of the significance and location of WHS at an all-time high, no wonder governments strategically choose which monuments to nominate as symbols of national character and culture and which ones not. While in some instances packaging WHS to cater to a world market appears to be subservient to the nationalistic needs and criteria of the individual countries in which the sites are to be found (Boniface and Fowler 1993), WHS are, par excellence, global heritage products. Every international visitor contributes to the globalisation of heritage by asserting the value of the site as universal and the right of general accessibility to it (Di Giovine 2008). However, the very concept of universal heritage is increasingly contested. After all, it privileges an idea originating in the West and requires an attitude towards culture that is also distinctly European in origin. Within the discourse of universal heritage, there is little room for specific cultural, political or religious positions that diverge from Western, secularist viewpoints. The fact that the very concept of heritage is underpinned by the globalisation of Western values has prompted challenges, resistance and misunderstandings (Salazar and Porter 2004; Porter and Salazar 2005).

Today, global heritage tourism largely continues to base policies around a Western-centric network of organisations and technologies. The intergovernmental agencies of UNESCO officially charged with the definition, recognition, designation and protection of World Heritage (especially the World Heritage Centre and its expert advisory groups such as ICOMOS) are often blamed for this bias. While they certainly play a role, it is rather a hesitant and ambiguous one. After all, the sites designated on the WH list represent those national choices and priorities that have successfully been lobbied for, rather than any international standard (Ashworth and Tunbridge 2000). In other words, organisations like UNESCO offer a forum for national representation rather than world governance. World heritage is 'the sum of scrutinised national heritages, a situation which has the potential to create competition given that heritage becomes an expression of national self-esteem' (Timothy and Boyd 2003: 15). Ironically, UNESCO's apolitical stance towards cultural conservation feeds directly into the heritage-tourism-development nexus created by many governments. Indeed, we should not forget that many countries, especially poor ones, see tourism as a major tool to develop, and that development in the eyes of those in power often equals erasing local, traditional cultural practices.[7]

Of course, world heritage is but one facet of the move towards globalisation and while a shared heritage is desired by certain countries, it is not a universal presumption. Moreover, UNESCO's idea of a WH list is not new. Various precursor listings have been compiled over the ages to catalogue the most spectacular natural and cultural heritage in the world. One of the first known inventories was the Seven Wonders of the Ancient World, based on guidebooks popular among Hellenic sightseers, including monuments located around the Mediterranean rim.[8] This ancient list inspired the creation of many similar rankings ever since. Recently, the Swiss-based New7Wonders Foundation invited people around the globe to cast their votes on the Internet for the New 7 Wonders of the World. Over 100 million people worldwide participated. On 7 July 2007, the foundation organised a televised declaration ceremony in which it announced the winners: the Great Wall (China), Petra (Jordan), Chichén Itzá (Mexico), the Statue of Christ Redeemer (Brazil), the Colosseum (Italy), Machu Picchu (Peru) and the Taj Mahal (India). The results were cleverly used by the winning countries to boost both national pride and international visitor numbers. For the same reasons, countries such as Canada, Poland, Portugal, Russia and Ukraine (who were not included in the final list) organised their own national Seven Wonders campaigns.

Interpreting local heritage for a global audience

Although seldom acknowledged, the globalisation of heritage through tourism can seriously influence its interpretation, both for locals and tourists. We should not forget that cultural heritage mainly has value because of the selective meaning that people ascribe to it, often through personal identification and attachment. The way people relate to a place is not so much caused by the specific site attributes but by the visitor's personal motivations and perceptions (Poria et al. 2003). Those who view a site as bound up with their own heritage are likely to behave significantly differently from others. A single heritage site can provoke varied degrees of under-standing – be it on a local, national, regional or even global scale. In fact, there is no heritage without interpretation, and the attached subjective meaning is always cul-turally (re)constructed and often contested, because 'society filters heritage through a value system that undoubtedly changes over time and space, and across society' (Timothy and Boyd 2003: 2). As Adams writes:

> In today's context of international tourism, 'heritage' and 'tradition' become all the more intensely rethought, rearticulated, and recreated and contested, both by insiders and outsider packagers, politicians, and visitors. Tourism does not simply impose disjunctures between the 'authentic past' and the 'invented past', as earlier researchers suggested, but rather blurs these artificial lines, creating new politically charged arenas in which competing ideas about heritage, ritual, and tradition are symbolically enacted.
>
> (Adams 2003: 93)

As a tourism construct, a wide variety of individuals and institutions attribute meaning and authenticity to heritage (Peleggi 1996).

The interpretation of heritage is important to defining, evoking and enhancing its meaning (Uzzell 1989). Making the different layers of multiple and shifting mean-ings and their dissonances accessible and understandable, for both local residents and tourists from varied backgrounds, requires carefully designed strategies of repre-sentation. Interpretative services are not a special favour to visitors; they are an essential part of the work of heritage management (see Figure 7.2). As Moscardo argues, 'successful interpretation is critical both for the effective management and conservation of built heritage sites and for sustainable tourism' (1996: 376). This is an extremely challenging task, because the desire to (re)present heritage for both

Figure 7.2 Aspiring heritage guides learning the tricks of the interpretation trade (Photo by the author)

domestic and international audiences often creates a tension around the selection of stories to be told and what is to be left untold (Salazar in press). Moreover, 'although the global heritage dialogue tends to present the built environment as an empty container, places of heritage remain places where real people live and where real conflicts may arise' (Al Sayyad 2001: 22).

What does the globalisation of heritage do to its interpretation? Alternative readings of heritage as imbued with local values and meanings risk being subsumed, and thus erased, by the universalist assertions of global heritage tourism. When the interpretation of heritage crosses boundaries and becomes entangled in the complex web of global tourism, it can have the effect of disembedding local (or nationally) produced senses of identity. Local tour guides, therefore, play an instrumental role in mediating the tension between ongoing processes of global standardisation and local differentiation. Paradoxically, they often seem to rely on fashionable global tourism tales to interpret and sell their cultural heritage as authentically 'local' (Salazar 2007). This is partly because tourists appear to appreciate interpretations that combine narratives about the particularities of a destination with well-known tourism imaginaries that are circulating globally. In tourism to developing countries, for example, marketing has long capitalised on cultural economies of the exotic and the primitive, each of which are to be discovered in the pre-modern, traditional. However, this does not mean that local guides merely reproduce normative global templates. Guiding is always to some extent improvised, creative and spontaneous, in this way defying complete standardisation. In the interaction with tourists, local guides become themselves creative producers of tourism rhetoric (Salazar in press).

Highly trained heritage guides not only benefit tourists but also the local community, by preparing and instructing visitors to be more culturally sensitive and ethical, follow minimal impact or responsible behaviour and encourage respect and proper consideration for local traditions and customs. UNESCO has recently also become aware of the importance of professional tour guiding and the organisation has taken a proactive role in benchmarking heritage interpretation, especially in Asia. Increased tourism activities at heritage sites tend to overlook the importance of transmitting knowledge about and learning the significance as well as the cultural value of such sites (Dioko and Unakul 2005). The UNESCO Asia and Pacific region office in Bangkok, Thailand, was among the first to acknowledge this. In 2005, it proposed, together with the Asian Academy of Heritage Management network, a regional-based programme for heritage tour guide training (UNESCO 2005). The Macao Institute for Tourism Studies is the first institution to offer a 'Cultural Heritage Specialist Guide Training and Certification Programme for UNESCO World Heritage Sites'. The programme aims to address several important challenges arising from the greater and more frequent interface between heritage and global tourism and how on-site tour guides specially trained in heritage guiding can play a central role in meeting these challenges. It is noteworthy that this is an example of a 'regional standards of excellence' practice, rather than an attempt to create a global benchmark.

Glocalising heritage: the case of central Java, Indonesia

Java is the fifth largest and most populated island of the Indonesian archipelago. The central region of Java comprises of two provinces: Central Java and the much smaller Yogyakarta Special Province. The earliest signs of habitation in this fertile volcanic area are prehistoric. From the seventh century the region was dominated by Hindu and Buddhist kingdoms, giving rise to the eighth-century Buddhist shrine of Borobudur, the ninth-century Hindu temple complex of Prambanan, and many other temples. Islam, coming mainly via India, gained ground in the inner areas of the island during the sixteenth century. The Dutch began to colonise the archipelago in the early seventeenth century. The British established a brief presence on Java under Sir Thomas Stamford Raffles (1811–16), but the Dutch retained control until Indonesia's independence 130 years later. When the Dutch reoccupied Jakarta after the Japanese occupation of Java during World War II (1946–49), Yogyakarta functioned as the stronghold of the independence movement by becoming the provisional capital of the newly declared Republic of Indonesia. In return for this unfailing support, the first Indonesian central government passed a law in 1950 granting Yogyakarta the status of Special Province and making its Sultan Governor for life.

Organised tourism to the centre of Java first developed under Dutch colonial rule, mainly through the *Vereeniging Toeristenverkeer* (Association of Tourist Traffic of the

Dutch East Indies), which opened an Official Tourist Bureau in Weltevreden (now Jakarta) in 1908. After independence, the new Indonesian government continued to promote international tourism, although President Sukarno's political rhetoric was markedly anti-Western. Under Major-General Suharto's New Order government (1966–98), long-term planning and a relatively stable environment for business transformed the country's tourism, and Yogyakarta became a major gateway to central and east Java, both for international and domestic visitors. By the mid-1990s, tourism had become Indonesia's third most important source of foreign revenue and Yogyakarta the second most visited destination after Bali.

While central Java offers a whole range of touristic activities, the main product is cultural heritage. The three Indonesian cultural sites on UNESCO's WH List – the Prambanan Temple Compounds (1991), the Borobudur Temple Compounds (1991) and Sangiran Early Man Site (1996) – are all located in central Java. Four others – the Yogyakarta Palace Complex, the Ratu Boko Temple Complex, the Sukuh Hindu Temple and the Great Mosque of Demak – are since 1995 on UNESCO's tentative list. The most common tour package includes visits to Borobudur, the Yogyakarta Palace and Prambanan. When time permits, tourists also have a chance to experience central Java's rich intangible cultural heritage, including performing arts (traditional court dances, Ramayana Ballet, shadow puppet plays and gamelan orchestra performances), traditional craftsmanship (woodcarving, batik design, the silverware from Kotagede and the pottery from Kasongan) and occasional ritual or festive events (such as the annual Sekaten and Labuhan festivals).

As Dahles points out in her study on the politics of cultural tourism in Indonesia,

> [T]he cultural heritage of the Yogyakarta area has shaped the (international) images of Indonesia, as government propaganda has used architectural structures like the temples and the sultan's palace and expressions of art like the Ramayana dance to promote Indonesian tourism world-wide.
>
> (Dahles 2001: 20)

This kind of image building particularly happened during the New Order era, when the central government (led by Javanese) strongly favoured central Java in its (re)invention of Indonesia, promoting it as the cultural heart of the nation. The current planning and development of heritage tourism in the area is in the hands of many authorities at various levels: city (Yogyakarta City Department of Tourism, Arts and Culture) and regency (Magelang, Sleman and Klaten Tourism Offices), provincial (Central Java and Yogyakarta Provincial Tourism Offices), Java (Jawa Promo), national (Ministry of Culture and Tourism), regional (ASEAN Committee on Trade and Tourism and APEC Tourism Working Group), and global (UNWTO and UNESCO) levels. Because policy makers at these different echelons have widely diverging interests, decisions taken at one level are often contested at another.

UNESCO has a long-standing history of involvement in central Java's heritage. In 1972, it launched a US$25 million safeguarding campaign to restore Borobudur, often listed as one of the seven forgotten wonders of the world. Concurrent with the

Figure 7.3 Local tour guide enacting part of the Ramayana story at Prambanan

elevation of Borobudur and Prambanan to WHS in 1991, UNESCO collaborated with UNDP and the former Indonesian Directorate General of Tourism in the ambitious 1991–94 'Cultural Tourism Development Central Java-Yogyakarta' project (UNESCO 1992). Since the May 2006 earthquake, UNESCO has been actively involved in the rehabilitation of the damaged Prambanan temple complex. Another influential global player in the area's heritage management is the non-profit World Monuments Fund, which listed Kotagede Heritage District in Yogyakarta on its 2008 World Monuments Watch list of 100 most endangered sites. Kotagede, which suffered severe damage after the 2006 earthquake, is also the current focus of the local Jogja Heritage Society.

It is no coincidence that sites such as Sangiran (prehistoric), Prambanan (Hindu) and Borobudur (Buddhist) appear on UNESCO's list of World Heritage, whereas Sukuh temple or the Sultan's Palace are not (yet) included. After all, the central government in Jakarta proposes sites to UNESCO and it is in its strategic interest to nominate politically 'safe' monuments. Sukuh temple, for instance, is a beautiful Hindu temple tucked away in the highlands of Central Java. It is unique, not only in overall design, but also in decoration: it is the only known erotic temple on Java. Around the temple, statues and reliefs of erect male members abound. Given the moral sensibilities of the majority Muslim population (and the increasing power of fundamentalists), Sukuh is not a site the Indonesian government would want to promote. The Sultan's Palace, on the other hand, is Muslim (or, at least, partly) but a place where current politics are being played out instead of a 'dead' heritage site, such as the Ratu Boko Hindu–Buddhist complex. The internationally little-known Mosque of Demak, the historical place from where Islam spread around Java, probably has more chance of being reclassified as world heritage than the Sultan's Palace. Such politics of heritage serve as a reminder that, ultimately, a WHS is the product of agency on the national level. Besides, the Indonesian government has its own national list of *cagar budaya* (heritage conservation).[9]

Central Java is not only passively undergoing outside influences in its heritage management, but also acting as a symbolic location where broader heritage tourism agendas are being set. As a fashionable venue for conventions, Yogyakarta has had its share of key conferences in this domain. In 1992, for instance, the International Conference on Cultural Tourism led to the Yogyakarta Declaration on National Cultures and Universal Tourism. This was followed up in 1995 by an Indonesian–Swiss Forum on Cultural and International Tourism and in 2006 by an UNWTO-sponsored International Conference on Cultural Tourism and Local Communities, leading to the Yogyakarta Declaration on Cultural Tourism, Local Communities and Poverty Alleviation. In 1994, the city hosted the APEC Tourism Working Group meeting and, in 2001, it welcomed the East Asia Inter-Regional Tourism Forum. In 2002, Yogyakarta housed the ASEAN Tourism Forum.

During the last decade, central Java's tourism has suffered from a whole series of unfortunate events in Indonesia and the wider region (Salazar in press). However, 2006 dealt a fatal blow to the already ailing industry. Between May and July of that year, the area had to endure numerous natural disasters, including multiple eruptions of Mt. Merapi (one of the most active volcanoes in the world), a minor tsunami (reminding Indonesians of the tragic 2004 tsunami in Aceh) and a major earthquake of 5.9 on the Richter Scale, killing around 6,000 people and leaving an estimated 1.5 million Javanese homeless.[10] Large numbers of tourists cancelled their trips to Java, exposing the fragility of the local tourism sector but also bringing to light the resilience of its workers. Prambanan was among those sites hit by the quake, along with parts of the Sultan's Palace. Borobudur did not suffer from the earthquake but had to be cleaned because the monument was covered under dark grey ash from Mt. Merapi's eruptions.

The disasters disclosed some of the local-to-global politics driving heritage tourism. It took almost a month before UNESCO sent international experts to measure the damage to Prambanan. During that time, the monument was closed to visitors. After the assessment, a newly built viewing platform (very similar to the ones erected after 11 September 2001 around Ground Zero in New York) allowed tourists to see the main temple complex from a safe distance, without being allowed to enter it. PT Taman Wisata, the state-owned enterprise managing the park, decided not to lower the entrance fees (US$10 for foreigners). Anticipating tourist complaints, many local tour operators decided to suspend trips to Prambanan. The few tourists who still came to visit did not want the service of a local guide (approximately U$5 extra) because they knew that they could not get near the main temples anyway. This left the local guides in a very precarious situation. Some of the security guards in charge of protecting the site offered foreign tourists to enter the damaged main complex anyway, in exchange for sizeable amounts of cash. The on-site guides knew about these practices but preferred to keep quiet.

The calamities became the feeding ground for new interpretative narratives and imaginaries (Salazar 2009). The adversity precipitated a spontaneous revitalisation of old Javanese myths and mystical beliefs, including the legend of Loro Jonggrang (see Figure 7.4).[11] In the weeks following the earthquake, the Prambanan guides

Figure 7.4 Rara Jonggrang or Prambanan? Local versus global interpretations of heritage (Photo by the author)

blamed UNESCO for keeping the main temples closed to the public (preventing them from earning their living). This translated into their narratives containing much fewer references to the organisation or to the officially sanctioned interpretations of the WHS. Through initiatives such as the 2008 Prambanan Camp for World Heritage Volunteers, the negative perception of UNESCO in Prambanan was somewhat adjusted. This project, in collaboration with the Archaeology Department and Provincial Tourism Office of Central Java, enabled international volunteers to assist the experts with the restoration of the temple and to increase the heritage awareness of local youth. The example of Prambanan illustrates how, in times of change, the local meaning and function of heritage can change too. The growing supralocal interdependence of heritage tourism is irreversible but variously received (Salazar in press). The global recognition by UNESCO, for instance, is used strategically when guiding for foreign tourists, but local guides clearly sensed and criticised the organisation's 'distance' in the period after the earthquake – not recognising that, often, national instances were to blame rather than international ones.

What's next?

As this chapter has illustrated, cultural heritage tourism is a double-edged sword. On the one hand, it can be a positive force to retain cultural values and to help mitigate threats. On the other hand, global tourism can become itself a menace to the sustainable management of heritage. Therefore, a good understanding of the tourism sector, its markets and trends is instrumental to sustainable heritage management (cf. Pedersen 2002). Those in charge of heritage sites clearly need to pay closer attention to reconciling the needs of the various parties involved, each with their own interests. Instead of one universally accepted meaning, the significance of heritage – be it natural or cultural, tangible or intangible – is characterised by pluriversatility. Heritage appropriation and interpretation are always enmeshed in complex webs of meaning, variously cherished and expressed by shareholders at different levels. Cultural heritage is, by nature, a unique and fragile non-renewable resource. Therefore, it is imperative to understand how to develop these sites sustainably while protecting and conserving them for the long term. If not, irreparable and irreversible damage can be done. Although often heralded as a likely solution to conservation and community development challenges, local staff and communities in poor countries do not always have the resources, experience or training they need in order to use tourism as an effective instrument for achieving these goals. The tools to provide coherent and sustainable heritage management are yet to be fully developed or effectively applied. As I have argued, heritage interpretation and (re)presentation by local tour guides play a key role in this.

To make local heritage workers more competitive in the current landscape of international labour circulation, standardisation seems to be the way to go. Even if there remain great local variations in qualifications, there is a global tendency to standardise, reinforcing the idea that tourism is a global practice. This chapter has argued that thinking of globalisation and local differentiation as being opposed to each other is not very helpful in understanding and explaining contemporary tourism. The constant (re)shaping of local heritage is in many respects part of and simultaneously occurring with the globalising process itself. By studying the daily practices of local guides and the way they (re)present and actively (re)construct local culture for a diversified audience of global tourists, we can learn a lot about how processes of globalisation and localisation are intimately intertwined and how this glocalisation is transforming culture – through tourism and other channels. Such studies bring to light that the processes of negotiation regarding the interpretation and (re)presentation of heritage are highly complex, multifaceted and flexible owing to the involvement of various parties with different interests in these interactions.

As global tourism continues to expand, heritage sites will be the source of historically unprecedented numbers of tourists. Most indicators suggest there will be a huge increase in tourism worldwide over the next ten years, virtually doubling the current numbers. It is estimated that China alone will produce 100 million outbound tourists by 2025. Interestingly, a large amount of the increased travel for leisure will be intraregional (rather than global). At any rate, the predicted growth of intraregional tourism – 1.2 billion intraregional arrivals per year by 2020 (WTO 2001) – will seriously change the global tourism landscape. For cultural heritage tourism, the challenges of global (and, ever more, regional) standardisation and local differentiation will take on new dimensions. While the management of heritage is usually the responsibility of a particular community or custodian group, the protection, conservation, interpretation and (re)presentation of the cultural diversity of any particular place or people are important challenges for us all.

Notes

1 Since the definition of heritage has been expanded to include not only material manifestations (monuments and objects that have been preserved over time) but also living expressions and the traditions that groups and communities have inherited from their ancestors and transmit to their descendants, the previously made distinction between heritage tourism and cultural tourism has become redundant.

2 While there is protest against standardisation at the global level, homogenising policies proposed by regional blocs – which are believed to be more culturally uniform – are perceived as less of a problem. This is particularly the case in Asia, the continent with the fastest growth rate of intra-regional tourism. APEC, for instance, is successfully developing its own Tourism Occupational Skill Standards while ASEAN is working on a Common Competency Standards for Tourism Professionals Framework.

3 The glocalisation concept is modelled on the Japanese notion *dochakuka* (becoming autochthonous), derived from *dochaku* (aboriginal, living on one's own land). This originally referred to the agricultural principle of adapting generally accepted farming techniques to local conditions. In the 1980s, the term was adopted by Japanese businesspeople to express global localisation or a global outlook adapted to local conditions. The marketing technique of melding the global inside the local quickly spread worldwide.

4 The cultural heritage sites are described as those monuments, groups of buildings or locales with historical, archaeological, aesthetic, scientific, ethnological or anthropological value.

5 See http://www.international.icomos.org/tourism_e.htm

6 With the promotion of sustainable tourism actions and improved tourism practices a concern at many WHS, the World Heritage Tourism Programme develops policies and processes for site management and for the states parties to the Convention to address this increasingly important management concern. It implements actions to preserve sites for future generations and contributes to sustainable development and intercultural dialogue. See http://whc.unesco.org/en/sustainabletourism/

7 Until the 1970s, such ideas and practices were common in the Western world as well. The all-pervasive ideology of modernisation equated traditional societies with underdevelopment and an inferior phase to full development.

8 The seven ancient wonders included the great pyramid of Giza (Egypt), the hanging gardens of Babylon (Iraq), the statue of Zeus at Olympia (Greece), the temple of Artemis at Ephesus (Turkey), the mausoleum of Maussollos at Halicarnassus (Turkey), the Colossus of Rhodes (Greece) and the lighthouse of Alexandria (Egypt). The only wonder that stood the test of time is the Great Pyramid of Giza, which was inscribed as a WHS in 1979 and is one of Egypt's major tourism attractions.

9 The national regulation concerning the preservation of cultural sites and objects (*Undang-Undang Nomor 5 Tahun 1992, Pemeliharaan Benda Benda dan Situs Benda Cagar Budaya*) was based on Dutch colonial law (*Monumenten Ordonantie, Staatsblad 1931, No. 238*).

10 Since the disasters also greatly affected my fieldwork, I wrote a public weblog entitled *Earthquake Disaster: An Anthropologist's Report from Yogyakarta, Indonesia*, with reflections as the events unfolded: http://www.museum.upenn.edu/new/research/blogs/earthquake_blog.shtml

11 According to local beliefs, the statue in the north chamber of the central Shiva shrine does not represent the Hindu goddess Durga but Loro Jonggrang (Javanese for slender virgin). Legend has it that she was a Javanese princess who agreed to marry a man she did not love if he could build her a temple ornamented with a thousand statues, between the setting and rising of the sun. When the man was about to fulfil her demand, she tried to trick him. He was so furious that he petrified her and she became the last (and most beautiful) of the thousand statues.

References

Adams, K.M. (2003) 'The politics of heritage in Southeast Asia: Interplaying the local and the global', *Indonesia and the Malay World*, 31: 91–107.

Al Sayyad, N. (ed.) (2001) *Consuming Tradition, Manufacturing Heritage: Global Norms and Urban Forms in the Age of Tourism*, London: Routledge.

Ashworth, G.J. and Tunbridge, J.E. (2000) *The Tourist-Historic City: Retrospect and Prospect of Managing the Heritage City*, Amsterdam: Pergamon.

Boniface, P. and Fowler, P. (1993) *Heritage and Tourism in 'the Global Village'*, London: Routledge.

Chang, T.C. (1999) 'Local uniqueness in the global village: Heritage tourism in Singapore', *Professional Geographer*, 51: 91–103.

Dahles, H. (2001) *Tourism, Heritage and National Culture in Java: Dilemmas of a Local Community*, Richmond: Curzon Press.

Di Giovine, M.A. (2008) *The Heritage-scape: UNESCO, World Heritage, and Tourism*, Lanham: Lexington Books.

Dioko, L.A. and Unakul, M.H. (2005) 'The need for specialized training in heritage tour guiding at Asia's world heritage sites: Preliminary findings on the challenges and opportunities', paper presented at PATA Educator's Forum, Macao, 16 April 2005.

Hampton, M.P. (2005) 'Heritage, local communities and economic development', *Annals of Tourism Research*, 32: 735–59.

McKercher, B. and Du Cros, H. (2002) *Cultural Tourism: The Partnership Between Tourism and Cultural Heritage Management*, New York: Haworth Hospitality Press.

Moscardo, G. (1996) 'Mindful visitors: Heritage and tourism', *Annals of Tourism Research*, 23: 376–97.

Nuryanti, W. (ed.) (1997) *Tourism and Heritage Management*, Yogyakarta: Gadjah Mada University Press.

NWHO (1999) *Sustainable Tourism and Cultural Heritage: A Review of Development Assistance and its Potential to Promote Sustainability*, Oslo: Nordic World Heritage Office.

Pedersen, A. (2002) *Managing Tourism at World Heritage Sites: A Practical Manual for World Heritage Site Managers*, Paris: UNESCO World Heritage Centre.

Peleggi, M. (1996) 'National heritage and global tourism in Thailand', *Annals of Tourism Research*, 23: 432–48.

Poria, Y., Butler, R. and Airey, D. (2003) 'The core of heritage tourism', *Annals of Tourism Research*, 30: 238–54.

Porter, B.W. and Salazar, N.B. (eds) (2005) 'Heritage Tourism, Conflict, and the Public Interest', Theme Issue, *International Journal of Heritage Studies* 11(5).

Robertson, R. (1995) 'Glocalization: Time-space and homogeneity-heterogeneity', in M. Featherstone, S. Lash and R. Robertson (eds) *Global Modernities*, London: Sage.

Salazar, N.B. (2005) 'Tourism and glocalization: "Local" tour guiding', *Annals of Tourism Research*, 32: 628–46.

——(2007) 'Towards a global culture of heritage interpretation? Evidence from Indonesia and Tanzania', *Tourism Recreation Research*, 32: 23–30.

——(2009) 'The world's, Asia's, Indonesia's or ours? Heritage interpretation and appropriation in times of change', paper presented at Heritage in Asia: Converging forces and conflicting values, National University of Singapore, Singapore, 8–10 January 2009.

——(In Press) *Envisioning Eden: Mobilizing Imaginaries in Tourism and Beyond*, Oxford: Berghahn.

Salazar, N.B. and Porter, B.W. (eds) (2004) 'Heritage and Tourism, PIA and Global Interests', Theme issue, *Anthropology in Action* 11(2/3).

Shackley, M.L. (ed.) (1998) *Visitor Management: Case studies from World Heritage Sites*, Oxford: Butterworth Heinemann.

Timothy, D.J. and Boyd, S.W. (2003) *Heritage Tourism*, Harlow: Prentice Hall.

——(2006) 'Heritage tourism in the 21st century: Valued traditions and new perspectives', *Journal of Heritage Tourism*, 1: 1–16.

Timothy, D.J. and Prideaux, B. (2004) 'Issues in heritage and culture in the Asia Pacific region', *Asia Pacific Journal of Tourism Research*, 9: 213–23.

UNESCO (1992) *Cultural Tourism Development Central Java – Yogyakarta: Final report*, Yogyakarta: UNESCO/UNDP/Directorate General of Tourism.

——(2005) *Heritage Tour Guide Training and Certification for UNESCO World Heritage Sites*, Bangkok: UNESCO Bangkok Office.

UNWTO (2008) *Tourism Highlights. 2008 Edition*, Madrid: United Nations World Tourism Organization.

Urry, J. (2002) *The Tourist Gaze*, London: Sage.

Uzzell, D.L. (ed.) (1989) *Heritage Interpretation*, London: Belhaven Press.

Wall, G. and Black, H. (2004) 'Global heritage and local problems: Some examples from Indonesia', *Current Issues in Tourism*, 7: 436–39.

WTO (2001) *Tourism 2020 Vision*, Madrid: World Tourism Organization.

WTTC (2008) *Progress and Priorities 2008/09*, London: World Travel and Tourism Council.

Chapter 8

The business of heritage and the private sector

Fiona Starr

In our increasingly commercial and globalising world, it is not surprising that the activities of the international private sector often intersect with the thousands of significant cultural heritage sites around the world. Some sites are recipients of philanthropic assistance that provides much-needed conservation resources, while other sites become passive players, caught up in the dealings of the private sector. The enormous socio-economic value of heritage sites means they are targeted as commercial resources, but their use for profit-driven purposes can potentially be at odds with the principles of heritage preservation.

A number of global trends are influencing how the private sector interacts with cultural heritage. Increasing costs of managing and conserving cultural heritage sites and the pressure of global market forces are accompanied by governments releasing some of their traditional responsibility for heritage places. These trends are influencing the privatisation of heritage conservation and management and are placing more pressure on the national and international private sector to provide support through public–private partnerships. In addition, the global increases in population and poverty are influencing a greater need for community use of the economic values of heritage resources, and other resources surrounding sites.

A range of threats such as mass tourism, pollution and climate change, combined with dwindling government resources and the potentially damaging encroachment of commercial activities, means the responsibility of the private sector is becoming indispensable to heritage conservation. These circumstances call for an examination of the relationship between heritage and the private sector, and how these two potentially incompatible fields of activity approach one another. Through four parts this chapter examines the variety of ways in which the international private sector interacts with cultural heritage, discussing the responsible and not-so-responsible aspects of the private sector–heritage relationship and considering new approaches to mobilising further private support and for ensuring fair and ethical use of heritage sites in relation to commercial activities and privatisation.

The chapter begins with a discussion of the various ways heritage is used for commercial purposes, and the difficulties that have emerged through association of profit-making activities with the ethics and values of heritage sites. It then presents an outline of the corporate social responsibility (CSR) movement, and reviews a number of examples of mutually-beneficial corporate-heritage relationships. Finally, the chapter discusses the ethics and challenges of private sector interaction with cultural heritage and how these might be addressed. It suggests that a stronger private sector application of the principles of CSR to heritage is required, which might be assisted by building a better business case for the effectiveness of cultural heritage partnerships to achieve CSR objectives.

Private sector and heritage: a difficult relationship?

Private enterprises interact with cultural heritage sites in a variety of ways, using the values and prestige associated with sites for the purposes of marketing and increasing profits, and through regular business activities, which may lead to the encroachment of urban development on cultural heritage sites. Even if controlled by enforced governmental and local regulations, the impacts of such commercial activities often incite considerable public discussion and opposition. The challenge is in finding a publicly and ethically acceptable balance between profit-making activities and the heritage values of a place.

Commercialism and corporate proximity to heritage sites

The proximity of corporate advertisements and premises to heritage sites can be contentious if a company profits through association with the site without returning revenue for conservation. For example, in 2007 a Starbucks franchise operating within the Forbidden City World Heritage site in Beijing was closed after public outcry (CNN.com 2000; BBC News 2007). Other multinational brands, however, operate freely in close proximity to World Heritage (WH) sites, such as the Pizza Hut restaurant adjacent to the Great Pyramids in Giza, Egypt (Figure 8.1). Food and beverage outlets are certainly needed to service the volume of visitors to such iconic sites, but the impact of the visibility and association of such commercial multinational brands for visitors attending heritage sites is often controversial. Even when corporate sponsorship deals support conservation at heritage sites, such as the proposed US$2.7 million deal for Coca-Cola vending machines to be installed throughout Venice, the resulting public outcry is still strong (Pisa 2009).

Large commercial premises and uncontrolled commercialism that stand to profit from proximity to cultural heritage sites are equally problematic. At the Terracotta Warriors archaeological site in Xi'an, China, visitors to the site have no choice but to walk through the Terracotta Warriors International Plaza shopping mall. As one visitor explained: 'I can't say I was surprised to see this commercialized exit extravaganza, but I was irked that we were forced to walk through it … After viewing such an ancient and sacred memorial, the barrage of souvenir stands and yells from store clerks just left me feeling grumpy' (Amabile 2007).

Figure 8.1 Pizza Hut restaurant adjacent to the Great Pyramids, Giza, Egypt, 2002 (Photo by the author)

Use of heritage sites for commercial events and films

Iconic cultural heritage sites are often sought after as dramatic and romantic locations for large events and filming. In 2000 at Machu Picchu, Peru, US publicity firm J. Walter Thompson filmed a commercial for Peruvian beer Cusquena, using the *Intihuatana*, a 15th-century granite sundial, as a makeshift bar. Worse still, a crane brought to the site for the filming toppled over and broke a part of the sundial, resulting in criminal charges being filed against the production company (BBC News 2000).

Even if the impacts of commercial activities at sites are minimised, and even if rent is paid to the management authority, questions of ethics and the use of heritage sites for commercial purposes are often raised. In October 2007 the Juyongguan section of the Great Wall of China was used as the location for an exclusive fashion show by Italian brand Fendi (Figure 8.2), aiming to break into the booming luxury market in China. One invitee said to the press: 'Beforehand, part of me was thinking, how can you justify using the Great Wall of China in this way?' (Borrelli-Persson 2007). Other comments posted on websites question if the event was appropriate: 'It seems like China is willing to sacrifice their history and monuments in order to make money and seem more western ... Does European high fashion belong on the Great Wall?' (Fabsugar 2007).

It is unknown if this event, which cost around US$10 million, involved a payment to the government-run China Great Wall Society, which granted permission

Figure 8.2 Fendi fashion show on the Juyongguan section of the Great Wall of China World Heritage site, October 2007 (Photo courtesy Associated Press)

to stage the event, or indeed if such a payment would have been used towards the conservation of the site. Staging such an event at this iconic place must certainly have had enormous marketing effects for the company, although perhaps returned few benefits to the site and local communities.

Ethical issues were also raised by the use of the Colosseum in Rome as the location for concerts by the likes of Paul McCartney (2003), Elton John (2005), and the MTV Europe Music Awards (2004). Giving heritage sites such a function in contemporary society certainly keeps them alive. However, the concerts raised public concerns about the vibrations from the amplified music damaging the ruins and the cheapening of the image of the place to promote commercial pop music. Adriano La Regina, head of the archaeological department, argued: 'It's debased, exploited, commercialized. An image (of Rome) that in the end will have less value because it will have lost its fascination, its integrity, its beauty' (Reuters 2004).

Similarly, cultural heritage sites are often chosen as dramatic and unique locations for big-budget films by major Hollywood production companies, although such use seems to raise less public debate than the examples above. More than a dozen WH sites have featured in the Indiana Jones film series, and more recently *Gladiator* (2000) (Dreamworks Pictures) and *Alexander* (2004) (Warner Bros) were both filmed at Ait Ben-Haddou in Morocco. *Tomb Raider* (2001) (Paramount Pictures) was filmed at Angkor, Cambodia, although the management authority established procedures to secure royalties for images of Angkor used commercially (APSARA 2000). Little information is publicly available about any payments made by production companies to site management for such use of the sites.

Use of heritage sites and their images for advertising

An advertisement by Nestlé has been displayed on the entrance ticket of the Imperial Palace Museum WH site in Beijing, and at the Temple of Heaven the Ganzhou Pharmaceutical Group logo is presented on signage. If the companies mentioned are granted rights to display their logos in this manner in return for site sponsorship (without any expectation from the company of such exposure), such arrangements might generally be considered acceptable. However, even if the revenue is directed towards the restoration of the site, the proximity of advertisements and association of unrelated brands competes with the heritage values of the sites. As Cori (2006) argues, such association with consumer brands is detrimental, undermining the WH image and the conservation cause. If the WH brand is more effectively defined, WH managers will be better placed to make informed selections about which corporate brands have values that are appropriate to associate with WH.

Government spending cuts and an attempt to find alternative sources of funding for restoration work in a number of European cities have led to the sale of advertising rights on heritage buildings, such as in Porto, Portugal (Figure 8.3) and, more controversially, in Venice, Italy. In 2008, advertisements were hung over restoration scaffolding of some of the most significant areas of Venice, resulting in public outcry

Figure 8.3 Advertising hoarding for Novo Seat Ibiza, on the restoration scaffolding of the 12th-century Episcopal Palace, Porto, Portugal, May 2008 (Photo by the author)

over the association of commercial brands with iconic buildings, and the commercialisation of one of the world's most famous heritage cities. A Lancia car advertisement was hung on the front of the Palazzo Ducale, a giant Rolex over the Biblioteca Nazionale Marciana in St Mark's Square and the façade of the Ca' Rezzonico palazzo was covered with a jeans advertisement.

In light of the €1.25 million cut from the Italian Ministry of Culture's budget over three years (Povoledo 2008), selling advertising space was a logical alternative to fund the necessary restorations, since just one of the advertisements in St Mark's square yields €3.5million (Hooper 2008). As one commentator admitted: 'I understand that on-going restoration really is needed, and someone has to pay for it'. Another observer argued ' ... some things should be beyond money ... visitors (who may only ever come once to this ethereal city) should not go away with the impression ... that Venice is just an extension to Disneyland or Vegas' (Beyond the Bridge 2008).

At the very least, allowing such advertising does finance conservation works. However, another form of advertising is a potentially large source of lost revenue and marketing for heritage conservation. The uncontrolled use of images of heritage sites for commercial advertising allows companies to profit from association of their brands with the values of heritage, without benefit to the sites. For example, the magazine and newspaper advertisements by watch company Vacheron Constantin, which depict iconic heritage sites such as Machu Picchu and the Eiffel Tower, play on the concept of heritage in relation to the age of the company and the value of its watches: 'When the lost city of the Incas was discovered in Peru, Vacheron Constantin was 156 years old'. Such associations between products and cultural heritage sites create unfair advantage for companies, and present missed opportunities for cultural heritage conservation, when more formal agreements with such companies might have mutually-beneficial co-branding effects.

Privatisation of heritage site management

The tendency of governments to reduce budgets for heritage management is resulting in the granting of concessions and privatisation of some state-owned cultural heritage. This can include administration (auditing, personnel, strategic planning), conservation projects, maintaining the collection, developing exhibitions, restaurant or café catering, cleaning and maintenance (Boorsma 1998).

Privatisation brings advantages to the management of heritage, potentially increasing efficiency and improving the quality of visitor services. However, it may also result in job losses and increased production costs and may be in conflict with the principles of free access to heritage. Questions of balance are raised and the public is often concerned that private sector involvement may allow for decisions to be made by ill-informed or biased managers, or breed abuses of trust and standards (Schuster 1998).

The appointment of Mario Resca, former chief of McDonald's in Italy, as the new chief of museums and archaeological sites is part of the controversial new approach in Italy. Despite public opposition to the appointment, the proposed approach of the new chief is to raise visitor numbers, create thousands of new museum jobs and make culture more popular through strategies such as selling filming rights and access for events at sites such as Pompeii and the Colosseum and Forum in Rome. Resca noted, 'I don't want to "McDonaldise" Italy's culture but we want multi-national companies to choose Italy to launch products like the iPod. It would be a fantastic opportunity for the company and good for Italy's image' (Squires 2008).

Another potential problem is corruption and the mismanagement of funds collected from ticketing. In 1999 Cambodian petrol/hotel company Sokimex was granted the right to control ticketing at Angkor, Cambodia, for a flat fee of US$1 million. The company was required to give the management authority, APSARA, half of the first US$3 million collected, and 70 per cent thereafter (EEPSEA 2006). The agreement was renewed in 2005, despite being disputed by the International Monetary Fund which repeatedly urged the government to use competitive bidding in granting the ticketing concession (Kay and Wasson 2005). In 2006 Radio Free Asia reported huge discrepancies between the tourist numbers that Sokimex reported and those counted by the government Tourism Department, suggesting Sokimex may have underpaid by tens of millions of dollars (Tyler 2007). It was estimated that in 2005 the revenue from tickets was anywhere between US$11 million to almost $44 million (De Lopez 2006), and the estimated amount being returned to APSARA for management is between 5 and 15 per cent (Howse et al. 1998; Kay and Wasson 2005), which may represent as little as US$500,000 per year. Many sites throughout Asia suffer from a similar lack of revenue being fed back into site conservation (UNESCO 2004).

In France, privatisation of services at heritage sites and museums is reasonably common, and seems to be cost-efficient and successful. This often includes receiving visitors, cultural entertainment activities, security and maintenance, souvenir shops and cafés, although very few public museums are entirely managed by private firms (Benhamou 1997). However, examples of privatisation in other countries suggest it is not so successful. In 2001 the government of Qufu, China, established the Confucius International Tourism Co. Ltd to manage eight heritage sites, including the WH listed temple, cemetery and mansion of Confucius (Chan and Ma 2004). Unfortunately, perhaps as a result of lack of conservation awareness and training, a company truck driver knocked over and damaged a precious stone tablet, and cleaners hosed down plaques and walls with water and brushed dirt from ancient surfaces, causing the paint to peel and humidity levels to rise.

Commercial activities impacting on cultural heritage

Through regular business activities companies in certain industries have direct impact on heritage sites, in particular the extractive industries, developers and tourism operators. Commercial operations such as mining or construction within close proximity to heritage sites can have potentially devastating impacts. Uranium mining in Australia's Kakadu National Park, inscribed on the World Heritage List for its natural and cultural values, presents a famous example. Although the mining leases predate the heritage listing, the activities of the mining companies, and the potential for contamination from radioactive waste, raised enormous public and political debate, since they threatened the protected environment, ancient Aboriginal sites and the livelihood of local communities.

Around the world, historic urban landscapes are increasingly being threatened by private developments, and risk losing their heritage values and thus inscription on heritage protection lists. Four hotel development projects have recently contravened height restrictions in Malaysia's historic George Town (Sulaiman 2009), threatening its WH status, and Saint Petersburg risks losing its WH status due to a proposal to build Europe's highest tower (at least 300 metres), as headquarters for Gazprom, one of the world's largest energy companies. The height and design of the proposed tower will have an enormous impact on the historic skyline, and if allowed to be built could create a precedent for the construction of further towers, compromising the outstanding heritage value of the city (Donnelly 2007).

Numerous studies have shown the damaging impacts of mass tourism at cultural heritage sites (McKercher and duCros 2002; Pedersen 2002; Radcliffe 2004; Smith 2007). Commercial businesses such as tour operators, hotels, transport providers and restaurants profit from the value and popularity of the sites that are attracting their tourist customers. At some heritage sites, such as Lijiang, in Yunnan, China, commercial development has caused a loss of authentic atmosphere, with encroachment and even displacement of the protected heritage areas by tourist-oriented commercial premises (Jing et al. 2009). In Lijiang Old Town, a Business Permission Certificate system was at least introduced in 2003 to ban unsympathetic businesses such as video shops, karaoke bars, internet cafés and discos in the core historic zones. Large tour groups, tour buses, and associated pollution from traffic brought to such sites by commercial tour operators also have immense impacts, requiring site managers to devise complex monitoring and tourism management plans. A variety of heritage tourism-related businesses depend on the attraction and future preservation of heritage in order to survive, yet very few tourism businesses offer any of their profits to conservation efforts.

These case studies have demonstrated the difficulties and concerns with private sector involvement with cultural heritage, suggesting that a greater private sector awareness and corporate responsibility for heritage conservation is still required. This awareness needs to be fostered by the heritage community and media, and solutions to the difficulties of such informal and uncontrolled use of heritage sites may be found through connecting with the global corporate social responsibility agenda and coercing the private sector into more structured, mutually beneficial relationships with heritage.

International business and its social responsibility

Corporate social responsibility (CSR) has been stimulated by globalisation, international trade and an intense public expectation for companies to not only be profitable, but also to operate legally, to behave ethically and to give something back to the community. By addressing social, cultural and environmental issues, companies aim to improve competitive advantage, align social and economic goals and improve long-term business prospects (Porter and Kramer 2003). CSR is most commonly demonstrated through cause promotion, cause-related marketing, corporate social marketing, corporate philanthropy, community volunteering and responsible business practices (Kotler and Lee 2005). Elkington's (1994) phrase 'Triple Bottom Line' has come into popular usage, implying that companies should work towards not one bottom line (profits), but three – economic, social and environmental performance.

Companies commit to CSR due to social pressures from NGOs and activist groups, the media, regulators and consumers, who can reward or punish companies by providing or withdrawing economic support (Valor 2005), and also for reasons of competition and management judgement about the long-term benefits to the company (Marsden and Andriof 1998). Through responsible behaviour, companies can potentially achieve a range of important business benefits, including improved public image and reputation, increased profitability, access to new markets, sustainability, greater consumer loyalty, licence to operate, higher employee morale, market positioning, risk profile management, ability to attract top job candidates, and improved investor relations (Roberts et al. 2002).

Of all these benefits, reputation enhancement is widely considered the primary cause of CSR, as demonstrated by a 2003 World Economic Forum survey and a Sustainable Asset Management survey (World Economic Forum 2004). A survey of senior executives of 1,200 firms worldwide (Economist Intelligence Unit 2008) indicated that 79 per cent of respondents ranked enhanced brand reputation as a 'very important' goal for their CSR programs, 18 per cent of firms thought that most of their customers would pay extra for a 'brand renowned for its commitment to sustainable development' and 37 per cent thought that at least a 'significant minority' of customers would pay more.

Since 2007 the Ethisphere Institute has examined the activities of 10,000 global companies to elect an annual list of the *World's Most Ethical Companies*, ranking companies according to CSR, innovation contributing to public well-being, strong leadership, ethics and governance. Ratings scales such as the Dow Jones Sustainability Index and the FTSE4Good, which publicise the social performance of companies, also create powerful incentives for good behaviour.

Through CSR activities, the private sector is addressing some of the major problems troubling our world, including hunger and poverty, global warming and climate change, HIV/AIDS, water shortages, illiteracy, shortages of education resources, biodiversity loss and environmental concerns. In 2008 socially responsible investment assets reached a figure of US$2.71 trillion (Greenbiz.com 2008) and more and more companies are budgeting large sums for corporate responsibility programs. Many firms employ designated CSR staff to report on their environmental and social impacts, while over a thousand multinational enterprises (MNE) have signed up to the United Nations Global Compact and increasing numbers are signing the World Economic Forum statement on Global Corporate Citizenship (2002). Responsible companies have also begun to adopt principles and codes of conduct such as the Global Sullivan Principles (1999) and the Equator Principles (2006), which set standards for assessing and managing social and environmental risk. The Millennium Development Goals, which promote sustainable development through targets to be achieved by 2015, are providing benchmarks and driving many CSR initiatives. Likewise, the Global Reporting Initiative requires companies to report annually on a range of impacts. Microfinance and socially responsible investing are providing seed funding and assisting communities in developing countries to build capacity and manage their own socio-economic growth.

The CSR agenda is not only central to business strategy now, but has been predicted to become a future driver of business growth. Developing and emerging markets will be the main source of growth for many MNEs, and as Cescau (2007) argues, the companies that make a positive contribution to economic growth and poverty reduction will be better placed to grow.

Corporate responsibility for cultural heritage

Neither the state nor the private sector can afford to act alone to protect heritage (Riley 1997), but it is also certain that public and NGO sources of funding are simply unable to contribute sufficient funds to protect the world's important heritage sites for the future. So the resources and influence of the private sector will need to have an increasingly important role into the 21st century, requiring the building of more extensive dialogue and trust between heritage agencies and the private sector.

Support for cultural heritage conservation is not typically high on the CSR agenda, even though it is surely a cause of interest to the stakeholders of many firms. A study of 100 MNEs listed on the Global *Fortune 500* found that while many codes of conduct mentioned environmental stewardship, ecosystems and historical landmarks rated very low in priority (Reich 2005). In recent years, however, some CSR initiatives have been influential in supporting cultural heritage conservation, hopefully representing the emergence of a new set of attitudes towards partnerships in this field.

Philanthropic partnerships and CSR initiatives often occur directly between cultural heritage sites and companies, although many are also managed by NGOs such as the World Monuments Fund (WMF) and heritage management bodies such as the UNESCO World Heritage Centre (WHC). Many successful partnerships have been initiated and managed by the WHC and its program PACT, or Partnerships for Conservation Initiative, launched in 2002, in response to increasing interest from international partners to support WH. The WHC has developed innovative private–public partnerships, in areas such as sustainable tourism, forests, cities, marine sites, education and awareness-raising.

Financing of conservation by cash donations is often through direct partnerships between companies and sites, and projects are co-managed by the partners. For example, French bank Crédit Agricole recently committed €1.4 million for restoration and re-opening of the historical rooms of the Château de Fontainebleau in France. Similarly, the construction group Vinci undertook restoration of the Hall of Mirrors at the Château de Versailles, the largest cultural philanthropy project ever realised in France. Using its expertise in construction and smaller companies specialising in restoration, Vinci financed the project to the order of €12 million.

Cash contributions are also frequently managed through NGOs such as the WMF. Through the Partners for Preservation program, the WMF has secured US$5 million from American Express for an international program to safeguard some of the world's most precious cultural heritage sites. This represents only the latest contribution from this company, which for over a decade has supported the WMF in its mission. In 1995, American Express was the founding sponsor of the World Monuments Watch List, and has since contributed US$10 million, which has assisted in leveraging $150 million from other sources (WMF 2005/6), for the preservation of 126 sites in 62 countries.

Many companies deal in services, products or expertise that can provide much-needed in-kind support for conservation. CSR initiatives that make use of core business in this way can often be more effective than requests for cash donations. Using its expertise in information technology, IBM has produced an online digital recreation of the Forbidden City in Beijing, entitled *Beyond Space and Time* (IBM 2005) and Hewlett Packard has provided in-kind support to produce the World Heritage maps for the World Heritage Centre.

A number of successful partnerships with media companies have involved awareness-raising of conservation issues, such as with German television company Sudwestrundfunk Media, and Japanese television stations NHK and TV Tokyo, through the production and screening of documentaries featuring well-known cultural sites. Companies from other industries also get involved in raising awareness, for example Vietnam Airlines, which features local tangible and intangible heritage in its in-flight magazine, *Heritage*. Singapore Airlines, which sponsors the conservation activities of the Global Heritage Fund, also features heritage conservation through in-flight films, publications and events, and provides free travel for Global Heritage Fund staff. The Heritage-Friendly Businesses scheme in Cambodia supports heritage preservation by contributing to education about heritage issues, supporting best-practice in tourism and non-involvement in the illegal antiquities trade.

Some companies are demonstrating responsibility for heritage through staff volunteering, although this still seems to be a largely untapped area. As part of its 'Local citizens' initiative, Diageo Korea has adopted a cultural heritage site, and company employees are encouraged to participate in volunteer programs to help preserve the site and raise awareness of conservation (CSR Globe 2008).

Fortunately an increasing number of tourism operators are encouraging responsible tourism behaviour and ethical commercial enterprise surrounding heritage sites. Jet Tours, EF Tours and Maison de la Chine have developed tours that promote sustainable and responsible tourism in and around WH sites, providing a few dollars from each tourist booking for site conservation. Since 2005, through the World Heritage Alliance, a partnership between Expedia and the United Nations Foundation, 50 tourism and hospitality companies have committed to sustainable business practices, support for local communities and educating travellers about the importance of conservation.

Government regulations, legal instruments, codes of ethics and public expectations are urging many companies to act responsibly, and to monitor activities when their core business impacts on heritage sites. For example, in 2003, 15 mining companies signed a pledge 'to recognize existing World Heritage properties as "no-go" areas' (WHC 2004). Environmental impact assessments (EIAs) require full inventories of cultural heritage resources under threat by development projects, and result in analysis of alternative project designs or sites that may eliminate or reduce impacts (Marriott 1997). Companies seeking finance from investment and development banks are required by the Equator Principles (2006) and the International Finance Corporation Performance Standards (No. 8) to produce an EIA to assess the impacts of projects on cultural heritage. The protective power of this instrument was recently demonstrated in the financing of the Ilisu Dam project in Turkey (Environmental Finance 2009). German, Swiss and Austrian export credit agencies suspended guarantees for the World Bank financing of the dam, since it failed to reach the Bank's minimum standards. While the Turkish Government claims the dam will encourage economic development and create jobs, it will also flood the ancient city of Hasankeyf and about 300 archaeological sites.

A further example is the planning of the West–East Pipeline Project in China by Shell, a US$8.5 billion project to bring gas from northwestern China to the developing cities in the east. Shell conducted EIAs and a social impact survey of 10,000 people, to engage a broad range of stakeholders in discussion about the impact of the pipeline which crosses the Great Wall of China at 12 locations, and passes close to four state-protected cultural heritage sites (Seymour 2004).

Not only does CSR have the potential to directly finance conservation projects, it can provide management skills and technical expertise, in-kind donations, technology, communications support, information, ideas and alternative perspectives. Through CSR companies may in future assist in identifying sites for inscription on heritage lists, support education programs and media campaigns, produce publications and exhibitions, allow for secondment of staff, and provide training in skills such as architectural conservation, urban planning, conservation, and condition reporting.

Ethics and challenges in heritage partnerships

As previously discussed, the association of the private sector with heritage can present a range of problems, particularly through advertising or use of sites for commercial purposes. However, the divergent interests of heritage and the private sector can also create a number of challenges and ethical issues within formal partnerships. For example, the intentions of a company in aligning itself with heritage may be less than altruistic. Such partnerships may in fact be motivated only by the desire to enhance goodwill towards the company and for lobbying government or other decision makers on issues of commercial interest to the company.

Also, through associating heritage with the private sector, heritage managers may give credibility to corporate partners whose commercial activities contradict the principles and values of cultural heritage. In the 1980s, the frescoes in the Sistine Chapel in the Vatican were restored with a grant of US$4.2 million from the Nippon Television Network Corporation (NTV). Although not in contradiction of the values of heritage, the television network was best known for its populist programming such as quiz shows and baseball coverage, perhaps an odd marriage with a site as reverent as the Sistine Chapel.

This partnership raised another important ethical issue – that of restricting access to a public heritage site. Although reporters, art historians and others with a genuine interest were allowed access, the restoration was financed in exchange for exclusive photographic and filming rights of the Chapel for NTV during the restoration process. There was widespread concern over the restoration, partly because the company did not publish any photographs during the process. It has been suggested that the company probably withheld the photos in order to release them later in the form of a large limited-edition two-volume coffee-table book. When finally produced, the book retailed for US$1,000, making the photos available only to the few who could afford to buy it. One commentator suggested it was the 'television company's attempt to capitalize on its investment' before its control over the photography lapsed (Kimmelman 1991).

In return for sponsorship or in-kind support, corporate logos are often displayed on heritage site signage, publications and websites. Such public acknowledgement of the support is essential, but must be done in a subtle and tasteful manner, or it risks being viewed by visitors as blatant advertising in conflict with the values of the site. In fact, attempts by companies to gain maximum exposure in such ways from partnerships can reflect negatively on the company, and be seen as an attempt to buy goodwill.

A good model for the acceptable use of corporate logos at sites is the display of the American Express logo on interpretive signage at sites supported by the company (Figure 8.4).

Figure 8.4 American Express logo (bottom right of photo) on interpretive signage at Ayutthaya, Thailand (Photo by the author)

Challenges in private sector heritage partnerships

Attracting partnerships and encouraging responsible behaviour from the private sector presents a range of challenges. Perhaps the first barrier is the debate within the private sector about the effectiveness of CSR. For many companies focused on the financial bottom line, CSR is still often regarded with cynicism, being criticised as a costly, public-relations-focused activity that does not address business objectives. *The Economist* worldwide survey of senior executives (Economist Intelligence Unit 2008) found that a major barrier to CSR was the difficulty in aligning social and environmental activities with corporate strategy (31 per cent). While cultural heritage is well recognised as a tool for sustainable development (concern for which is one aspect of corporate strategy), it does not yet seem to be considered by the private sector as such.

Of all the causes that the private sector may support through CSR, heritage and the arts were on average rated lowest in priority in an online international survey of corporate attitudes towards heritage partnerships recently conducted by the author. Corporate respondents noted that the challenges they had experienced in relation to heritage were specific to heritage partnerships, rather than typical of partnerships in general. Some respondents reported problems with cultural differences, excessive legal/administration work, long lead times and lack of partner transparency. There were also difficulties with both internal and partner bureaucracy, and some dissatisfaction with the management of projects by an intermediary, the choice of allocation of company funds, and the limited degree of company input allowed regarding the allocation of funds.

Many cultural heritage sites are in developing countries, where local companies are financially unable to provide support. These sites would benefit enormously from the assistance of foreign companies, but, as Erika Harms notes, many companies simply do not know how to go about international partnerships (UN Foundation 2002). International partnerships also present problems due to cultural differences and communication barriers. Encouraging the private sector to invest in poor countries is also difficult because of perceptions of high risk due to political instability and corruption, the risk of expropriation, and inadequate or absent legal frameworks to enforce laws and contracts (Brainard and Lafleur 2005). Other problems include the lack of infrastructure to implement projects and manage funds and suppression of the media. Some of these issues can be addressed by the management of partnerships by intermediaries such as the WHC, which provides insurance that funds will be properly managed. However, the involvement of intermediaries may also create problems of communication.

Heritage must compete for limited resources with a multitude of charitable causes which have also earned a greater profile through the CSR movement. As Bommelaer (2008) notes, French companies have begun to rationalise their approach to philanthropic patronage for museums and heritage. For example, Jean-Paul Claverie, responsible for philanthropy at the luxury brands group LVMH, notes that the group does not plan to give up, but to invest each Euro more meaningfully. In addition, François de Mazières of the Cité du patrimoine et de l'architecture notes that the regular partners of the organisation are suffering from the crisis, so it is important for the organisation to continue attracting them by programming exhibitions of interest to the private sector and by approaching partnerships with a more commercial attitude.

Private and public partners often have differences in types and levels of resources and competencies, and are seeking different outcomes and benefits. For example, the long lead times required for many heritage projects can be challenging to many corporate partners, which are more accustomed to shorter time-frames for projects. Joanna Serna-Sullivan of the WHC notes that such lead times may also result in mis-timing where conservation projects require funding at a time when companies are less able to provide support. Alternatively, CSR programs and corporate budgets may be available at times when conservation bodies are unable to act immediately on their projects (Serna-Sullivan 2008). The extensive legal paper work required before securing a contract with a sponsor may also be a deterrent (Lehnert 2004). Guidelines need to be developed that could ensure alignment on common goals, outlining responsibilities and roles, ensuring accountability and transparency, and no unfair advantage or exclusivity. There is a need for greater sharing and learning from experience, to evaluate future partnerships before initiation.

Addressing the challenges

Perhaps the first approach to attracting greater private sector responsibility for heritage is to draw attention to the need for conservation support, in order to stimulate voluntary CSR initiatives. A second major approach is to make a strong business case for heritage conservation support to show how responsibility for heritage addresses CSR objectives. As discussed above, CSR is motivated by a range of factors, in particular three main points which will be discussed here: the ability of an initiative to create shared value, its ability to address the sustainable development agenda, and its ability to provide corporate benefits such as reputation enhancement and increasing visibility and rapport with existing and emerging markets.

Porter and Kramer (2006) argue that companies must only undertake projects that have the potential to achieve a convergence of interests or 'shared value' – projects that improve competitive positioning for the company, but also promote social and environmental development. The recent survey-based research conducted by the author suggests that cultural heritage partnerships create shared value, producing benefits for all parties involved and clearly addressing sustainable development goals. These include direct and indirect benefits for the historic fabric of the site, its visitors, the local community, and the supportive company.

Projects supported by well-known brands potentially have a social marketing effect on visitors and the general public, increasing visitor understanding of the value of a site and influencing a greater appreciation for the need to behave respectfully while visiting. Visitors also stand to benefit individually from CSR, since building consolidation projects increase visitor safety and interpretive signage and publications greatly improve visitor understanding of a site.

CSR support for conservation that allows for preservation and sustainable use of the site by the local community and the tourism industry can be effective in assisting poverty alleviation and sustainable development goals. Cultural heritage and its conservation can often bring economic benefits through cultural tourism and employment, but also social benefits such as establishing identity and pride, promoting social inclusion and regenerating local communities. Preservation itself creates jobs for labourers, craftsmen, conservators, architects, archaeologists and engineers and often provides training for local people in skills vital to the ongoing conservation and management of sites (Starr, in press). This helps to build the capacity of the local community and a sense of ownership amongst residents. In addition, when cultural heritage is conserved and used in a sustainable way by tourists and the local community, it remains available as a sustainable income source for present and future generations.

Companies are publicly challenged to address sustainable development issues and are searching for projects to support that fulfil their triple bottom line objectives, which they do by considering whether their involvement will be effective both for the recipient and their own business goals. Heritage must therefore make itself visible by demonstrating how its support can have multidirectional benefits, and make a substantial contribution to socio-economic development. Through playing the sustainable development card in this way, heritage conservationists can appeal to the private sector agenda to address socio-economic development issues through CSR initiatives (Starr 2008).

Finally, in relation to encouraging private enterprise to be responsible for heritage, the recent research by the author confirms that the association of companies with heritage sites can have a positive effect on corporate reputation and branding, the key driver of CSR initiatives. Cultural heritage is a unique and rewarding cause with which companies can align themselves. Responsibility for heritage can act as a marketing tool, allowing companies to achieve good publicity that is not available in the marketplace. Such free access to media coverage has been shown to have even greater credibility than commercial publicity pursuits (O'Hagan and Harvey 2000; d'Astous and Bitz 1995).

In addition to reputation enhancement, conservation of cultural heritage facilitates competitive positioning, allowing companies to engage with emerging markets through gaining a positive presence in local communities, or to consolidate relationships and exposure within existing markets. Heritage initiatives also provide tangible proof that a company is committed to the livelihoods of local communities. For example, BHP has supported the production of a series of documentaries highlighting the rich cultural heritage of the Sahara desert, where the company is extracting oil and gas (BHP 2006). Companies also support heritage sites of interest to their existing local target markets, such as the Jindal Steel Corporation providing funding for the conservation of the Chandramuleshwar Temple of Hampi. In addition, Portuguese concrete company CIMPOR funded the conservation of frescoes in the Convento do Cristo, in Tomar, Portugal, and Standard Chartered (Nepal) Ltd has been involved with a restoration project at Durbar Square, Kathmandu, Nepal.

Cultural heritage partnerships also offer financial incentives for companies, directly addressing the economic bottom line required to motivate CSR. In some countries, such as the US, philanthropic contributions to registered non-profit organisations are tax-exempt. In 2003 the French government adopted new measures for better tax incentives for private donors and foundations, although Morel (2005) questions whether these measures are sufficient to influence CSR, arguing that it may be used by already active arts donors, but do little to encourage new donors. Her study of corporate executives in Lille, France, revealed that tax discounts were far from the primary motivations for patronage, but that deductions did help with justifying support for cultural projects to senior executives.

Addressing the challenges experienced by players within private-heritage partnerships needs to be project-specific and further solutions to such issues may become available in the future when more partnership evaluations are undertaken. Improved management and planning and greater transparency will hopefully prevent some of the ethical problems, imbalances of interest and the unfair financial advantage that the private sector can gain from aligning itself with heritage.

Private financing and the direction of heritage conservation

The re-direction of heritage financing away from the public sector towards NGOs and the private sector may be changing the way we preserve, manage and interpret heritage, in that corporate goals may be affecting how funding or resources are spent within heritage partnerships. As Alexander (1996) notes in relation to art museum philanthropy, companies want to sponsor art that has wide public appeal. This bias may also be reflected in the way companies are attracted to cultural heritage sites, leaving lesser-known or less significant sites without support. For example, the restoration of the Sistine Chapel has been financed by a large Japanese enterprise, but such companies are not taking any interest in the thousands of churches that are falling into decay. Frangialli (1998) argues that this imbalance also causes a bias in visitor numbers to better-known and better-preserved monuments, and a creaming-off effect of private sponsorship, causing a drop in the quality of tourist services, higher prices, congestion, queues, and degradation of sites.

The privatisation of site management and conservation projects also raises the question of the quality standards of conservation work being done. In order for quality control to be achieved, UNESCO requires that conservation works on WH sites are undertaken using professional expertise recognised by the organisation, and previously tested conservation techniques. However, when private funding becomes available for conservation, such standards cannot always be upheld. For example, at the ancient city of Apamea and other archaeological sites in Syria, scientifically controversial conservation works were financed by entrepreneur Osman Aidi, Chair of Cham Palace Hotels. The funds were not managed through UNESCO, since the private donor decided not to partner with UNESCO as it was considered too constraining and expensive. Thus conservation works were implemented according to his own standards in a scientifically questionable manner (UNESCO 2002).

The World Monuments Watch lists cultural heritage sites most in need of conservation support, and is used by the World Monuments Fund and its private sponsors to make an annual selection of sites to receive funding. Since 1995 the WMF Watch program has awarded 354 grants to 177 sites in 71 countries (WMF 2007). Thus some private funds are being distributed fairly and evenly across a range of countries and types of sites. However, when private partners engage in individual partnerships with sites, their motivations may relate more to the aims of the company to engage with specific markets, or to raise their profile within a community for political or financial reasons. In this way, the choice of sites to receive conservation support is largely being determined by private or market-driven interests. It has also been argued that in a similar manner tax incentives to stimulate support for culture are transferring the decision-making process about the direction of cultural resources to the private sector and away from the public (Throsby 1998).

Conclusion

This chapter has provided an outline of the various ways the global private sector interacts with cultural heritage, using case studies from around the world to demonstrate that greater responsibility is required from the private sector and suggesting that this can be achieved through presenting a stronger business case for the ways heritage conservation can address corporate social responsibility objectives. This requires a better understanding of CSR from the heritage sector and a raised awareness of the conservation needs of heritage in the private sector. There may also be lessons to be learned from the ways the private sector interacts with other sectors.

When companies become associated with heritage, not only do they address the public expectation to be responsible for sustainable development, they create multidirectional benefits. These form a strong business case for cultural heritage managers to present to potential corporate partners, and for CSR managers to justify support for heritage in the boardroom.

Global recession has caused dwindling private resources and government cuts to heritage and the arts worldwide, so more than ever heritage needs to provide new and interesting opportunities for the private sector to get involved to meet its own CSR objectives. This may be by launching new and imaginative projects which make news, produce films, books, pamphlets, and educational material, by reviewing and evaluating successful partnerships, building conservation schemes and through the enthusiasm and networks of young people.

When greater dialogue is achieved between the private sector and heritage, new types of CSR for heritage may become possible. For example, there may be potential for heritage sites to benefit from microfinance and socially responsible investing. For example, at the CultureBank in Mali, cultural objects have been used as collateral for local small business loans at 3 per cent interest per month. This microcredit initiative provides individuals with ongoing, and increasingly larger, loans, as against the finite, small profits gained from selling cultural heritage objects. By housing the deposited objects in a museum, the heritage is conserved, and the loans counteract the looting of artifacts (Deubel 2002).

In order to continue to attract corporate funding and partnerships in years to come heritage conservationists will need to stay well informed of the CSR movement and be willing to adapt approaches according to shifting corporate agendas. For CSR projects to be sustainable and attractive, conservation project outcomes must be aligned with business strategy. The credibility and benefits of cultural heritage partnerships must be framed in relation to recognised CSR outcomes, using the language that is employed in annual CSR reports. To give credibility to heritage conservation as a worthy recipient for CSR, private sector partnerships must be approached with the CSR agenda at the forefront of proposals.

Bibliography

Alexander, V. D. (1996) *Museums and Money: The Impact of Funding on Exhibitions, Scholars and Management*, Bloomington: Indiana University Press.

Amabile, K. (2007) 'Chinese Buffet – Part 18: Xi'an', <http://www.gadling.com/2007/08/22/chinese-buffet-part-18-xian-excursion-day-two/print/> (accessed 25 January 2009).

APSARA (2000) 'International Film Production', *Yashodara*, 3 (July–Dec).

BBC News (2000) 'Fury at sacred site damage', *BBC News*, <http://news.bbc.co.uk/2/hi/americas/923415.stm> (accessed 12 March 2009).

BBC News (2007) 'Forbidden City Starbucks Replaced', *BBC News*, <http://news.bbc.co.uk/go/pr/fr/-/2/hi/asia-pacific/7010181.stm> (accessed 24 September 2007).

Benhamou, F. (1997) 'France and the case of museums', paper presented to the CIRCLE Round Table. *Privatization/Desetatization and Culture: Limitations or Opportunities for Cultural Development in Europe?* Amsterdam: Boekmanstichting.

Beyond the Bridge (2008) 'Sacred and profane', <http://beyondthebridge.wordpress.com/2008/11/17/sacred-and-profane/> (accessed 20 January 2009).

BHP (2006) 'BHP Sahara film project', <http://hsecreport.bhpbilliton.com/2004/repository/caseStudies/environment21.asp> (accessed 13 October 2006).

Bommelaer, C. (2008) 'Les entreprises mécènes recentrent leur action', *Le Figaro*, 28 November 2008.

Boorsma, P. (1998) 'Privatising the Muse "and all that Jazz"', in Boorsma, P., Van Hemel, A. and Van Der Wielen, N. (eds) *Privatisation and Culture*, Dordrecht: Kluwer Publishing.

Borrelli-Persson, L. (2007) 'A walk on the wild side: Fendi makes fashion history on the Great Wall', <http://www.style.com/peopleparties/parties/scoop/102207FEND> (accessed 20 March 2008).

Brainard, L. and Lafleur, V. (2005) *Expanding Enterprise: Lifting the Poor: The Private Sector in the Fight Against Global Poverty, Brookings Blum Roundtable*, Washington DC: The Brookings Institution.

Cescau, P. (2007) 'Beyond corporate responsibility: social innovation and sustainable development as drivers of business growth', *2007 INDEVOR Alumni Forum*. Fontainebleau, France: INSEAD.

Chan, W.-Y. and Ma, S.-Y. (2004) 'Heritage preservation and sustainability of china's development', *Sustainable Development*, 12: 15–31.

CNN.com (2000) 'Starbucks brews storm in China's Forbidden City', <http://www.cnn.com/2000/FOOD/news/12/11/china.starbucks.reut/> (accessed 10 February 2008).

Cori, P. (2006) 'Branding World Heritage: A sustainable approach for global tourism', PhD thesis, Bangkok: University of Silpakorn.

CSR Globe (2008) 'Diageo CSR Profile, CSR Globe', <http://www.csrglobe.com/login/companies/diageo.html> (accessed 26 September 2008).

D'Astous, A. and Bitz, P. (1995) 'Consumer evaluations of sponsorship programmes' *Journal of Marketing Research*, 29: 6–22.

De Lopez, T. (2006) 'Towards sustainable development in Angkor, Cambodia: Social, environmental and financial aspects of conserving cultural heritage', *EEPSEA Research Report*. Singapore: Economy and Environment Program for Southeast Asia.

Donnelly, B. (2007) 'Russian city risks its world heritage status over Scots-designed tower', *The Herald*, 17 December 2008, <http://www.theherald.co.uk/news/news/display.var.1908261.0.Russian_city_risks_its_world_heritage_status_over_Scotsdesigned_tower.php> (accessed 25 January 2009).

Economist Intelligence Unit (2008) 'Doing Good: Business and the Sustainability Challenge', <http://www.sustainability.com/aboutsustainability/news-article.asp?id=1346> (accessed 20 November 2008).

EEPSEA (2006) 'Rags Among Archaeological Riches', in EEPSEA (ed.) *EEPSEA Policy Brief*. Singapore: Economy and Environment Program for Southeast Asia.

Environmental Finance (2009) 'Credit agencies force Ilisu suspension', <http://www.environmental-finance.com/onlinews/0108exp.html> (accessed 6 February 2009).

Fabsugar (2007) 'Fabtv: Fendi on the Great Wall of China', <http://www.fabsugar.com/725847> (accessed 10 January 2009).

Frangialli, F. (1998) 'The Role of Private Financing in Sustainable Cultural Development', Washington: World Bank.

Grenbiz.com (2008) 'Socially Responsible Investment Assets Top $2.71T', <http://www.wbcsd.org/plugins/DocSearch/details.asp?type=DocDet&ObjectId=Mjg4ODk> (accessed 20 December 2008).

Hooper, J. (2008) 'Outrage in Venice as giant ads smother cultural jewels', *The Guardian*, 22 November 2008.

Howse, J. M., Eagle, S., Boffa, F., De Lambert, R., McCraken, I., Macmillan, D., Gray, I., Townley, G., Henderson, D., Ashwell, D., Turnbull, G., Steele, M. and Duke, N. (1998) *Angkor Forest Rehabilitation and Landscape Enhancement Project*, Auckland: Fraser Thomas and Boffa Miskell.

IBM (2005) 'Forbidden City: Beyond space and time', <http://www-05.ibm.com/cy/events/press/1.html> (accessed 10 January 2009).

Jamali, D. and Mirshak, R. (2007) 'Corporate Social Responsibility (CSR): Theory and practice in developing country context', *Journal of Business Ethics*, 72: 243–62.

Jing, F., Logan, W. and Kaldun, B. (2009) Mission Report: Advisory Mission to the Old Town of Lijiang World Heritage Property, China, 24–30 November 2008, unpublished report, Paris: UNESCO World Heritage Centre.

Kay, K. and Wasson, E. (2005) 'IMF, resort owner dispute contract renewal', *Cambodia Daily (Phnom Penh)*, 7 September, 12.

Kimmelman, M. (1991) 'Finding God in a double fold out', *The New York Times*, 8 December 1991.

Kotler, P. and Lee, N. (2005) *Corporate Social Responsibility: Doing the Most Good for Your Company and Your Cause*, Hoboken, N.J.: Wiley.

Lehnert, R. (2004) 'New money needed for world's ancient monuments', <http://www.globalheritagefund.org/news/conservation_news/new_money_june_29_2004.asp > (accessed 15 October 2008).

Marriott, B. B. (1997) *Practical Guide to Environmental Impact Assessment*, New York: McGraw-Hill.

Marsden, C. and Andriof, J. (1998) 'Towards an understanding of corporate citizenship and how to influence it', *Citizenship Studies*, 2: 329–52.

McKercher, B. and du Cros, H. (2002) *Cultural Tourism: The Partnership Between Tourism and Cultural Heritage Management*, New York: Haworth Hospitality Press.

Morel, C. (2005) 'Will businesses ever become legitimate partners in the financing of the arts in France?', *International Journal of Cultural Policy*, 11: 199–213.

O'Hagan, J. and Harvey, D. (2000) 'Why do Companies Sponsor Arts Events? Some Evidence of a Proposed Classification', *Journal of Cultural Economics*, 24: 205–24.

Pedersen, A. (2002) *Managing Tourism at World Heritage Sites*. Paris: UNESCO World Heritage Centre.

Pisa, N. (2009) 'Outrage as Coca-Cola gets £1.75m deal to sponsor Venice', <http://www.dailymail.co.uk/news/worldnews/article-1153348/Outrage-Coca-Cola-gets-1–75m-deal-sponsor-Venice – And-install-dozens-vending-machines-city.html> (accessed 17 March 2009).

Porter, M. and Kramer, M. R. (2003) 'The competitive advantage of corporate philanthropy', *Harvard Business Review on Corporate Responsibility*. Boston: Harvard Business School.

Porter, M. and Kramer, M. R. (2006) 'Strategy & society: The link between competitive advantage and corporate social responsibility', *Harvard Business Review*, 84: 78–92.

Povoledo, E. (2008) 'Cheeseburgers get into the mix in the Italian debate on museums', *The New York Times*, 21 November 2008.

Radcliffe, L. (2004) 'Catch them while you can', *Newsweek* (Atlantic Edition), 143 (7): 64.

Reich, S. (2005) 'When firms behave "responsibly", are the roots national or global?', *International Social Science Journal*, 57: 509–28.

Reuters (2004) 'MTV Colosseum concert worries Romans', *Amusement Business*, 18 November 2004.

Riley, C. A. (1997) 'When public meets private', in Schuster, M., De Monchaux, J. and Riley, C. A. (eds) *Preserving the Built Heritage: Tools for Implementation*, Hanover and London: University Press of New England.

Roberts, S., Keeble, J. and Brown, D. (2002) The Business Case for Corporate Citizenship. Arthur D. Little, <http://www.adlittle.com/insights/studies/pdf/corporate_citizenship.pdf> (accessed 7 January 2008).

Schuster, J. M. (1998) 'Beyond privatization: the hybridization of museums and the built heritage', in Boorsma, P., Van Hemel, A. and Van Der Wielen, N. (eds) *Privatization and Culture*. Dordrecht: Kluwer Publishing.

Serna-Sullivan, J. (2008) Personal communication, June 2008, UNESCO World Heritage Centre, Paris.

Seymour, M. (2004) 'Partnerships to support sustainable development and conservation: the West-East Pipeline Project, China', *Conservation Biology*, 18: 613–15.

Smith, J. (2007) 'Tourist invasion threatens to ruin glories of Angkor Wat', *The Observer*, 25 February 2007.

Squires, N. (2008) 'McDonald's boss in charge of Italy's museums', *The Daily Telegraph*, 1 December 2008.

Starr, F. (2008) 'Corporate responsibility and World Heritage conservation: playing the sustainable development card', in Amoeda, R. S. L., Pinheiro, C., Pinheiro, P. and Pinheiro, J. (eds) *World Heritage and Sustainable Development*, Barcelos, Portugal: Greenlines Institute for Sustainable Development.

Starr, F. (in press) 'Poverty alleviation through World Heritage conservation', in Albert, M-T., Richon, M., Vinals, M-J. and Whitcomb, A. (eds) *The Impact of the International Designation on Local Communities*, World Heritage Papers Series, Paris: UNESCO World Heritage Centre.

Sulaiman, Y. (2009) 'Penang's Tourism Dilemma: To build or retain its UNESCO status', <http://www.eturbonews.com/8481/penang-tourisms-dilemma-build-or-retain-its-unesco-status> (accessed 26 March 2009).

Throsby, D. (1998) 'Rethinking the State's Role: privatization, economics and cultural policy', in Boorsma, P., Van Hemel, A. and Van Der Wielen, N. (eds) *Privatization and Culture*, Dordrecht: Kluwer Publishing.

Tyler, L. (2007) 'Trampled temples', <http://www.geographical.co.uk/Features/Trampled_temples_Sep07.html> (accessed 15 March 2008).

UN Foundation (2002) 'UNF: Setting the standard for World Heritage partnerships' <http://whc.unesco.org/venice2002/archives/interviews/interview_15.htm> (accessed 13 October 2006).

UNESCO (2002) Rapport sur les projets, archives of the former Unit for mobilization of Human, Technical and Financial Resources, Cultural Heritage Division, Culture Sector of UNESCO.

UNESCO (2004) *Impact: Tourism and Heritage Site Management in the World Heritage Town of Luang Prabang, Lao PDR*, Bangkok: UNESCO.

Valor, C. (2005) 'Corporate social responsibility and corporate citizenship: towards corporate accountability', *Business and Society Review*, 110: 191–212.

WHC (2004) '"No-go" mining pledge', *World Heritage Review*, 34: 52.

WMF (2005/6) 'World Monuments Fund at 40', *ICON*, Winter 2005/6: 10–16.

WMF (2007) Annual Report, 2006. New York, World Monuments Fund.

World Economic Forum (2004) *Values and Value: Communicating the Strategic Importance of Corporate Citizenship to Investors*, Geneva: World Economic Forum.

Part III

The future of the past: twenty-first-century challenges

Chapter 9

Cultural heritage and the global environmental crisis

Colin Long and Anita Smith

In a book about heritage and globalisation there can perhaps be no more relevant issue than climate change. Climate change leaves no nation untouched, although some will feel the impacts more than others. Despite – perhaps because of – its global significance, efforts to deal with climate change have taken on many of the characteristics of the global system: international agreement is difficult to achieve in the face of governments' efforts to protect their own perceived national interests; history, particularly the unhappy record of Western exploitation of the developing world, and the differential history of national industrialisation, weighs heavily, if often unspoken, on negotiations; global disparities of wealth and development opportunities shape national attitudes and condition responses; ideological differences run like scarcely concealed fissures through international forums; other challenges – economic crises and perceived international security threats – continue to draw heavily on the resources of national governments and international agencies and distract from the urgent need to address both the causes and effects of climate change.

In the rapidly expanding discourse about heritage and climate change we can already discern certain patterns that replicate existing social, economic and political relations, as well as existing approaches to heritage practice: much of the best work is coming out of Europe; most of it is concentrated on tangible heritage, and is site-specific; and there is a heavy emphasis on technical responses to climate change, with a focus on understanding the physical threats and working out how to deal with them. For example English Heritage (2008) has recently released a report arguing that retention and conservation of the historic built fabric rather than construction of new dwellings, along with the upgrading of the energy efficiency of traditional buildings, is an important mitigation measure, assisting in meeting targets for reduction in CO_2. The report also details the potential or likely impacts on the historic environment of predicted increasing temperatures and variability in rainfall patterns and associated storm events. Coupled with increasing coastal erosion these environmental impacts threaten historic buildings and archaeological sites through, among other things, heightened risk of flooding, ground subsidence and the accelerated decay of stonework. The warming climate is also likely to make some of Britain's historically significant tree plantings and gardens difficult to conserve.

The 2008 report follows the publication of a series of guides, including ones on shoreline management planning and historic heritage (English Heritage 2006); improving the energy efficiency of historic buildings (English Heritage 2007) and case studies on the effects of wetting and drying on historic fabric (Cassar and Hawkings 2007).

These and other similar programs are making a strong contribution to debates on mitigation strategies; developing a corpus of such information will be essential to conservation in the coming decades. However, they build on the existing, well-developed and institutionalised heritage conservation and management processes in the developed world. In this chapter we wish to look beyond this technical, site-specific or impact-specific approach to the current and predicted effects that the global environmental crisis is likely to have on cultural heritage in general. In this we emphasise the effects of climate change on cultural heritage in the broadest sense, on intangible heritage and in fact, in the case of many small island states, for instance, on whole cultures. We recognise that while technical approaches are useful in the conservation of fabric, on their own they fall short of protection and con-servation for much of the heritage of the developing world and retain too much control in the hands of heritage or climate change 'experts'. This encourages an approach that says: climate change will have the following effects on the environ-ment in the area that your heritage site is located; you should introduce the fol-lowing technical measures to cope with it. In some cases, for specific sites, this may be the right approach but it will not account for either the varied impacts that cli-mate change is having on the heritage of developed and developing countries or for the ability of communities to protect their heritage in the face of these impacts. In much of the world resources simply do not exist for communities to hire 'experts': it will be up to locals, often drawing on generations of lived experience and traditional knowledge, to deal with environmental change. Indeed, provided communities can maintain their resilience, this may in fact produce the better results, by drawing on the resources of whole communities and recognising cultural heritage – tangible and intangible – as integral to and not simply a 'superstructural' element of societies. For some communities adapting to climate change will equate to cultural survival and require society-wide mobilisations.

The point that technical solutions are important but insufficient to manage the threats to heritage from climate change draws on a growing awareness that the environmental crisis more broadly is unlikely to be amenable to a technological fix, although such a hope remains thoroughly ingrained in the cultural and political mindset of many people, including perhaps most politicians, in much of the world. In the later parts of this chapter we suggest ways in which a particular kind of heritage practice – one that is aware of the limitations of technical approaches – can contribute to environmental sustainability more generally. What is required, we argue, is a questioning of what is perhaps now the dominant approach to heritage, the instrumental view of it as a resource for economic development and growth. Such a view accords with the technical approach to heritage and both are equally problematic.

Figure 9.1 Fagaloa Bay, Upolu, Samoa, 2006. A sea wall constructed in 2005 to hold back encroaching seas. Similar sea walls have been constructed along many parts of the north coast of Upolu in response to increasing inundation (Photo by the Anita Smith)

Climate change, heritage and local communities

Most work on climate change and heritage tends to see cultural and natural heritage as a potential or current 'victim', subject to the impacts of climate change and in need of protection or rescue. While natural heritage or the natural environment is often at the centre of both climate change modelling and impact assessment, cultural heritage rarely features in international or scientific discussions about climate change unless these arise from an agency, such as the UNESCO World Heritage Centre, that is specifically involved in cultural heritage conservation. Our approach, in contrast, is to subsume both under the broad rubric of 'development' within the wider context of approaches that emphasise poverty reduction, social justice, and development practice (IISD et al. 2003). What is required, we believe, is a rethinking of the way that climate change and heritage are conceived. We want to see them approached not as separate technical fields of research and policy development, but as integral considerations for sound development practice, through examination of how local communities, heritage preservation and climate change intersect. In this way we can direct attention away from climate change as a threat to buildings and structures to climate change as a threat to the livelihoods and cultures of the people who give those buildings, structures and other cultural expressions life.

In this we draw on approaches that stress adaptation and the building of cultural resilience, approaches that are animating much of the discourse and practice around climate change in the development community (IISD et al. 2003; IPCC 2007; Working Group on Climate Change and Development 2007). Adaptation is defined as:

> the ability to respond and adjust to actual or potential impacts of changing climate conditions in ways that moderate harm or take advantage of any positive opportunities that the climate may afford. It includes policies and measures to reduce exposure to climate variability and extremes, and the strengthening of adaptive capacity.
>
> (IISD et al. 2003: 5)

This approach starts from the premise that climate change has advanced to the extent that we must now start working out how to cope with and adapt to its effects. Even should CO_2 emissions be immediately and substantially reduced at a global scale, which unfortunately appears unlikely in the near future, the process of global warming and its impacts will continue for many years. While urgent mitigation strategies for the reduction of greenhouse gases must continue, so should the development of strategies for adaptation to climate change.

The most recent assessment report from the Intergovernmental Panel on Climate Change (IPCC) emphasises that the adaptive capacity of communities is intimately connected to social and economic development, and is therefore not evenly distributed across and within societies (Wilbanks et al. 2007: Chapter 7). The report highlights the disproportionately greater impact climate change is predicted to have on the poor, on traditional societies and on indigenous peoples, especially where communities rely on subsistence agriculture. From a development perspective, central to adaptation is recognition that poor people's livelihoods are often precarious and therefore it is through building cultural resilience in general that a community's capacity to successfully adapt to climate change will be enhanced. Natural disasters

Figure 9.2 Niue Island, 2004. During cyclone Heta in 2004 the force of the giant waves threw this coral boulder, nearly three metres in diameter, up the 20-metre-high cliff that surrounds the island and inland another 20 metres to land on this house platform (Photo by Anita Smith)

and other sudden shocks can have a major impact on incomes. Climate change is already having such an effect, and this is likely to increase as temperatures rise. Numerous long-term changes in climate, including changes in Arctic temperatures and ice, widespread changes in precipitation amounts, ocean salinity, wind patterns and aspects of extreme weather including droughts, heavy precipitation, heat waves and the increasing intensity of tropical cyclones, have been observed. Of course not all of the effects of climate change will take the form of sudden shocks like storms or more intense cyclones. Problems may manifest only incrementally: less rainfall over many years, or slowly rising sea levels, or the gradual spread of pests and disease, for instance. Whatever the case, the point is that already vulnerable people and communities are especially vulnerable to climate change.

Four regions are identified by the IPCC as especially vulnerable to the effects of climate change, both because of the predicted nature of the environmental impacts and the social and economic circumstances of the population who live in them:

the Arctic, because of the impacts of high rates of projected warming on natural systems and human communities;

Africa, because of low adaptive capacity and the severity of projected climate change impacts;

small islands, where there is high exposure of population and infrastructure to projected climate change impacts;

Asian and African megadeltas, due to large populations and high exposure to sea level rise, storm surges and river flooding

(IPCC 2007: 9)

Climate change exacerbates existing problems, such as water and food shortages, agricultural production difficulties such as crop failure, drought, salinity, over-grazing, arable land shortages, and market distortions, and the spread of disease and intensification of other health issues, all of which contribute to and maintain inequalities that exist between the developing and developed world. The vulnerability of poor communities in general is compounded for those who live in the high-risk areas noted above and especially the coastal and river flood plains, the low-lying deltas in Africa and Asia and the small island nations. The capacity of communities to adapt to current and predicted effects of climate change is dependent on a society's productive base, including natural and human-made capital assets, social networks and entitlements, human capital, institutions, governance, national income, health and level of technological capability (Wilbanks et al. 2007: 727–31).

Indeed, because adaptive capacity is so closely linked to social and economic development, the importance of empowering local communities to deal with climate change cannot be understated. In short:

the reduction of vulnerabilities and the improvement of resilience of poor people to withstand the impacts of climate change will improve their security: that is, the extent to which they can live their lives and conduct their livelihoods free from threats.

(IISD et al. 2003: 6)

For our purposes we are interested in the intersection of climate change, heritage and vulnerable communities. We see the role of heritage in this equation in two ways: first, as a source of income; and second as a form of capital – 'cultural capital' – for poor people and communities without substantial access to financial capital. In this second sense we do not see culture as valuable only when it enters the exchange process (in this regard the term 'capital' is a little misleading, but given we want to emphasise culture's role as a resource on which people can draw, we think the term useful). Cultural capital can serve as a resource to give social meaning and stability to communities – as the cultural underpinning of communities – without being used as a commodity in any sense. Any threat to the maintenance of this sort of cultural capital represents a major threat to these people's and communities' livelihoods. What we are interested in, therefore, is how climate change is likely to affect the cultural underpinnings of poor people's livelihoods – it is through this lens that we consider the impacts on heritage assets, rather than seeing the impacts on heritage assets in isolation from the cultural and social contexts in which those assets originate and which give them meaning. This has the added advantage of putting the focus on people as the creators, maintainers and beneficiaries of heritage. But it will require a different approach to climate change as it affects local communities, as the International Institute for Sustainable Development points out:

> For too long the whole climate change debate has focused at the global level, both in terms of global climate and in relation to the global economic and political system. When considering adaptation, starting from this perspective misses the point. Adaptation is about – and must build from – the actions of people, especially the poorest people who are the most vulnerable and most likely to actively adapt.
>
> (IISD et al., 2003: 1)

In fact poor people who have strong and vibrant cultural heritage assets (whether tangible or intangible) are actually better positioned than many other poor people, especially those living in parlous physical and social conditions in war-torn cities, or in unhealthy slums. It should be recognised that these cultural and heritage assets are valuable, and even more so to poor people. In many cases it will be their only real capital. However, ensuring the voices of vulnerable communities are heard and their needs met will be difficult: as so often in the world system, national wealth and political power determine the level of attention received.

> Knowledge of their natural surroundings leads many of these peoples to wisely conclude that the only way to adapt is to reclaim, restore and promote their traditional, ancestral ways of life, while distancing and differentiating themselves from the conventional proposals which they question ... The many solutions they seek include ecological agriculture, traditional medicine, sustainable soil and water management, the construction of decent housing, and affordable alternative energies.
>
> (Friends of the Earth 2007: 3)

Although traditional and indigenous communities may in general be more vulnerable to climate change, these communities are not and have never been passive in the face of environmental changes, and the intelligence and flexibility of traditional systems of land use are cultural responses to social, cultural and environmental change in the past (IUCN 2007). Traditional knowledge systems have only recently begun to be recognised within international climate change discourse as powerful tools for monitoring climate change at the local level and for the development and implementation of sustainable and successful adaptation strategies, linked to sustainable development. The abstraction of climate science and the large scale at which scientific modelling takes place means this discourse is often less effective in provoking local responses than

> personal observations and experiences [which] evoke deeply felt emotions, as familiar signs of seasonal changes become decoupled and traditional knowledge

of the weather becomes invalidated. Scientific causal explanations of climate changes may be seen as removed and abstract: invisible things are being put out into the atmosphere by anonymous corporations and states. As a consequence, people may feel powerless and/or not responsible for combating climate changes, despite their own vivid experiences of climate change impacts.

(Salik and Byg 2007: 18)

Indigenous and local communities observe environmental changes at the local level, at a scale that cannot be predicted by the large-scale models which the IPCC and other global agencies use to monitor and predict impacts (Salik and Byg 2007). Of note are several studies of Inuit observations of recent environmental change in the Arctic, in particular the observations of a group of elders and hunters of Nunvat that the weather is *Uggianaqtuq* or behaving in unexpected ways with associated changes in animal populations and the timing of their movements (Fox 2003). Unfortunately such detailed studies are still few in number but they provide sufficient data on local environmental changes observed by local and Indigenous communities to argue for the value of local knowledge not just in monitoring climate change but in adaptation. As the aforementioned study recognises, local traditional and Indigenous knowledge of the environment and its changing characteristics is not simply an alternative information source to be utilised as data in the development of scientific models, but is the intangible cultural heritage of these communities and needs to be respected as such. In relation to the adaptive capacity of Indigenous peoples, Berkes and Jolly (2001) concluded that cultural and ecological adaptations of the Inuvialuit of the Canadian Arctic, which have enabled them to live in their highly variable and uncertain environment, represent long-term adaptive strategies for climate change:

> Switching species and adjusting the 'where, when, and how' of hunting are examples of shorter-term responses. On the other hand, adaptations such as flexibility in seasonal hunting patterns, traditional knowledge that allows the community to diversify hunting activities, networks for sharing food and other resources, and intercommunity trade are longer-term, culturally ingrained mechanisms.
>
> (Berkes and Jolly 2001: 18)

Similarly, the traditional knowledge systems that have enabled Pacific Island communities to thrive in the Oceanic environment provide mechanisms for adaptation to climate change and extreme weather events. The most recent assessment report of the IPCC identifies small island states around the world as being especially vulnerable to the effects of climate change, sea-level rise and extreme events. People from small island communities in the Pacific Ocean are likely to become some of the world's first 'sea-level refugees'. Sea-level rise, increasing storm activity and associated coastal erosion are reducing the size of small islands in the Pacific where at least 50 per cent of the populations live within 1.5km of the coast, the location of almost all infrastructure and capital cities. The small island ecosystems are especially vulnerable to environmental degradation and have a high coastline-to-land area, so damage from rising sea levels, wave action and storms are magnified, with increasing salt water incursion into often limited fresh water in coastal areas making subsistence gardening and commercial agriculture less productive. Current evidence suggests cyclonic activity will become increasingly pronounced, with cyclones of longer duration and greater intensity (Barnett 2005: 204).

Notwithstanding this, Pacific Island societies are remarkably well attuned to the relatively large variations in environmental conditions that have occurred in the recent and more distant past, with the associated high resilience fostering an ability to cope with natural environmental changes. Archaeological evidence demonstrates that although communities in the Pacific Islands have experienced short- and long-term environmental changes due to fluctuations in temperature and rainfall patterns and the impacts of catastrophic events including volcanic eruptions, tsunamis and cyclones (Allen 2006), the flexibility and resilience of the Pacific Island social systems and their long-established strategies for dealing with climate variability have enabled communities to live in the Oceanic environment for over three millennia. For example, across the Pacific traditional resource management systems, such as *ra'ui* in the Cook Islands, allow delineated and enforceable control over the gathering or collecting of particular food or plants at particular times of the year or in certain places (Tiraa 2006) and provide a culturally embedded system of conservation for adaptation to short- and long-term environmental impacts of climate change on natural resources.

In short, local communities are often best placed to determine the appropriate responses to local impacts and have a right to do so in an informed manner, protecting their tangible and intangible heritage within their cultural and social frameworks. A recent IUCN report (Macchi et al. 2008) has argued that climate change adaptation by Indigenous and traditional peoples rests on reducing factors that increase their vulnerability, such as poverty and inequality, marginalisation, poor health and nutrition, coupled with enhancing their resilience through strengthening traditional economies and social and economic networks that encourage cooperation and reciprocation, self-reliance, mutual aid and local production. This would also entail, and draw on, an associated cultural revitalisation.

It is important to note that we do not reject the importance of technological or scientific approaches to climate change adaptation. Our point is that such approaches stand a much better chance of success if they are also culturally appropriate. Adaptation strategies imposed from outside may be technologically possible but culturally undesirable. As Foale (2008: 33) argues in relation to the protection of marine environments in Melanesia, rather than the current international approach of protecting 'Biodiversity Hotspots', an approach to conservation that emphasises maintenance of ecological functions in the interest of sustaining food security and cash benefits from reef-associated resources would be more in line with Millennium Development Goals for participatory natural resource and ecosystem management systems that deliver pro-poor outcomes. Such an approach has the potential to embrace traditional knowledge of marine resources and their management and recognises the rights of the traditional owners of these resources.

The Capacity Building to enable the Development of Adaptation Measures in Pacific Island Countries (CBDAMPIC) project was one of the first projects in the Pacific to support adaptation implementation at the village level. Completed in 2006, the project involved sixteen villages in several Pacific Island countries in climate change impact assessment and community-based adaptation options. The aim was to incorporate adaptation into existing village decision-making processes and contribute to building the resilience of communities to climate-related risks, including through construction of sea-walls, relocation of villages, and the introduction of water-saving devices, thereby improving livelihoods and alleviating poverty by aligning climate change adaptation with sustainable development principles.

Alongside such community-based and traditional approaches there is also a need for culturally appropriate education materials about climate change and human impacts on the environment to assist communities in understanding those impacts within their culturally diverse world views (cf. Foale 2008: 34). To assist in this information sharing, in 2007 the United Nations Framework Convention on Climate Change Secretariat established a database of Local Coping Strategies as a means to ensure

> transfer of long-standing coping strategies/mechanisms, knowledge and experience from communities that have had to adapt to specific hazards or climatic conditions to communities that may just be starting to experience such conditions as a result of climate change.
>
> (UNFCCC 2000)

In practice, provided that communities consent to the dissemination of their local traditional knowledge, this is also a form of protection of cultural heritage through documentation.

However, most Indigenous communities no longer rely exclusively on their traditional resources and all are tied to non-traditional economic, social and political systems that limit their flexibility in responding to environmental change through traditional mechanisms. Returning to the example of the Inuit communities: although, as discussed above, their long history of adaptation to changing environmental conditions does enhance community resilience to climate change, their flexibility to respond to climate variability and unpredictability has been reduced by settlement in permanent communities, associated loss of traditional resource bases and breakdown in the transfer of traditional knowledge to the young (Ford et al. 2006).

In the Pacific region, the first 'climate change refugees' are likely to be people from the tiny low-lying Pacific Island nation of Tuvalu. Here the community is already experiencing increasing coastal erosion and rising of the salt water table, with serious negative consequences for staple root crops (Corlett 2008). Should mitigation strategies be too slow or too late to halt climate change before it makes life untenable for communities in places like Tuvalu, the low-lying deltas of Asia and elsewhere, the IPCC (2007: 56) recognises that the destruction of heritage as part of the overall environmental impacts will take place on a large scale. Effects on cultural heritage will include damage to physical fabric, and loss of traditional practices and associations with place. Strategies to relocate communities will be needed. At this stage there has been little consideration of how the protection of cultural heritage will be incorporated into the development of these strategies. While movable cultural heritage can in theory be transported, the loss of place associated with historical and cultural identity, natural and cultural resources and impacts on cultural practices in general, as well as social networks and cultural knowledge, are likely to be great. Programs to reduce these impacts will need to be implemented long in advance of any forced migration of communities from areas that climate change has rendered uninhabitable.

Programs for recording of traditional knowledge and customary practices of peoples, such as the cultural mapping project being undertaken by the Fiji Government, may provide a model framework for the development of useful tools to protect cultural heritage and cultural knowledge should climate change necessitate abandonment or relocation. Fiji's program, established in 2004, is creating a national inventory of traditional knowledge and expressions of culture in all 14 provinces of Fiji (Ministry of Fijian Affairs, Culture and Heritage 2007). The documented knowledge is held in a database that respects and protects the ownership of knowledge through restricting access to traditional custodians of the knowledge. The long-term benefit is protection of cultural heritage through the recording process and the building of cultural resilience through reinvigorating cultural knowledge, especially in relation to traditional understandings and uses of natural and cultural resources.

Similarly, the UNESCO Endangered Languages Program seeks to conserve languages that are at risk of extinction and to revitalise their use within the speaker community. Many of the languages considered at risk are those of minorities and/or marginalised groups. The program recognises that among a range of capacity-building measures, strengthening the speaker community by improving living conditions and respect for human rights are important elements in the conservation of the language that sit alongside the need to document and record the language itself (UNESCO 2003).

Climate change, culture and human rights

The recognition of the likely need for abandonment of certain particularly vulnerable places in the face of climate change raises several difficult but very important issues about the rights of affected communities. The world already faces an intractable refugee problem, which will be exacerbated by climate change refugees. Already the President of the Indian Ocean nation of the Maldives – most of which is less than one metre above sea level – has been reported as expressing interest in buying land in another country to relocate his nation's citizens (Henley 2008). Corlett (2008: ch. 3) argues that a system independent of the existing international refugee protection system is needed to deal with people displaced by environmental problems like climate change. But protection from climate-related displacement must be founded on an objective means of assessing when a particular place becomes uninhabitable. There are empirical issues at stake here. How do you determine and measure climate-related factors leading to displacement? How will they be separated from other factors, including other environmental factors, which may lead to dislocation? At what point does a physical environment become so degraded that it is no longer capable of sustaining a humane existence?

The answers to questions like these rely not just on some sort of scientific observation. They are value laden. Indeed, they point to a question of an altogether higher order: what is a humane existence?

(Corlett 2008: 50)

Corlett points out that the existing international human rights framework can provide some assistance in answering this question: the UN Declaration on Human Rights, the International Covenant on Civil and Political Rights, and the International Covenant on Economic, Social and Cultural Rights, and others.

While the limitations of the international human rights framework are acknowledged (Cordes-Holland 2007), it will be interesting to see what role it might play in mitigating and managing the effects of climate change. Cultural rights have always been hard to legislate for, or to protect in international agreements (Langfield et al. 2009), and the task is fraught with difficulties: finding a suitable middle ground between cultural relativism and cultural imperialism poses real problems. As we have argued in this chapter, managing climate change requires more than just technological solutions. It requires an assertion of the validity and effectiveness of local understandings, traditional knowledge systems and community participation. It requires, in other words, an acknowledgement of the power of culture. But it also requires an acknowledgement that culture is vulnerable to climate change. In either case, we believe there will be a heightened emphasis on culture as a human right – as a right threatened by climate change, and as a right whose expression can help communities to adapt to climate change.

There are two potential ramifications of this. First, there is likely to be an expansion of the concept of human rights to take account of the threats to the environment and cultures from climate change and other forms of environmental degradation. The protection of the environment will take on more of the character of other rights assertions, especially given the indivisibility of cultural heritage and the natural environment asserted by most traditional and Indigenous communities. The right to live in a clean, safe and sustainable environment will become just as pressing as the right to live free of oppression. Further, there will be an awareness of the close connection between environmental and cultural rights, that the destruction of the environment is the destruction of cultural resources or cultural heritage.

Second, it may become increasingly common to use international rights instruments in the defence of environmental and cultural rights. For instance, could States Parties to the World Heritage Convention be held to be in breach of their obligations to protect their World Heritage properties from climate change? Could it be argued that, for example, refusing to introduce sufficiently stringent CO_2 emission reduction targets represents a threat to Australia's Great Barrier Reef and Kakadu National Park? Could displacement of peoples due to sea-level rise represent an infringement of various human rights instruments by the nations most responsible for CO_2 emissions, and leave nations and political leaders vulnerable to charges of human rights abuses? In a foreshadowing of the potential use of international instruments in protecting cultural heritage, in 2005 the Inuit people of Alaska and Canada filed a petition in the Inter-American Commission on Human Rights (IACHR), 'alleging that the failure of the United States to curtail its [greenhouse gas] emissions constitutes a violation of [Inuit] rights and freedoms protected by regional and international human rights law'. The petition alleges the infringement of a number of rights:

> First, the Inuit's right to enjoy their culture, particularly their subsistence way of life, is violated by the widespread environmental change that is occurring.
>
> Meanwhile, the right to use and enjoy traditional Inuit lands is allegedly violated because large tracts of Inuit lands are fundamentally changing, in some areas becoming inaccessible. A particular problem is the disappearance of sea ice, which is used by the Inuit to travel and hunt, and is now often thin and unsafe.
>
> The Inuit's right to enjoy their property is allegedly infringed because climate change has reduced the value of both the Inuit's personal property – including hides, snowmobiles, and dog sleds – as well as their 'cultural intellectual property', namely their traditional knowledge, which is now often 'unreliable or inaccurate as a result of climate change'. In addition, Inuit rights to health and life are being impacted by new pressures on the Inuit to maintain their traditional diet, as well as increasing numbers of life-threatening accidents caused by changes to ice, snow and land. Rights of the Inuit to residence and movement, and to inviolability of the home, are also allegedly infringed because of threats to the physical integrity of their homes. Storm surges, permafrost melt and erosion are destroying coastal homes and communities, whilst in inland areas, slumping and landslides are threatening homes and infrastructure.
>
> (Cordes-Holland 2007)

While the Inuit petition was ultimately rejected by the IACHR, the Commission did invite the chief petitioner, Sheila Watt-Coutier, to provide testimony on the connection between human rights and climate change (Watt-Coutier, undated c. 2007). This is one of the more prominent examples of a growing push to treat climate change as a human rights issue, with a particular focus on the impacts on cultural rights of Indigenous peoples. There are a number of areas of international human rights law, specifically the International Covenant on Civil and Political Rights, that may be infringed by climate change, including: the right of minorities to enjoy their culture; the right of self-determination; the right to life; the right to protection of privacy, family and the home; the right to freedom of residence and movement (Cordes-Holland 2007).

Concern about the impact of climate change on World Heritage sites has focused on natural sites, for obvious reasons. Under Article 11(4) of the World Heritage Convention, a number of sites – Sagarmatha National Park in Nepal, Huascaran National Park in Peru, the Great Barrier Reef and Greater Blue Mountains Area in Australia, Belize's Barrier Reef Reserve System, the Waterton-Glacier International Peace Park in the United States and Canada – have been the subject of petitions to include them on the 'List of World Heritage in Danger' because of their particular vulnerability to the effects of climate change (Huggins 2007). All of these sites are listed for their natural values, but most also have extremely important cultural significance for local people. Australia's Great Barrier Reef is a good example. Recent debate about the country's response to climate change has seen critics of the government's weak CO_2 emission targets charge the government with putting the reef in danger. The reef's environmental values have become a part of the nation's broader cultural identity. Its significance is anchored in Australians' strong physical and cultural attachment to the sea – the vast majority of the island continent's population lives close to the coast – and their perception – however flawed in reality it might be – of Australia as a place with a unique and pristine environment. The reef and the adjacent Wet Tropics World Heritage area are also important places to local Indigenous communities who have drawn on their resources for millennia and built sophisticated cultural understandings of them.

Huggins (2007) argues that the World Heritage Convention imposes obligations on States Parties to protect World Heritage sites within their own jurisdictions, and those in other countries, from climate change. Article 5 of the Convention obliges States Parties to 'endeavor, in so far as possible', to counteract dangers that threaten their cultural or natural heritage and to 'take appropriate legal, scientific, technical, administrative and financial measures necessary for the identification, protection, conservation, presentation and rehabilitation of this heritage'. This includes, Huggins maintains, 'a duty on States Parties to commit to "deep cuts" in GHG emissions'. She concludes: 'if the Convention is to remain an effective tool for protecting and conserving sites of universal value for future generations States Parties must engage in extensive mitigation strategies without delay'.

Despite the increasingly clear danger that climate change poses to World Heritage sites there have been to date no sites added to the World Heritage In Danger list for this reason. It is in fact quite difficult and rare for sites to be listed on the List of World Heritage Sites in Danger. The World Heritage Committee is unable to list sites without the consent of the relevant State Party and, given the prestige that World Heritage sites are seen to accord the nations in which they are situated, such consent is infrequently forthcoming. The World Heritage Convention has been one of the most successful and popular of the UN bodies' international instruments, and there is considerable reluctance to introduce controversial issues into its ambit for fear of destroying the cooperation and accord that has characterised its implementation until now.

While threatened communities and groups will no doubt continue to explore international legal avenues in their efforts to combat climate change and its effects, it is worth remaining cognisant of the limitations of legal action to deal with what is essentially a political issue. Ultimately the risks associated with climate change will only be tackled if sufficient people in individual countries can convince their governments through political processes – construed in the broadest sense – that it is the population's will that action be taken, and that there will be a political cost for inaction. Indeed, heavy reliance on legal strategies can sometimes have a negative effect on political campaigns, if legal action is seen as a substitute for other kinds of activism, since legal processes are largely slow, expensive and exclusive of non-legally trained individuals. Legal action can only ever be one tactic employed by political campaigns, not the primary focus.

Heritage and sustainability

The processes of the World Heritage Convention provide some scope for the intervention of heritage as a profession and a practice into the effort to combat climate change and cope with its impacts. But there are other ways in which heritage practitioners can exert a more substantial influence on the climate change debate than they have to date. Indeed, if we are to think about adaptation strategies and building cultural reliance in the ways that we have called for, there is a pressing need to move the discourse beyond scientific considerations and outside the prism (prison) of economic growth. What is required above all else is a new way of thinking about our world, about the way we use its resources and the effect we have on our cultural and natural environments. It is in the development of such a new way of thinking that we believe heritage preservation can play a very important role.

Our claim for the integration of climate change, heritage and development practice demands a reassessment of the role of heritage in *economic* development strategies. Contemporary heritage conservation has its origins in the late-nineteenth-century reaction against the destructiveness of industrial capitalism. It was an inevitable reaction to, but also a manifestation of, the ethic of relentless progress that characterised the second half of the nineteenth century. One becomes particularly conscious of the legacies of the past when they are under threat. It was the destruction of war and the additional damage to historic buildings and structures during post-war reconstruction that stimulated the rise of heritage consciousness and a heritage profession in the second half of the twentieth century. The great international heritage instruments – the World Heritage Convention and the Venice Charter – emerged in this context. Heritage was being preserved *from* potential destruction. It needed special laws to protect it since it was largely not valued sufficiently by the market (or, sometimes, by local communities) to survive in a free market system. The iron law of capitalist real estate markets – 'highest and best use' should prevail – had to be ameliorated by citizen protest and regulatory intervention. There grew, thus, a strong view that heritage preservation and heritage professionals were 'anti-development'.

Over the past few decades, to counter this view, and to assert the political relevance of their field, many heritage policy makers have sought to demonstrate that heritage – or heritage places – are just as commodifiable, just as capable of stimulating economic growth and jobs as any other 'industry'. Thus heritage economics is a burgeoning field, heritage is now seen as a primary resource for the tourism industry, and town planners seek to regenerate declining industrial areas through 'investing in heritage' (European Association of Historic Towns and Regions 2007).

The defensive preservation model, then, has given way to a 'wise use' approach. UNESCO and other agencies, Boccardi points out, have come to believe that

> heritage, both cultural and natural, can and should positively contribute to sustainable development. In this perspective, cultural heritage properties should be protected not only for their intrinsic value, but because they constitute an important asset to sustain the economic growth and social development of communities.
>
> (Boccardi 2007: 6–7)

There is increasing evidence that the balance between preservation and economic growth is extremely difficult to achieve. More accurate would be to place heritage preservation and social development, on the one hand, in tension with economic growth on the other. As Askew argues in this volume, the way that nation-states use the World Heritage system to further their own development and political agendas often has very little to do with the preservation of heritage for its 'intrinsic value'. At national and local levels it is increasingly common to make the case for heritage preservation as a form of *economic* development – often as a form of tourism development. It seems clear, though, that in many cases there is a real tension between economic growth and heritage preservation. However, our point is a somewhat different one. It is possible to ensure that economic development does not harm the immediate heritage preservation needs of heritage sites. But should heritage preservation advocates be engaged in the whole process of encouraging economic growth at all? This question will no doubt come as a shock to many readers. Perhaps we can put it in a different, more open, way: what role can heritage play in the creation of sustainable societies?

Our point is to call for a different way of thinking, one that draws on and emphasises the adaptation approach to climate change that we discussed in the first part of this chapter. That is, it is a way of thinking that is entirely compatible with the emphasis on local understanding and solutions, Indigenous knowledge, poverty alleviation and social justice that makes up the essence of our approach to climate change and heritage. This involves the decoupling of heritage preservation from processes of commodification, and an emphasis on the *conservative* essence of heritage – that is, the idea of heritage as the opposite of never-ending growth, renewal, waste and consumption, being embedded in a specific society rather than an 'expression' of that society that can be protected and preserved in isolation from it.

In order to sustain such a new way of thinking an awareness of the differential developmental needs of different parts of the world is required. Our heritage practice needs to be more nuanced and more varied according to the needs of particular regions and localities. In Britain, Australia, Europe or other parts of the developed world heritage practice should concentrate on the sustainable use of historic resources – natural, built and cultural – as substitutes for the consumption of new, scarce resources – the first beginnings of such an approach are starting to be made in the UK and other places, as we indicated at the start of this chapter. Economic activity related to heritage preservation should be a substitute for other unsustainable forms of economic activity – not just an addition to the overall rate of growth. On the other hand, in Africa or Southeast Asia, or other developing parts of the world, there may be more overt emphasis on absolute growth in economic activity, although, again, long-term sustainability should be a key feature.

Conclusion

In many ways the environmental and heritage movements share common impulses. They are both conservative in the true sense of the word: that is, interested in the preservation of what has been passed on from previous generations. They also have similar origins as movements and as shapers of public policy. In most Western countries, at least, both environmentalism and heritage protection started as grass roots movements that dragged governments – often kicking and screaming – along with them. Resistance from governments and other elites was, and in many cases remains, dogged. It seems clear from the slow pace of international negotiations around climate change treaties and from the nearly universally poor response of national governments to the climate crisis that governments and policy elites cannot be relied on to take the necessary measures to avert disaster: they will need to be pushed by grass roots movements and by ordinary citizens.

The field of heritage preservation is rarely seen as a hotbed of political or social activism. Its strong middle-class, antiquarian and high-culture roots are never far from the surface. But at various times and in various places, claims for the preservation of heritage have combined with broader social and political claims to provide a radical critique of contemporary societies. The Green Bans movement in Australia in the early 1970s, when building workers and their trade union joined with resident and heritage groups to challenge the massive redevelopment and 'modernisation' of Sydney and Melbourne, is one example (Burgmann and Burgmann 1998). The claims of Indigenous peoples in many countries, including the Inuit of North America, the Orong Asli of Malaysia, and the Mirrar People of Australia's Northern Territory, for recognition of their cultural and land-use rights over the development agendas of modern industrial states, are another. Recognising the strengths of local communities, especially in particularly vulnerable places such as small island states, as lying in their cultural knowledge of their environments is important to enabling adaptation to climate change. Heritage practitioners can play a major role in defending the cultural rights of local and Indigenous communities, perhaps in partnership with human rights advocates, using international human rights or heritage instruments.

Ultimately, though, we believe that in the struggle against climate change heritage practitioners can make their most worthwhile contribution by arguing for a de-commodified form of heritage practice that emphasises the involvement of local communities and recognition of their cultural resources; that resists being coopted into economic growth strategies unless they supplant other forms of unsustainable economic development; that focuses on heritage as an alternative way of viewing resources and their use (emphasising *conservation* of resources). By doing so we will not only improve heritage practice, but contribute to the broader effort of creating a sustainable society.

Bibliography

Allen, M. (2006) 'New Ideas about Late Holocene Climate Variability in the Central Pacific', *Current Anthropology* 47(3): 521–35.

Barnett, Jon (2005) 'Titanic States? Impacts and responses to climate change in the Pacific Islands', *Journal of International Affairs* 59(1): 203–19.

Berkes, F. and Jolly, D. (2001) 'Adapting to climate change: social-ecological resilience in a Canadian western Arctic community', *Conservation Ecology* 5(2): 18.

Boccardi, Giovanni (2007) 'World Heritage and Sustainability: Concern for social, economic and environmental aspects within the policies and processes of the World Heritage Convention', MSc. Built Environment: Sustainable Heritage report, University College London.

Burgmann, M. and Burgmann, V. (1998) *Green Bans, Red Union: Environmental Activism and the New South Wales Builders Labourers Federation*, Sydney: University of New South Wales Press.

Cassar, M. and Hawkings, C. (eds) (2007) *Engineering Historic Futures*, Stakeholders Dissemination and Scientific Research Report. London: University College London, Centre for Sustainable Heritage.

Cordes-Holland, Owen (2007) 'The sinking of the Strait: the implications of climate change for Torres Strait Islanders' human rights protected by the *ICCPR*', *Melbourne Journal of International Law*, vol. 9 (2), <http://www.austlii.edu.au/au/journals/MelbJIL/2008/16.html>.

Corlett, David (2008) *Stormy Weather: The Challenge of Climate Change and Displacement*, Sydney: UNSW Press.

Daly, Cathy (2008) 'Climate Change and World Heritage: A Vulnerability Assessment of Bruna Boinne, Ireland', Master of Arts Thesis in World Heritage Studies, Brandenburg Technical University.

English Heritage (2006) *Shoreline Management Plan Review and the Historic Environment*, English Heritage Guidance, London: English Heritage.

English Heritage (2007) *Cutting Down on Carbon: Improving the Energy Efficiency of Historic Buildings*, Summary of Government Historic Estates Unit Annual Seminar, Building Research Establishment, Garston, 9 October 2007 (www.helm.org.uk/ climatechange).

English Heritage (2008) *Climate Change and the Historic Environment*, London: English Heritage.

European Association of Historic Towns and Regions (EAHTR) (2007) *Inherit: Investing in Heritage*, EAHTR, Norwich.

Foale, Simon (2008) 'Conserving Melanesia's coral reef heritage in the face of climate change': [Paper in: Global Climate Change and Cultural Heritage. McIntyre-Tamwoy, Susan (ed.).] [online] *Historic Environment*, v.21, no.1, March: 30–36.

Fox, S. (2003) *When the weather is uggianaqtuq: Inuit observations of environmental change*, Boulder, Colorado USA: University of Colorado Geography Department Cartography Lab. Distributed by National Snow and Ice Data Center. CD-ROM.

Henley, Jon (2008) 'The last days of paradise', *The Guardian*, Tuesday 11 November, <http://www.guardian.co.uk/environment/2008/nov/11/climatechange-endangered-habitats-maldives>.

Hoivik, Susan (2008) 'Change is inherent in all things: global warming and World Heritage sites', in Kurt Luger and Karlheinz Wohler (eds) *Welterbe und Tourismus: Schutzen und Nutzen aus einer Perspektive der Nachhaltigkeit*, Innsbruck, Studienverlag: 305–23.

Huggins, Anna (2007) 'Protecting world heritage sites from the adverse impacts of climate change: obligations for states parties to the World Heritage Convention', *Australian International Law Journal*, vol. 14: 121–36.

International Institute for Sustainable Development (IISD), IUCN – The World Conservation Union and Stockholm Environment Institute – Boston Centre (SEI-B) (2003) *Livelihoods and Climate Change: Combining Disaster Risk Reduction, Natural Resource Management and Climate Change Adaptation in a New Approach to the Reduction of Vulnerability and Poverty*, Manitoba, IISD.

IPCC (2007) *Climate Change 2007: Synthesis Report. Summary for Policymakers*. <http://www.ipcc.ch/pdf/assessment-report/ar4/syr/ar4_syr_spm.pdf>.

Langfield M., Logan, W.S. and Nic Craith, M. (eds) (2009) *Cultural Diversity, Heritage and Human Rights*, London: Routledge.

Ministry of Fijian Affairs, Culture and Heritage (2007) *Intangible Cultural Heritage in Fiji*, DVD. Suva: Institute of Fijian Language and Culture.

Reuveny, R. (2008) 'Econmigration and violent conflict: case studies and public policy implications'. *Human Ecology* 36:1–13.

Salik, J. and Byg, A. (2007) *Indigenous Peoples and Climate Change*, Oxford: Tyndall Centre for Climate Change Research.

Terrill, Greg (2008) 'Climate change: how should the World Heritage Convention respond', *International Journal of Heritage Studies*, 14:5: 388–404.

Tiraa, A. (2006) 'Ra'ui in the Cook Islands – today's context in Rarotonga', SPC Traditional *Marine Resources management and Knowledge Information Bulletin* 19:11–15.

UNESCO Ad Hoc Expert Group on Endangered Languages (2003) *Language Vitality and Endangerment*, Paris: UNESCO.

United Nations Framework Convention on Climate Change (2007). Local coping strategies data base, <http://maindb.unfccc.int/public/adaptation/>

Watt-Coutier, Sheila (undated, c. 2007) *Global Warming and Human Rights*, Earthjustice and The Centre for International Environmental Law, <http://www.earthjustice.org/library/references/Background-for-IAHRC.pdf>.

Wilbanks, T.J., P. Romero Lankao, M. Bao, F. Berkhout, S. Cairncross, J.-P. Ceron, M. Kapshe, R. Muir-Wood and R. Zapata-Marti (2007) 'Industry, settlement and society', in M.L. Parry, O.F. Canziani, J.P. Palutikof, P.J. van der Linden and C.E. Hanson (eds) *Climate Change 2007: Impacts, Adaptation and Vulnerability. Contribution of Working Group II to the Fourth Assessment Report of the Intergovernmental Panel on Climate Change*, Cambridge: Cambridge University Press, UK: 357–90.

Working Group on Climate Change and Development (2007) *Up in smoke? Asia and the Pacific. The threat from climate change to human development and the environment*, The fifth report from the Working Group on Climate Change and Development, International Institute for Environment and Development and New Economics Foundation, London.

Chapter 10

Conflict heritage and expert failure

Lynn Meskell

Archaeology's engagement with politics and its larger framing within global developments are direct outgrowths of a specific disciplinary trajectory that has slowly embraced interventions from social theory, politics, philosophy, feminism and indigenous scholarship. During the 1980s and 1990s many archaeologists deepened their awareness and application of social theory, while the 1990s and 2000s were marked by recognition of the field's sociopolitical embedding. In recent years practitioners have become increasingly concerned with the ethical implications of their research and, more importantly, the politics of fieldwork and collaborations with local people, descendants, indigenous groups and other communities of connection (e.g. Hall 2005; Hodder 1998; Joyce 2005; Lilley and Williams 2005; Meskell 2005a, 2005b; Smith 2004; Watkins 2004; Zimmerman et al. 2003). Ethics itself has become the subject of numerous volumes (e.g. Lynott and Wylie 2000; Meskell and Pels 2005; Messenger 1999; Vitelli and Colwell-Chanthaphonh 2006), as had politics and nationalism before that, and these were not simply Euro-American trends but were more often driven by archaeologists from Latin America, Australasia, Africa and the Middle East (see Abdi 2001; Funari 2004; Ndoro 2001; Politis 2001; Scham and Yahya 2003; Shepherd 2002).

The new millennium brought with it a new set of concerns for archaeologists and heritage practitioners. It is no longer possible to take refuge in the past or in the comfort that the subjects of our research are dead and buried. Rather than a circumscribed set of practices archaeologists find themselves ever broadening out to embrace the discourses and impacts of environmentalism, protectionism, international law, or to confront the modalities of war and conflict. This expansion underlines a cosmopolitan engagement that follows from the discipline's first forays into sociopolitics during the 1980s, and stretches ever more widely into the larger, international political arenas in which we are all enmeshed. The interest in archaeology in conflict zones and the potential of heritage in post-conflict reconciliatory contexts have similarly gathered scholarly momentum over the past decade (Bernbeck and Pollock 1996; Colwell-Chanthaphonh 2003, 2006; González-Ruibal 2005; Meskell 2006; Rowlands 1999; Tunbridge and Ashworth 1996). These subjects have not only become the topics of research, but of new degree courses and training programs internationally.

In the following I provide two case studies that outline the dilemmas for both heritage practitioners and citizens in and around conflict zones. The first example is drawn from Afghanistan – which is hardly a post-conflict zone at the time of writing, although international efforts to rebuild have been mobilised over the past few years. The second case focuses upon Luxor, Egypt – an ongoing internal conflict zone where heritage has been at the core of a struggle between locals and the state for decades. Both show how archaeology is deployed, almost in military fashion, against the very people who live in those areas and who have most to win or lose in decisions as how best to use the past in the future.

Rhetorics of rescue

To illustrate the complex conflict situations in which archaeologists and their objects of study are increasingly embroiled, it may be instructive to think through the dramatic recent developments in and around Afghanistan. Specifically, this example underscores that proliferating global rhetorics of helping, saving, and preservation ultimately serve a limited good of our own invention. Notions of conserving and protecting might seem to embody cosmopolitan principles, but in fact typically serve international goals that may at times be at odds with local cultures and communities. Prior studies of heritage often take for granted that archaeologists and others must conserve at all costs, that *things* trump people at every turn, that the discipline is inherently doing good by *saving* the past for future generations. The case of Afghanistan is key, since the destruction of the Bamiyan Buddhas formed a nodal point in what was to become the United States' declared war on terror, and media coverage and debate around cultural properties subsequently became part of a political arsenal. In the aftermath of September 11, the matter of Afghan heritage was publicly deployed for political ends. The president and the chairman of the World Monuments Watch explicitly juxtaposed the destruction of the World Trade Center with the Taliban erasure of the Bamiyan Buddhas (Perry and Burnham 2001). For international heritage agencies, the Buddhas were global patrimony and their erasure subsequently stood for symbolic violence, loss, and the intolerance and 'barbarity' of the Taliban regime. In Afghanistan there was vocal concern over international exclusion, escalating poverty and religious difference, and outrage that ancient statues were considered more important than the desperate plight of living people (Meskell 2002; Romey 2006). This was a clear instance where moral censure, followed by military intervention, was brought to bear on one nation whose relationship to its material past fell outside the bounds of Western acceptability.

The category 'World Heritage' is a supposed global good, yet it is often used to culturally demonise certain polities with which the West has irreconcilable differences. The notion of World Heritage, as understood in humanitarian terms, potentially betrays a 'hypocritical neutrality, behind which the domination by another conception of the good (precisely the secular ethos of equality) is merely taking refuge' (Habermas 2005: 24). Such moves direct attention at other nations rather than addressing illegalities or violations at home. Recently we have seen the language of sanctions being used to combat looting in Iraq, although we know that the largest market for illegal antiquities remains the United States (Eck and Gerstenblith 2003). In addition, UNESCO has publicly mobilised anti-Islamic sentiments to criticise Afghanistan, stating that 'due to prolonged armed conflict and *fanaticism* much of Afghanistan's outstanding cultural heritage has been destroyed' (my emphasis).[1] The fetishisation of the Bamiyan destruction and its linkages to international agendas has been explored elsewhere (Colwell-Chanthaphonh 2003; Meskell 2002). Bamiyan may provide a dramatic example, but it also begs the question in more mundane settings of whether archaeologists are stewards or arbitrators of other people's pasts. Increasingly, archaeologists are recognising their moral and ethical situatedness since our projects are typically organised around the well-being of communities, the survival of esteemed heritages, and competing notions of the good.

Archaeology, heritage, conservation and culture have increasingly entered the political frame in the past decade. UNESCO's intervention in Afghanistan exemplifies the widespread programmatic desire to create disciplined heritage subjects by developing didactic programs of governance. Ulf Hannerz (2006: 79) describes UNESCO's strategies as 'cultural engineering' based on nation-state logics and global governance. In Afghanistan UNESCO's policy is to 'help re-establish the links between the populations concerned and their cultural history, helping them to develop a sense of common ownership of monuments that represent the cultural identity of different segments of society'.[2] Archaeological materials are thus seen as recuperative objects directly serving the 'nation-building process within the framework of the UN and international concerted efforts for rehabilitating Afghanistan'. For Paul Gilroy (2005: 59), 'the discourse of human rights supplies the principal way in which this shared human nature can be made accessible to political debate and legal rationality', yet under the rubric of 'humanitarianism these particular moral sensibilities can promote and justify intervention in other people's sovereign territory on the grounds that their ailing or incompetent national state has failed to measure up to the levels of good practice that merit recognition as civilized'. Universal rights talk potentially masks local understandings of what constitutes heritage in the first instance, plus what constitutes the appropriate strategies for conservation and development for potential futures, as they are cross-cut by nation, culture, religions, wealth, international profile and so on. According to the UN Secretary-General's dictum, 'Our challenge is to help the Afghans help themselves',[3] while policies and activities for the safeguarding of Afghanistan's cultural heritage focus on training and capacity-building activities premised upon the preservation of their own histories. Here culture is being instrumentalised through internationally sanctioned modes of salvation, betterment and development. In large part, non-Western cultures cannot escape the secularisation and pluralism of worldviews stemming from modernisation, and their cultural individuality against a capitalist world culture is severely curtailed (Habermas 2005: 28). What is disturbing here is that Afghanistan has recently slipped from academic attention, like the previous case of Ayodhya, India (Bernbeck and Pollock 1996, 2004). Our minds have turned to Iraq and the international safeguarding of antiquities there and the shadowy practices of looting and transnational trade (e.g. Bernhardsson 2006). Archaeologists and heritage practitioners are very fickle when it comes to research subjects of import and there is an inherent politicisation surrounding the kinds of causes we are willing to take up (or have thrust upon us) at specific historical moments.

Finally, we have to ask whether the safeguarding in Afghanistan specifically serves the nation or, more probably, benefits the world as understood by Euro-American constituencies. UNESCO recommendations stress preservation first and foremost within the new Afghan constitution, and endorse projects that raise awareness and instantiate values around cultural heritage via educational curricula and through public information. National elites must be similarly co-opted through the creation of an 'Inter-ministerial Committee on Cultural and Natural Heritage and Development to be established in Kabul in order to enhance the awareness of cabinet members and those policy makers whose decisions would have an impact on the cultural heritage of Afghanistan'. Local communities must be brought into the fold and educated about the value of preservation efforts, in order to ensure the sustainability of projects. Paralleling the language of global biodiversity and conservation, the creation of heritage registers, threats of endangerment and loss, and the push for community involvement are all markers of pragmatic concerns about the most effective ways to ensure conservation on the one hand, and socio-economic management and intervention on the other (Hayden 2003: 59–60). If the didactic route fails in Afghanistan, there are always military options. One recommendation argues for a 'special security force to protect Afghan sites with the support of the international community'. Why is it that the material past so often trumps living people?

Using the rhetoric of development through heritage, UNESCO champions 'the immediate needs of the Afghan population and, where feasible, incorporates strategies to ensure that rehabilitation activities provide opportunities for economic regeneration, and the creation of sustainable livelihoods. Where feasible, cultural rehabilitation should be closely coordinated with ongoing humanitarian activities in a given area.' At this juncture the discourses of international aid and rescuing monuments coalesce, and with those efforts come all the caveats that accompany the politics of humanitarian intervention. This is not a form of cosmopolitan intervention many in this volume would advocate, since it does not stem from invitation, dialogue and negotiation, but rather from imposition, invasion and neo-imperialism. The question of why the United States chose to intervene in Afghanistan and Iraq and not in countries like Sudan, for instance, is a moot point. In these contexts very different interpretations of international law have subsequently divided Western nations and, in light of the law's perceived failure, the hegemonic imposition of global liberal order is supposedly justified (Fine 2006; Habermas 2003). While Afghanistan may seem a dramatic case in point, other more mundane sites of rescue and management proliferate, such as the forced relocation of resident communities at Qurna, Egypt (Meskell 2005c; see Mitchell 2002) and Petra, Jordan (Massad 2001) for the purposes of tourism development, with the participation and sanctioning of international heritage authorities and archaeologists. In both contexts the communities of Qurna or Petra resisted such moves, since their livelihoods, traditions and connections to place were all threatened. In the case of Egypt violence was employed against its citizens over many decades in the name of preserving the nation's heritage. These examples lie at the intersection of culture and politics and are inextricably tied to matters of locality, identity and the management of cultural experience (Hannerz 2006: 71).

In the main, the politics of heritage protection has been traditionally mobilised from a Euro-American platform based on the presumed universalism of something called 'World Heritage', the logic of which has widespread effects in international and localised settings (see also Labadi 2007). Most effects could be seen as direct outcomes of the now familiar global processes of development, neoliberalism, and governmentality with their attendant array of concerns. Those who ultimately benefit are generally state authorities that can showcase pristine archaeology, the transnational companies whose business is tourism, and those who might gain employment in the process. Many more have something to lose in these new configurations of heritage and tourism, namely the immediate residents and stakeholders who happen to live amidst the ruins, as we will see next.

Expert failure in Egypt

It is to the specifics of Qurna that I now turn. During the 1990s I excavated for two seasons in what is called the Valley of the Nobles, the archaeological substrate of the modern village of Qurna. In fact each once existed side-by-side, ancient cemetery and modern village in a symbiotic and congenial relationship. The situation I documented through the 1990s and into the early 2000s (Meskell 2001; 2005c) has now come full circle to a series of forced removals and violent erasures.

During this last decade or more I have followed the local people of Qurna in their desperate attempts to reclaim their homes and their only source of income. This struggle involved diverse local groups and top-down global pressures stemming from notions of shared World Heritage and bolstered by UNESCO recommendations. Working there for several field seasons, I understand the perceived threats of destruction, the escalating pressures of tourism and the fractious relationships between the national government, archaeologists, tourists and Qurnawis.

Certainly, archaeologists working in Egypt generally assume that their priorities for research are primary and that the considerations of local people are secondary. Often the latter have been considered a hindrance to archaeology's project: a sentiment subsequently reinforced by sectors of the Egyptian government as well. Moreover, archaeology is inextricably linked to tourism and thus substantial economic injections for a 'developing' country. Ironically, the economic gains have been concentrated largely in the hands of Western companies operating within the new global arena. This renders suspect the notion that the majority of ordinary Egyptians really benefit from large-scale tourist expenditure. It similarly results in the prioritisation of foreign desires for commodification and leisure over local concerns and standards of living. The case study of the relocation of the community at Qurna is the most salient instance of this power imbalance. More dramatically, perhaps, in 1997 violence erupted when Islamic militants attacked foreign tourists at the nearby Temple of Hatshepsut (Meskell 2005c). This dramatic episode graphically recentred the interconnection between sites of heritage as places of contestation, foreign interventions in the form of archaeologists and tourists, and larger national tensions surrounding religion and nationhood.

From late in 2006 and into 2007 the forced removals and demolitions have been scaled up, culminating in a final solution to decades of concern about the villagers and their livelihoods. Yet as Timothy Mitchell documents, there has been more than a century of attempted relocation at Qurna. In 1996 the people of Qurna, threatened with the eviction and demolition of their homes, wrote a petition stating that they 'have become threatened in their homes, we have become agonized with fear, while our houses are demolished above our heads and we are driven from our homeland. The pretext for all this is that we damage and do harm to tourism and that we threaten the safety of the monuments. We do not understand who has fabricated these rumours. We come from the monuments and by the monuments we exist. Our livelihood is from tourism' (Mitchell 2000, 2002). Fear for one's life has been replaced by the fear of a damaged past.

In recent years the Egyptian authorities have deployed bulldozers, armed police, tourism investors, US and World Bank consultants: quite clearly the heritage industry has made use of violence in achieving its goals. In various attempts over the years people have been killed and others injured. In 1998 the head of the Luxor City Council was quoted in *Al-Ahram* as saying that the shanty town of Old Qurna would have to be depopulated because 'you can't afford to have this heritage wasted because of informal houses being built in an uncivilised manner' (quoted in Mitchell 2000). Qurna is not an isolated instance: the Egyptian government historically has attempted to move families away from the pyramid at Meidum, the temples in Esna and Edfu and from around the Great Pyramids in Giza. Several years ago Egyptian officials succeeded in removing from Qurna some 1,300 families who lived in tradi-tional mud-brick houses directly on top of the Tombs of the Nobles, which constitute a major tourist attraction. The Qurnawis are now housed in newly-built concrete buildings at a nearby village set up largely by Egypt's Armed Forces.

In December 2006 Qurna witnessed perhaps its largest crowd to 'watch an over-elaborate ceremony taking place on a hill opposite the village. Local officials brought in two busloads of journalists to witness the proceedings, which began with groups of schoolchildren in Pharaonic dress performing to the beat of drums. Once the children were done, visiting mayors, governors and council heads gave speech after speech to the attentive television cameras' (quoted in Steele 2007). They were there to witness the final razing of Qurna village, the last remaining houses that stood defiantly against the government's wilful destruction of a modern heritage. In the final stages of the spectacle, a select few residents were handed the deeds of their new houses. Then came the destruction crews. Four homes were symbolically reduced to rubble as the cameras flashed. One British reporter cynically referred to Qurna as the 'Valley of the Bulldozers' (Popham 2007).

Archaeologists, including the Director of Egypt's Supreme Council of Antiquities (SCA), Zahi Hawass, have publicly criticised the Qurnawis. Arguing that their alleged illegal looting is not the only issue, he stated that the presence of humans and animals living in tombs is even more of a threat to whatever antiquities may remain. 'Terrible damage has been done to the tombs of Gurna [*sic*] ... the fact that archaeology is regaining its rights here is the dream of my life' (quoted in Steele 2007). Other Egyptian authorities claim that there are some 950 tombs beneath the ground, though what reconnaissance this is based upon is unclear. One vocal opponent of the destruction, also a member of the SCA, holds a very different view. Naguib Amin (pers. comm.) witnessed the demolition and argues that 'even if we do not consider the primary issue of the people living there, from a strictly archaeological point of view what has happened is terrible, as bulldozers have slashed through layers and layers of archaeological remains, probably going back to pharaonic times, as it is now clear that people lived on those hills for thousands of years. So not even archaeology can justify what has been done to Qurna, and I am not holding my breath about "exciting discoveries". What was there to discover and learn is gone.' He forcefully explains that UNESCO never communicated effectively with the state authorities, the World Heritage Convention was not understood in Egypt, copious reports were generated but not implemented, there was no concrete management policy, that UNESCO failed in 'teaching' or even working with the Egyptian authorities, and so on. He asserts that the 'know-how remains the exclusive property of exclusive organizations in Vienna, Rome and Paris' and there has been what he brilliantly calls 'expert failure' on both sides.

At Qurna and elsewhere we see the dominant discourses of development, capacity building, conservation, sustainability and heritage tourism. What must be sublated in the present by the former residents of Qurna is promised to be recouped by future generations, while international elites and the adequately resourced will be able to enjoy the spoils of heritage and conservation in the present in the form of cultural tourism and archaeological research. Such promissory strategies ultimately de-privilege indigenous and minority communities, often disempowered constituencies whose land, livelihood and legacies are threatened. This is the case not only in Egypt but also in Iraq and Afghanistan and in very different contexts like South Africa where black communities have been removed from ancestral lands for the purposes of national parks and conservation tourism (Meskell 2005a). Collectively archaeologists must take seriously the intellectual foundations and political economies of something called 'heritage', the legal, political and ethical strata that underlie implicit tensions over access, preservation and control of the material past in a volatile present.

Implications for the archaeological present

Studies of the archaeological present have lately evinced the local dimension, while at the same time demonstrating global relevance, including the impact of global networks and forces, and the implications of international efforts, whether aid, development, protectionism, humanitarianism, and so on. Both ends of the spectrum, local and global, have their limitations if considered in isolation and do not fully consider the 'processes of self-transformation in which new cultural forms take place and where new spaces of discourse open up leading to a transformation in the social world' (Delanty 2006: 44). How the world is imagined in particular places varies greatly.

Archaeologists are beginning to examine the ways in which local and national heritage politics are made and unmade through international discourses and regulations, how transnational bodies and organisations such as UNESCO, the World Bank, conservation and funding agencies, and even the United States' 'war on terror' are brought into play in local arenas (see papers in Meskell 2008). Balancing appeals to universalism with cultural diversity remains a critical tension that underlies much of the existing literature on heritage and our engagements as practitioners. These strange proximities and multiplicities are experienced in particular regions and locales in distinct ways, even though the organisational directives might aspire to a presumed universality and neutrality. More importantly, salvage politics are often united by incentives of common goods, they are promise-based, future driven and depend upon networks of participation, discipline and sacrifice that discursively create desirable heritage citizens (see Hayden 2003). In an Orwellian tone, interventionist policies that control the past also serve to predict future outcomes, promising sustainable development, betterment and socio-economic uplift.

We must now take seriously the intellectual foundations and political economies of 'heritage', the legal, political and ethical strata that underlie implicit tensions over access, preservation and control of the material past in a volatile present. This entails questioning the translatability of such terms and practices across a wide array of sites and locations. It requires practitioners to reveal the discursive production, consumption and governing of other people's pasts through examination of the participants, organisations, stakeholders, beneficiaries, and victims.

Notes

1 Online. Available HTTP: <http://portal.unesco.org/culture/en/ev.php-URL_ID=18277& URL_DO = DO_TOPIC&URL_SECTION = 201.html> See <http://whc.unesco.org/en/ activities/2> (accessed 29 October 2008).

2 Online. Available HTTP: <http://portal.unesco.org/culture/en/ev.php-URL_ID= 24246&URL_DO = DO_TOPIC&URL_SECTION = 201.html> (see the section on Culture and Afghanistan) (accessed 29 October 2008).

3 See <http://www.islamabad.mfa.gov.af/cultural-affairs.asp> and <http://www.un.org/ News/dh/latest/afghan/sg-tokyo21.htm> (accessed 29 October 2008).

References

Abdi, K. (2001) 'Nationalism, politics, and the development of archaeology in Iran', *American Journal of Archaeology*, 105: 51–76.

Bernbeck, R. and Pollock, S. (1996) 'Ayodhya, archaeology, and identity', *Current Anthropology*, 37: 138–42.

——(2004) 'The political economy of archaeological practice and the production of heritage in the Middle East', in L. M. Meskell and R. W. Preucel (eds) *A Companion to Social Archaeology*, Oxford: Blackwell: 335–52.

Bernhardsson, M.T. (2006) *Reclaiming a Plundered Past: Archaeology and Nation Building in Modern Iraq*, Austin: University of Texas Press.

Colwell-Chanthaphonh, C. (2003) 'Dismembering/disremembering the Buddhas: renderings on the internet during the Afghan purge of the past', *Journal of Social Archaeology*, 3: 75–98.

Delanty, G. (2006) 'The cosmopolitan imagination: critical cosmopolitanism and social theory', *The British Journal of Sociology*, 57: 25–47.

Eck, D.W. and Gerstenblith, P. (2003) 'International cultural property', *International Lawyer*, 37: 565–73.

Fine, R. (2006) 'Cosmopolitanism and violence: difficulties of judgment', *The British Journal of Sociology*, 57: 49–66.

Funari, P.P.A. (2004) 'The archaeological study of the African diaspora in Brazil', in T. Falola and A. Ogundiran (eds) *The Archaeology of Atlantic Africa and the African Diaspora*, Studies in African History and the Diaspora series by University of Rochester Press.

Gilroy, P. (2005) *Postcolonial Melancholia*, New York: Columbia University Press.

González-Ruibal, A. (2005) 'The need for a decaying past: An archaeology of oblivion in Galicia (NW Spain)', *Home Cultures*, 2: 129–52.

——(2006) 'The dream of reason: an archaeology of the failures of modernity in Ethiopia', *Journal of Social Archaeology*, 6.

Habermas, J. (2003) 'Interpreting the fall of a monument', *Constellations*, 10: 36–70.

——(2005) 'Equal treatment of cultures and the limits of postmodern liberalism', *The Journal of Political Philosophy*, 13: 1–28.

Hall, M. (2005) 'Situational ethics and engaged practice: the case of archaeology in Africa', in L. M. Meskell and P. Pels (eds) *Embedding Ethics: Shifting the Boundaries of the Anthropological Profession*, Oxford: Berg: 169–94.

Hannerz, U. (2006) 'Cosmopolitanism', in J. Vincent and D. Nugent (eds) *A Companion to the Anthropology of Politics*, Oxford: Blackwell: 69–85.

Hayden, C. (2003) *When Nature Goes Public: The Making and Unmaking of Bioprospecting in Mexico*, Princeton: Princeton University Press.

Hodder, I. (1998) 'The past and passion and play: Çatalhöyük as a site of conflict in the construction of multiple pasts', in L. M. Meskell (ed.) *Archaeology Under Fire: Nationalism, Politics and Heritage in the Eastern Mediterranean and Middle East*, London: Routledge: 124–39.

Joyce, R.A. (2005) 'Solid histories for fragile nations: archaeology as cultural patrimony', in L. M. Meskell and P. Pels (eds) *Embedding Ethics*, Oxford: Berg: 253–73.

Labadi, S. (2007) 'Representations of the nation and cultural diversity in discourses on World Heritage', *Journal of Social Archaeology*, 7: 147–70.

Lilley, I. and Williams, M. (2005) 'Archaeological and indigenous significance: a view from Australia', in C. Mathers, T. Darvill and B. Little (eds) *Heritage of Value, Archaeology of Renown: Reshaping Archaeological Assessment and Significance*, Gainesville: University of Florida Press: 227–47.

Lynott, M. J. and Wylie, A. (eds) (2000) *Ethics in American Archaeology*, Washington, D.C.: Society for American Archaeology.

Massad, J.A. (2001) *Colonial Effects*, New York: Columbia University Press.

Meskell, L.M. (2001) 'The practice and politics of archaeology in Egypt', in A.M. Cantwell, E. Friedlander and M.L. Tram (eds) *Ethics and Anthropology: Facing Future Issues in Human Biology, Globalism, and Cultural Property*, New York: Annals of the New York Academy of Sciences: 146–69.

——(2002) 'Negative heritage and past mastering in archaeology', *Anthropological Quarterly*, 75: 557–74.

——(2005a) 'Archaeological ethnography: conversations around Kruger National Park', *Archaeologies: Journal of the World Archaeology Congress*, 1: 83–102.

——(2005b) 'Recognition, restitution and the potentials of postcolonial liberalism for South African heritage', *South African Archaeological Bulletin*, 60: 72–78.

——(2005c) 'Sites of violence: terrorism, tourism and heritage in the archaeological present', in L. M. Meskell and P. Pels (eds) *Embedding Ethics*, Oxford: Berg: 123–46.

——(2006) 'Trauma culture: remembering and forgetting in the new South Africa', in D. Bell, (ed.) *Memory, Trauma, and World Politics*, New York: Palgrave Macmillan: 157–74.

——(ed.) (2009) *Cosmopolitan Archaeologies*, Durham: Duke University Press.

Meskell, L.M. and Pels, P. (eds) (2005) *Embedding Ethics*, Oxford: Berg.

Messenger, P.M. (ed.) (1999) *The Ethics of Collecting Cultural Property*, Albuquerque: University of New Mexico Press.

Mitchell, T. (2000) 'Making the nation: the politics of heritage in Egypt', in N. A. Sayyad (ed.) *Global Forms/Urban Norms: On the Manufacture and Consumption of Traditions in the Built Environment*, London: E & F Spon/Routledge.

——(2002) *Rule of Experts*, Berkely: University of California Press.

Ndoro, W. (2001) *Your Monument Our Shrine: the Preservation of Great Zimbabwe*, Uppsala: Studies in African Archaeology 19, Uppsala University.

Perry, M. and Burnham, B. (2001) 'A critical mission – the World Monuments Watch', in *World Monuments Watch: 100 Most Endangered Sites 2002*: 3–4.

Politis, G. (2001) 'On archaeological praxis, gender bias and indigenous peoples in South America', *Journal of Social Archaeology*, 1: 90–107.

Popham, P. (2007) 'Valley of the bulldozers: Death on the Nile', *Independent* Online Edition vol. 20, March 2007. Available HTTP: <http://news.independent.co.uk/world/africa/article2374347.ece:>.

Romey, K. (2006) 'The race to save Afghan culture', in K. D. Vitelli and C. Colwell-Chanthaphonh (eds) *Archaeological Ethics*, Oxford: Altamira: 81–90.

Rowlands, M. (1999) 'Remembering to forget: sublimation as sacrifice in war memorials', in A. Forty and S. Küchler (eds) *The Art of Forgetting*, Oxford: Berg: 129–45.

Scham, S. and Yahya, A. (2003) 'Heritage and reconciliation', *Journal of Social Archaeology*, 3: 399–416.

Shepherd, N. (2002) 'The politics of archaeology in Africa', *Annual Review of Anthropology*, 31: 189–209.

Smith, C. (2004) *Country, Kin and Culture: Survival of an Australian Aboriginal Community*, Adelaide: Wakefield Press.

Steele, C. (2007) 'It's settled then', in *Egypt Today*, 28/4, February, Online. Available HTTP: <www.egypttoday.com/article.aspx?ArticleID=7166>.

Tunbridge, J. E., and Ashworth, G. (1996) *Dissonant Heritage: The Management of the Past as a Resource in Conflict*, Chichester: John Wiley and Sons.

Vitelli, K. D. and Colwell-Chanthaphonh, C. (eds) (2006) *Archaeological Ethics*, Walnut Creek: AltaMira Press.

Watkins, J. (2004) 'Becoming American or becoming Indian? NAGPRA, Kennewick, and cultural affiliation', *Journal of Social Archaeology*, 4: 60–80.

Zimmerman, L.J., Vitelli, K.D., Hollowell-Zimmer, J. and Maurer, R.D. (eds) (2003) *Ethical Issues in Archaeology*, Walnut Creek: AltaMira Press.

Chapter 11

Material heritage and poverty reduction

Kathryn Lafrenz Samuels

There can be no doubt that the ever-increasing fascination with heritage and its material forms is part and parcel of the process we call globalisation. A yearning for roots, tied to specific material places, embodies a nostalgia fashioned in the face of the apparent rootlessness and destabilising rapidity of global flows. With this widening perspective of the global contexts of material heritage, and how material heritage actively constructs these global contexts as well, the prominence of the socio-economic character of archaeological goods and material heritage is brought into sharper relief. We can see more clearly how archaeology and heritage operate within a political economy of resource management, cultural property, land tenure, development, propertied interests, the antiquities trade, tourism, traditional craft reproductions, and global structural inequalities. In the background, quietly negotiating and structuring these broader socio-economic and political relationships, is the spectre of poverty. Material heritage has a deep and complicated relationship with poverty. So pervasive is this indicator of inequality that it is taken for granted that such inequalities form a permanent part of the global landscape. At the same time, poverty is rendered less threatening by treating it as a technical problem, to be fixed through expertise. Therefore as poverty and heritage become bundled together in a nexus of concerns within development and heritage management, material heritage is increasingly mobilised within projects that purport to tackle this technical problem of poverty.

Here I argue that these mobilisations have less to do with a critical engagement with poverty, and the inequalities it represents, and more to do with the creation of new arenas for competing political and economic interests that seek to appropriate economically viable heritage resources. Often this is achieved through the travelling, formalistic rationalities of development organisations, which work to territorialise poverty and material heritage in innovative ways, to align community responsibilities with global risk, and to depoliticise poverty by positioning it as a 'local' problem, while the contributions of broad political economic structures to poverty are obscured (Craig and Porter 2006; Deleuze and Guattari 1983). Archaeology and heritage are particularly suited for this globalising project, of bridging 'the travelling' and 'the placed', the deterritorialised with the (re)territorialised, the flows of future-oriented progress with the boundaries of tradition-oriented parochialism. They act as the material embodiment of place, specific histories, diversity, and indigenous identities, while also embraced as World Heritage, under cosmopolitan ethics, for consumption in global tourism. Material heritage therefore provides the physical lynchpin for mediating these twinned processes of movement and rootedness. Having previously discussed these twinned processes elsewhere, with a focus on the travelling nature of development expertise in heritage management (Lafrenz Samuels 2009), in this chapter I wish to address the other side of the same coin: how poverty is situated as a local affair through the development of material heritage, in the specific case of urban conservation and rehabilitation projects in the Fez Medina, Morocco.

Situating poverty reduction through heritage management as a globalising project

The inadequacies of any portrayal of globalisation as an inexorable process of spatialising hegemony, of the global consuming the local, is highlighted by the sheer diversity and range of actors involved in heritage and development projects, with their competing interests and sometimes unexpected alliances. Instead what we are seeing are the proliferation of spatialities and territorialisations, situating material heritage with poverty in unique articulations of rootedness and travelling expertise. Critiques have deconstructed the process of globalisation to reveal instead a superficial network of ties between elites and experts, with experts often deriving from the ranks of economic elites (Cassarino 2004; Friedman 2007; Harvey 2005; Mehta 2001; Mitchell 2002; Quarles van Ufford et al. 2003; Van der Berg and Quarles van Ufford 2005). Included within these webs of relations are the networks of experts forming the structure of development organisations and greasing the wheels of poverty-reduction projects. Experts such as heritage managers, archaeologists, conservators, and historic preservationists of course also comprise these same networks.

Flowing through it all, according to Harvey (2005: 188) and Friedman (2007), are the ideologies of neoliberalism and cosmopolitanism, which can serve as a justification or kind of mask for the institutionalisation and maintenance of elite power and expert knowledge. A specifically Western form of advanced liberal ('neoliberal') democracy, the hallmark of neoliberalism is rule through internalised self-regulating techniques of governance, techniques which mimic market mechanisms and promote the centrality of civil society at the expense of the nation-state. The discourse on 'cosmopolitanism', meanwhile, imagines all humanity belonging to a single community of global citizens, who share an appreciation for diversity and seek consensus in the face of differing values (cf. Meskell 2009). Analyses of globalisation and development (Anders 2005; Ferguson and Gupta 2002; Gupta 1995; Gupta and Ferguson 1992; Hibou 2000; Mosse 2005a) have criticised neoliberal strategies as downplaying and neutralising the power of the state in relation to the global and local – strategies that are moreover reflected in much of the academic scholarship on the topic. Hence the turn to the 'transnational' rather than the 'international' as the realm of global relations. In a similar vein, Tsing (2000) calls for attention to how the category of 'the global' is produced through globalising projects – such as development and expertise, for our purposes here – while Graeber (2002: 1224) questions how the celebration in much of the academic literature of 'fractures and flows' and local resistance to the global draws attention away 'from the current attempt to impose the largest and most totalizing framework in world history – the world market – on just about everything'.

My point here is that expertise and the production of knowledge about globalisation are very much part of a globalising project. Understanding globalisation and development as intimately tied to the production of expert knowledge highlights the recursive nature of scholarship on development, and calls into question our own contribution to, and complicity within, the mobilisation of heritage onto the global stage through development projects. If we want to understand the connection between material heritage and poverty reduction, and how poverty is situated as a 'local' problem more generally, we must therefore come to terms with the central role played by the expert practices and projects of heritage. Heritage management is not the handmaiden to anything here, I argue, or some side project to the larger business of promoting economic growth, but rather the very technique, or *modus operandi*, of intervention and resource appropriation.

Poverty and the poverty of definitions

A major hurdle to understanding the relationship between poverty and material heritage is that poverty suffers from a problem of definition. Development economists, policy makers and grassroots activists struggle over questions of what poverty is, how to measure it, and what parameters or threshold criteria to use. As a result, there is little agreement on the best ways to alleviate poverty. Overall, there are three general approaches to defining and measuring poverty: income and expenditure, resources, and capability.

The most widely used approach, looking at income and expenditure, is favoured by many economists because it yields precise calculations, but is unable to measure well-being or quality of life due to its one-dimensionality (Robeyns 2005: 30). Expenditure measures tend to grossly underestimate poverty, as does the cost of a minimum basket of commodities, a commonly used poverty line measure (Bush 2007: 15–16; Fergany 2002). The $1 a day measure for the poverty line is also misleading because it is shorthand for the purchasing-power parity of $1.08 in the United States in 1993. That is, someone is considered poor if living on less than could be bought with $1.08 in the United States in 1993. Moreover, poverty estimates are very sensitive, when using such methods, to where the poverty-line is drawn: by the $1 per day measure poverty dropped worldwide from 40 to 21 per cent during 1981–2001, but by the $2 per day measure poverty significantly increased (Robeyns 2005: 31–32).

A diversity of resource approaches is employed, including GNP per capita and Rawlsian social primary goods (Rawls 1971, 1993). Following on this, the capabilities approach (Sen 1999) emphasises that Rawlsian goods and services will only get us so far, as what we really need to understand is how effectively people are able to use these goods and services, and thus the extent to which people can generate capabilities from them. The definition of poverty used by the United Nations Development Programme (UNDP) is derived from the capability approach, defining poverty as a 'deprivation of human capability of essential opportunities and choices needed for the well being of an individual, household or community' (UNDP 2002: 94). For the purposes of understanding the link between archaeology and poverty, the resources and capabilities approaches would likely grant us the greatest insights, and could be roughly coupled with, on the one hand, discussions within archaeology on material as cultural property or, on the other, material as the medium for identification, post-conflict reconciliation, or in rights-based claims for recognition.

However, my real purpose in outlining these various approaches is to demonstrate just how diverse the positions on poverty are within development. This has important consequences for understanding the precariousness of thought behind using material heritage to reduce poverty. In tandem with this definitional instability, moreover, poverty is once again the latest buzzword within development circles. This time around the focus of development energies for global financing institutions, led by the World Bank, is on Poverty Reduction Strategies, in the documentary genre of the Poverty Reduction Strategy Paper (PRSP). The new brand of poverty includes an emphasis upon 'donor harmonisation', so that the efforts of international organisations such as the United Nations Development Programme (UNDP), bi-lateral donors, NGOs and national governments are organised around the formulation and implementation of the objectives set out in PRSPs (Craig and Porter 2006). The struggles over a definition of poverty are very much caught up within the PRSP process, which consists of strategies on the part of development agencies to portray a gentler version of structural adjustment, sensitive to social vulnerability and exclusion. The backlash against the 'hard conditionality' of structural adjustment policies of the 1980s and 1990s spawned this new generation of 'soft conditionality' policies, centred around notions of 'good governance'.

Policies for 'good governance' typify neoliberal governance in its operation through indirect mechanisms of rule and prescription for economic liberalisation and privatisation (Anders 2005; Mosse 2005a, 2005b). 'Good governance' policies also follow the lead of New Institutional Economics (NIE), with its focus on transaction costs, market imperfections (such as imperfect knowledge), and institutional change for capacity building. Importantly for NIE, institutions are conceived as sets of rules structuring behaviour, so that the instruments of control have been reconfigured from the external conditions once set by structural adjustment to internal modes of self-monitoring and self-discipline under 'good governance' (Barry 1996; Burchell, Gordon and Miller 1991; Foucault 1991; Mosse 2005b). Hibou (2000) traces this shift in conditionality and discourse for sub-Saharan Africa at the World Bank, to show how the importance of the nation-state is again centre-stage, as the Bank realises that its policies 'may have contributed to the deterioration of countries' institutional infrastructures by exacerbating the fragmentation of central power' (2000: 210). However, now the effect is a 'privatisation' of the state that blurs the boundaries between public and private, state and civil society.

The decentralised and internalised techniques of 'good governance' work as indirect mechanisms for transnational control over resources, finances, and social policy, via the production of 'expert' knowledge, particularly in the field of environmental management, and its bureaucratic offshoot heritage management (Agrawal 2005; Byrne 1991; Caffyn and Jobbins 2003; Goldman 2001a, 2001b, 2005; Heynen et al. 2007; Mehta 2001; Mitchell 2002; Moore 2001). Therefore, 'good governance' is necessary for understanding how material heritage is developed for poverty reduction because it acts as the specific institutional strategy and focal point of discourse for mobilising heritage in development projects. It is the tool of experts in appropriating resources and raising material heritage to the global stage, while at the same time poverty is generated because of this resource appropriation. Good governance, according to Bush (2007: xiv), is therefore a red herring, drawing attention away from the fact that poverty is generated from difficulty in accessing and controlling resources. Poverty occurs exactly *because of* incorporation into the global community and market (2007: 20).

Localising poverty through material heritage in the Fez Medina

The connection between archaeology and poverty is nowhere made more evident than in World Bank projects that seek to develop material heritage for the reduction of poverty and economic growth. The Middle East and North Africa (MENA) is promoted by the World Bank as the model region for how development projects in cultural heritage should work. MENA is therefore the flagship, and proving ground, for developmental projects in cultural heritage. Yet the region is also considered by development experts to embody a distinctive constellation of Western concerns – security, terrorism, failed states, and the promotion of democracy – that could be rectified through economic growth. Cultural heritage is thus seen as integrating MENA into the world economy through cultural tourism and the generation of other revenue from material heritage. Yet investment in the region remains very low: total net flows of Foreign Direct Investment (FDI, a measure of integration into the world economy) from 1975 to 2000 was barely 1 per cent. Moreover, according to World Bank statistics, the MENA region has relatively low poverty rates and good income distribution levels compared to other regions. This begs the question of why donors and the West are so intent on 'developing' the region, except to enact economic reform as a means to political reform (Bush 2007; Harrigan et al. 2006). The development of cultural heritage projects in MENA (and its designation as the model region) must be understood as political projects, with poverty acting as the specific technique of intervention.

The Medina of Fez was the first historic site in Morocco inscribed on the World Heritage List, in 1981, and is regarded as the best preserved 'medieval' historic centre in MENA. Four years after its inscription on the World Heritage List, UNESCO launched a campaign to save the city from further deterioration. However, the preliminary stages of the project were focused more on urban planning, specifically on

Figure 11.1 Overlooking the Fez Medina (Fez el Bali) from Borj Sud (Photo by the author)

developing access for the provision of services (e.g. sanitation and emergency services) unavailable to most Medina residents due to the narrow winding streets. While such issues of access were the primary concern of some national agencies in Morocco, UNESCO objected to the first feasibility study, conducted in 1991 and financed by the UNDP, which cut wide swathes through the historic buildings of the Medina. Moreover, UNESCO was unable to raise the money necessary for improvements, so the World Bank was invited to join the campaign to provide loans, coordinate further financing, and provide expertise in implementing a large-scale development project. The government of Morocco and the World Bank prepared a new urban improvement plan that focused more specifically on the cultural heritage of the Medina, while also aiming at reducing poverty (Bouchenaki and Lévi-Strauss 1998; Carson, Mitchell and Conaway 2002: 120; Cernea 2001a: 70–71; Hardouin 1983; UNESCO 1987).

Over the years, numerous institutional bodies and organisations have gathered around the Fez campaign. In addition to the World Bank and UNESCO, these include the Getty Foundation, the Center for Urban Studies at Harvard University, Fez University, foreign governments acting as bilateral donors (Italy, Japan, Saudi Arabia), the *Fonds Arabe pour le Développement Économique et Social*, various Moroccan national government agencies, in addition to a diversity of other regional and local actors. This diversity at the local level is due in part to the 1983 decentralisation of government. Local actors included the regional government (the *Wilaya*), city prefecture, Fez Medina Council, ADER-Fèz (*Agence pour la dédensification et la réhabilitation de la Médina de Fès*, a local conservation agency, with the status of *société anonyme*), and a panoply of other NGOs and local civic groups (Carson, Mitchell and Conaway 2002: 120; Darles and Lagrange 1996; Serageldin 2001: 240; 2004: 55). For example, the actors involved in the renovation of one building alone – the Ibn Danan synagogue – included the Danan family, the World Monuments

Fund, the Directorate for Cultural Heritage of the Moroccan Ministry of Cultural Affairs, the Council of Jewish Communities, the Judeo-Moroccan Heritage Foundation, and the Fez Medina Council (Danan 1998; Kosansky 2002: 374; Lévi-Strauss 2001: 379; Lévy 1998).

Figure 11.2 Inside the Fez Medina (Photo by the author)

Fez is characterised by the World Bank as 'a pocket of concentrated, abject mass poverty' (Cernea 2001a: 71), with 36 per cent of residents living in poverty. This is a much higher rate than the national poverty averages for urban (10.4 per cent) and rural (28.7 per cent) areas. Under the World Bank's tutelage, the reduction of poverty in the Fez Medina is sought primarily by creating jobs, raising property prices, and raising living standards. Of these three aims, the creation of jobs was foreseen to have the most immediate and direct result for the poor. The project was forecast to generate 8,000–10,000 jobs over a period of fifteen years, but these are mainly temporary, informal, construction jobs and measured in person/work-years (Cernea 2001a; 2001b; Serageldin 2001: 242; World Bank 1997, 1999). In the final World Bank report on the Fez project these projections were recognised as overly optimistic, and in the end only 1,000 person/work-years were created (Bigio 2007; World Bank 2006). Indeed, for poverty alleviation the project outcomes as a whole were rated as unsatisfactory (World Bank 2006: 7).

The project's failure in creating jobs was deemed the result of a lack of cooperation and organisation at the local level. While ADER-Fès was appointed the executing agency for the World Bank project, and put in charge of creating a department to administer these jobs, the municipal government held the financing and preferred to contract out the rehabilitation and clearing work, 'which provided sub-optimal services in a climate of limited competition and inflated prices', rather than hand over the duties to ADER-Fès (World Bank 2006: 7–9). During the project period the municipal governments underwent major restructuring, effectively combining six local governments into one, and ADER-Fès was unable to take over responsibility of project monitoring and evaluation until the final two and a half years of the project, due to its own financing and bankruptcy problems (World Bank 2006: 4; n.d.: 45). One of the project's aims was to strengthen local institutions and foster cooperation, but the institutional restructuring foreseen under such aims for 'capacity building' and 'good governance' had an overall negative effect on the project. In the pursuit of political reorganisation and reform, the poverty reduction component of the Fez project went by the wayside. Thus we are left with the question of what exactly the project was supposed to achieve, when conflicting components of the project suggest that political reform, according to neoliberal visions of good governance, was more important than poverty alleviation, even though poverty was showcased as the municipal reason for international involvement.

The decentralisation of governance creates a system of decentralised responsibility, which ultimately directs responsibility and accountability vertically down to the local level. While the World Bank takes some limited responsibility for the project's failure, due to its project design and over-ambitious and over-optimistic expectations, the weight of blame is placed on ADER-Fès and the municipal government. This sentiment, placing responsibility for the success or failure of the rehabilitation on the local communities, is voiced again and again in the literature on the Fez campaign (Bronson 1993; Touri 1998; Work 1993; World Bank 1997, 1998, 2006). As a former municipal authority stated, in the parlance of international organisations:

> it is towards the mobilization of the principal actors of the city to which efforts must now be directed … [T]he population could take over its own environment not only as users but as custodians of a heritage to be developed and passed on to future generations. Therefore, it is genuine 'governance' that should be established to ensure the adequate safeguarding of this more than 1000-year-old city.
>
> (Filali Baba 1998: 7)

Misrecognised here is the requirement that local governance structures and operations align with the global way of doing business. In the Fez project this disjuncture is seen most clearly in the World Bank's procurement procedures, which the municipal government repeatedly sought to circumvent, versus the permit processes in Moroccan bureaucracy, regarded as time-consuming and superfluous by the World Bank. The same sort of misrecognition is evident in the attitudes towards property, where local modes and regimes of ownership are expected to mirror the neoliberal norms of property rights encouraged by international organisations, and the onus lies with the local when they do not. Frustration is repeatedly voiced over the difficulty in identifying owners, the pervasiveness of religious endowments (*habous*), and the fragmentary and overlapping ownership patterns with numerous co-owners of primary and subsidiary rights (Serageldin 2001, 2004; World Bank 1998, 1999).

The success of the project was argued to hinge on the participation of the local community, specifically through their private investments to augment the public and donated funds, but in the end such privately financed rehabilitation efforts did not materialise (World Bank n.d., 1997, 1998, 2006). The responsibility of the local community for the rehabilitation efforts was also framed in moralistic overtones which stress the recognition of the value of heritage, and education of the next generation to realise this value, all in the face of decay and destruction:

> In order to win each World Heritage town's struggle against the erosion and eventual destruction of its historic wealth (through poverty, pollution, natural disasters, armed conflict, etc.) every single man and woman should be motivated to help educate in this spirit the world's children, future decision makers, by encouraging them to develop lasting ties with the World Heritage so that it becomes 'their own'.
>
> (UNESCO 1993: 12)

Importantly, poverty is scripted as the cause of decay, not only in the degradation and loss of wealth in the form of material heritage, but also as an impoverished awareness of the value of this heritage, in which 'cultural riches are lost, and the people are impoverished in their self understanding and lifestyle' (Work 1993: 2). As a result, poverty is implicated in the aims of the Fez campaign not only through seeking its reduction via the creation of jobs in labour-intensive rehabilitation efforts, but also in locating poverty as the primary reason for needing urban rehabilitation in the first place. Poverty is the source of urban decay, at the same time that treatment of this urban decay provides a means for alleviating poverty.

Indeed, the poverty of the Fez Medina sits squarely within a discourse on decay, with decay begetting poverty and poverty begetting decay in a self-fulfilling circle of blame that spins off centrifugally the contributions of broader economic and structural inequalities to the production of poverty. Through the slippage of poverty with decay, in a concomitant 'fall from splendour to squalor' (Work 1993: 3), the well-being of the local community is elided with the material constitution of its architectural heritage. Because of this, the 'poverty' which the Fez campaign seeks to address is easily transferred into a concern with the revitalisation of the material heritage, rather than the communities living in and amongst these historic remains. An easy conversion is made whereby the renovation of houses – the material refashioning of decay into preservation – automatically alleviates the socio-economic inequalities of diminished resource access and constricted capabilities. The material realities of decay do have a profound and straightforward effect on the well-being of individuals, since every year residents are trapped under the collapse of deteriorated housing (World Bank 2006). The recent minaret collapse in Meknes is a tragic reminder of these realities. However, the Fez project constructed an exaggerated equation of people and their livelihoods with material and its state of preservation, which creates a determinedly narrow approach to understanding poverty. Such an approach applies a more or less preservationist logic to living communities and thus constrains their present-day needs and future aspirations – in effect, their capabilities – within potentially anachronistic and petrified lifeways.

In the Fez campaign, the responsibility placed at the feet of the local communities works to locate poverty as a local problem, not only by equating the local community with the material degradation of their built environment, but also by situating the impoverished inhabitants as active creators of this decay. Moreover, the current residents of the Medina, responsible for the decay, are set within a trope of urban wealth versus rural poverty, which also effectively shifts attention away from inequalities at the global level, back to inequalities at the regional level. The investment in and development of the *ville nouvelle* began under colonial rule and continued following the independence of Morocco, with the wealthy urban population of Fez increasingly choosing to move out of the Medina into the surrounding neighbourhoods. Following this was an influx of rural populations to the Medina, motivated by drought and declining rural economic opportunities and attracted by the cheaper rents, with 8,000 new residents arriving to the Medina every year from 1975 to 1982 (Porter 2003). 'Deserted by the better-off, the old city was caught in a downward spiral of poverty' (Darles and Lagrange 1996: 39). This demographic shift, with the flight of the wealthy urbanites and arrival of the impoverished rural dwellers, and subsequent overcrowding, is cited as a leading cause of the decay and material degradation of the Medina (e.g. Touri 1998; World Bank 1997). Likewise, the urban elite are accorded the power and agency to save the urban fabric: 'following the departure of the inhabitants of urban origin, the change which has occurred has left the city without a voice, without an elite which can defend its interests or sustain its memory' (Filali Baba 1998: 7). The original feasibility study rejected by UNESCO, which focused on issues of access to the Medina, was modeled on the assumption that the solution was to attract the wealthy and middle-class residents of the *ville nouvelle* back into the Medina (Bouchenaki and Lévi-Strauss 1998: 37).

The replacement of the Medina population with rural, largely Berber, inhabitants, whose poverty required more and more families to squeeze into residences, resulted in an overcrowding and dividing up of living space referred to as '*oukalisation*' or '*fondouqalisation*' by urban planners and preservationists (Touri 1998: 10; McGuinness 2005). Population densities reach over 1,000 inhabitants per hectare in some quarters of the Medina. Moreover, some of the first heritage legislation passed in Morocco, in 1912, concerned the protection of historic madrassas in the Fez Medina from the deteriorating effects of overcrowding (Ameziane and Lazrak 1998: 14–15). In fact, ADER-Fès was created in 1981 for the purpose of addressing the problems of over-crowding through the proposed relocation outside the Medina of some 50,000 inhabitants, in order to 'dedensify' the living space (Bronson 1993: 4; Porter 2003: 131). *Dédensification* has also been translated by ADER-Fès itself as 'slum clearance' (ADER-Fès 2001).

The Fez campaign was aimed at reducing the poverty of the Medina, as a material space, and not necessarily its current inhabitants. This is seen most clearly in the project's aim to raise property prices, which seeks to attract wealthy Fassi residents, foreigners, and tourists back into the Medina, thus reversing the demographic shift that is cited as the cause of deterioration and poverty. Grants and microcredit financing were offered to attract private rehabilitation efforts, and 50 new boutique hotels and six tourist circuits were created (Bigio 2007; Larbi 2007; McGuinness 2006, personal communication; World Bank 1998, 2006). While World Heritage designation of a site or city draws increasing attention from tourists (Ashworth and Tunbridge 1990; Carson, Mitchell and Conaway 2002; Drost 1996), according to Serageldin (2001: 238–39; 2004: 53) 'the population is very conservative, and their absorptive capacity for foreign visitors is quite limited'. Yet most of the World Bank's studies on the economic benefits of urban rehabilitation in the Fez Medina were focused on tourist perspectives and revenue (Carson et al. 1997; Carson, Mitchell and Conaway 2002; Dixon 1999). Fez also has a long history of tourism, developed in and inherited from colonialism, during which the decay of the Medina was encouraged so as to more perfectly reflect, in the colonial imagination, its 'medieval' origins (Porter 2000).

This colonial decay of the Medina, which yields its own sort of preservationist logic in preserving the Medina's medieval character, highlights that such decay is not simply the result of poverty or a technical problem to be solved. This decay has a history; it is a heritage in its own right, of colonial legacies, which continue on into the present and serve as the very point of continuing interventions. The colonial legacy is further managed so as to gloss over the origins of the decay, a history of dispossession deriving from colonial rule and its continuing effects. This poverty, decay and dispossession are therefore presented as the fault not of colonial govern-ance, but of the local populace. This conclusion is further supported by identifying poverty with the material constitution of the Medina, and not its population. The poverty of the Fez Medina is a poverty situated in a place, not a condition of its people. Therefore, the poverty is best reduced, according to this logic, by moving out the undesirable inhabitants, who have little appreciation of the value of the Medina's material heritage and are active agents in the Medina's decay, and bringing in wealthier Fassi and tourists.

In an article on imperialism's affinity for decay, and using decay as an analytic for understanding imperialism and its effects, Stoler (2008: 211) argues that the point of research is not 'to mount a charge that every injustice of the contemporary world has imperial roots but, rather, to delineate the specific ways in which waste accumulates, where debris falls, and what constitutes "the rot that remains"'. Material heritage, I argue, is one specific locus where the debris of empire accumulates and, moreover, is actively managed. Research on the connections between poverty and material heritage therefore present an opportunity for further understanding the specific ways in which colonial legacies live on in the present, and how material heritage is key to reproducing these legacies.

References

ADER-Fès (2001) 'Fes Medina: using local craftsmen in rehabilitation', *Turath* (2).

Agrawal, A. (2005) *Environmentality: Technologies of Government and the Making of Subjects*, Durham: Duke University Press.

Ameziane, M.H. and Lazrak, A. (1998) 'The Madrassas of Fez: a constantly evolving heritage', in T. Ettayeb, (ed.) *International Campaign for Safeguard of the Medina of Fez*, Paris: UNESCO: 11–15.

Anders, G. (2005) 'Good governance as technology: towards an ethnography of the Bretton Woods Institutions', in D. Mosse and D. Lewis (eds) *The Aid Effect: Giving and Governing in International Development*, London: Pluto Press: 37–60.

Appadurai, A. (1986) 'Introduction: commodities and the politics of value', in A. Appadurai (ed.) *The Social Life of Things: Commodities in Cultural Perspective*, Cambridge: Cambridge University Press: 3–63.

Ashworth, G.J. and Tunbridge, J.E. (1990) *The Tourist-Historic City*, New York: Belhaven Press.

Barry, A. (1996) *Foucault and Political Reason: Liberalism, Neo-Liberalism, and Rationalities of Government*, Chicago: University of Chicago Press.

Bigio, A. (2007) *Fes Medina Rehabilitation, Morocco*, Presented at 'Dialogue on Cultural Heritage in Sustainable Development', April 16, 2007, World Bank, Washington D.C. Available online at <http://siteresources.worldbank.org/INTCHD/Resources/430063–1177358417057/Anthony_Bigio.pdf>

Bouchenaki, M. and Lévi-Strauss, L. (1998) 'Urban Identities and Imported Models', in T. Ettayeb (ed.) *International Campaign for Safeguard of the Medina of Fez*, Paris: UNESCO: 34–38.

Bronson, S.D. (1993) *Mission Report: Fès, Morocco, 5–13 September 1993*, Rome: ICCROM.

Burchell, G., Gordon, C. and Miller, P. (1991) *The Foucault Effect: Studies in Governmentality*, Chicago: University of Chicago Press.

Bush, R. (2007) *Poverty and Neoliberalism: Persistence and Reproduction in the Global South*, London/Ann Arbor: Pluto Press.

Byrne, D. (1991) 'Western hegemony in archaeological heritage management', *History and Anthropology* 5: 269–276.

Caffyn, A., and Jobbins, G. (2003) 'Governance capacity and stakeholder interaction in the development and management of coastal tourism: examples from Morocco and Tunisia', *Journal of Sustainable Tourism* 11 (2/3): 224–245.

Carson, R.T., Mitchell, R.C. Conaway, M.B. and Navrud, S. (1997) *Non-Moroccan Values for Rehabilitating the Fes Medina*, Washington, D.C.: World Bank Report.

Carson, R.T., Mitchell, R.C. Conaway, M.B. (2002) 'Economic Benefits to Foreigners Visiting Morocco Accruing from the Rehabilitation of the Fes Medina', in S. Navrud and R. C. Ready (eds) *Valuing Cultural Heritage: Applying Environmental Valuation Techniques to Historic Buildings, Monuments and Artifacts*, Cheltenham: Edward Elgar: 118–141.

Cassarino, J-P. (2004) 'Participatory development and liberal reforms in Tunisia: the gradual incorporation of some economic networks', in S. Heydermann (ed.) *Networks of Privilege in the Middle East: The Politics of Economic Reform Revisited, New York: Palgrave: 223–242.*

Cernea, M.M. (2001a) 'At The Cutting Edge: Cultural Patrimony Protection through Development Projects', in I. Serageldin, E. Shluger and J. Martin-Brown (eds) *Historic Cities and Sacred Sites: Cultural Roots for Urban Futures*, Washington, D.C.: World Bank: 67–88.

——(2001b) *Cultural Heritage and Development: A Framework for Action in the Middle East and North Africa*, Washington, D.C.: World Bank.

Craig, D. and Porter, D. (2006) *Development Beyond Neoliberalism: Governance, Poverty Reduction and Political Economy*, London/New York: Routledge.

Danan, B. (1998) 'The Danan Synagogue of Fez will be restored', in T. Ettayeb (ed.) *International Campaign for Safeguard of the Medina of Fez*, Paris: UNESCO: 27–29.

Darles, G. and Lagrange, N. (1996) 'The Medina in Fez: crafting a future for the past', *The UNESCO Courier*, October 1996: 36–39.

Deleuze, G. and Guattari, F. (1983) *Anti-Oedipus: Capitalism and Schizophrenia*, Minneapolis: University of Minnesota Press.

Dixon, J. (1999) 'Valuing the Benefits of Restoring the City of Fes Medina', in *ICCROM Forum: Valuing Heritage Beyond Economics* (Rome, September 30–October 2 1999), Rome: ICCROM.

Drost, A. (1996) 'Developing sustainable tourism for Word Heritage sites', *Annals of Tourism Research* 23: 479–492.

Fergany, N. (2002) 'Poverty and Unemployment in Rural Egypt', in R. Bush (ed.) *Counter revolution in Egypt's Ccountryside: land and farmers in the era of economic Reform*, London/New York: Zed Books: 211–232.

Ferguson, J. (1999) *Expectations of Modernity: Myth and Meanings of Urban Life on the Zambian Copperbelt*. Berkeley: University of California Press.

Ferguson, J. and Gupta, A. (2002) 'Spatializing States: towards an ethnography of neoliberal governmentality', *American Ethnologist* 29: 981–1002.

Filali Baba, A. (1998) 'The specificity of the Medina of Fez', in T. Ettayeb (ed.) *International Campaign for Safeguard of the Medina of Fez*, Paris: UNESCO: 6–7.

Foucault, M. (1991) 'Governmentality', in G. Burchell, C. Gordon and P. Miller (eds) *The Foucault Effect: Studies in Governmentality*, Chicago: University of Chicago Press: 87–104.

Friedman, J. (2007) 'Globalisation', in D. Nugent and J. Vincent (eds) *A Companion to the Anthropology of Politics*, Malden, MA: Blackwell: 179–197.

Goldman, M. (2001a) 'Constructing an environmental state: eco-governmentality and other transnational practices of a "green" World Bank', *Social Problems* 48 (4): 499–523.

——(2001b) 'The birth of a discipline: producing authoritative green knowledge, World Bank-style', *Ethnography* 2: 191–217.

——(2005) *Imperial Nature: The World Bank and Struggles for Social Justice in the Age of Globalisation*, New Haven: Yale University Press.

Gordillo, G. (2002) 'The dialectic of estrangement: memory and the production of places of wealth and poverty in the Argentinean Chaco', *Cultural Anthropology* 17 (1): 3–31.

Graeber, D. (2002) 'The anthropology of globalisation (with notes on neomedievalism, and the end of the chinese model of the state)', *American Anthropologist* 104: 1222–1227.

Gupta, A. (1995) 'Blurred boundaries: the discourse of corruption, the culture of politics, and the imagined state', *American Ethnologist* 22: 375–402.

Gupta, A. and Ferguson, J. (1992) 'Beyond culture: space, identity, and the politics of difference', *Cultural Anthropology* 7: 6–23.

Hardouin, J. (1983) *Bilan de la Campagne Internationale Pour la Sauvegarde de Fes*, Paris: UNESCO.

Harrigan, J., Wang, C. and El-Said, H. (2006) 'The politics of IMF and World Bank lending: will it backfire in the Middle East and North Africa?', in A. Paloni and M. Zanardi (eds) *The IMF, World Bank and Policy Reform*, London/New York: Routledge: 64–99.

Harvey, D. (2005) *A Brief History of Neoliberalism*, Oxford: Oxford University Press.

Heynen, N., McCarthy, J., Prudham, S. and Robbins, P. (eds) (2007) *Neoliberal Environments: False Promises and Unnatural Consequences*, London/New York: Routledge.

Hibou, B. (2000) 'The political economy of the World Bank's discourse from economic catechism to missionary deeds and misdeeds', *Les Etudes du CERI* 39.

Kosansky, O. (2002) 'Tourism, charity, and profit: the movement of money in Moroccan Jewish pilgrimage', *Cultural Anthropology* 17 (3): 359–400.

Lafrenz Samuels, K. (2009) 'Trajectories of development: international heritage management of archaeology in the Middle East and North Africa', *Archaeologies: Journal of the World Archaeological Congress* 5(1): 68–91.

Larbi, H. (2007) *Cultural Heritage and Development: A Framework for Action in the Middle East and North Africa*, presented at 'Dialogue on Cultural Heritage in Sustainable Development', April 16, 2007, World Bank, Washington D.C. Available online at <http://siteresources.worldbank.org/INTCHD/Resources/430063-1177358417057/Hedi_Larbi.pdf>

Lévi-Strauss, L. (2001) 'Sacred Places and Historic Cities: Preservation Governance and Practicalities', in I. Serageldin, E. Schluger and J. Martin-Brown (eds) *Historic Cities and Sacred Sites: Cultural Roots for Urban Futures*, Washington, D.C.: World Bank: 375–381.

Lévy, S. (1998) 'The Danan Synagogue of Fez will be Saved', in T. Ettayeb (ed.) *International Campaign for Safeguard of the Medina of Fez*, Paris: UNESCO: 25–26.

Mauss, M. (1990) [1925] *The Gift: The Form and Reason for Exchange in Archaic Societies*, translated by W. D. Halls, New York: W.W. Norton.

McGuinness, J. (2005) 'A Textual Enactment of Community: On Discourse Analysis, the News Media and a Social Housing Project in Tunisia in the 1990s', *The Journal of North African Studies* 10(1): 1–18.

—— (2006) 'Errances vers un Orient imaginaire? Les polymigrants de la Médina de Fès (2000–2005)', *Revue de l'Institut des Belles-Lettres Arabes* 198: 179–208.

Mehta, L. (2001) 'The World Bank and its Emerging Knowledge Empire', *Human Organization* 60 (2):189–196.

Meskell, L. (ed.) (2009) *Cosmopolitan Archaeologies*, Durham: Duke University Press.

Mitchell, T. (2002) *Rule of Experts: Egypt: Techno-Politics, Modernity*, Berkeley: University of California Press.

Moore, S.F. (2001) 'The International Production of Authoritative Knowledge: The Case of Drought-Stricken West Africa', *Ethnography* 2 (2):161–189.

Mosse, D. (2005a) *Cultivating Development: An Ethnography of Aid Policy and Practice*, London: Pluto.

——(2005b) 'Global governance and the ethnography of international aid', in D. Mosse and D. Lewis (eds) *The Aid Effect: Giving and Governing in International Development*, London: Pluto: 1–36.

Porter, G.D. (2000) 'The city's many uses: cultural tourism, the sacred monarchy and the preservation of Fez's Medina', *The Journal of North African Studies* 5 (2): 59–88.

——(2003) 'Unwitting actors: the preservation of Fez's cultural heritage', *Radical History Review* 86: 123–148.

Quarles van Ufford, P., Kumar, A. and Mosse, D. (2003) 'Interventions in Development: Towards a New Moral Understanding of our Experiences and an Agenda for the Future', in P. Quarles van Ufford and A. K. Giri (eds) *A Moral Critique of Development: In Search of Global Responsibilities*, London/New York: Routledge: 3–40.

Rawls, J. (1971) *A Theory of Justice*, Cambridge, MA: Belknap Press.

——(1993) *Political Liberalism*, New York: Columbia University Press.

Robeyns, I. (2005) 'Assessing global poverty and inequality: income, resources, and capabilities', in C. Barry and T. W. Pogge (eds) *Global Institutions and Responsibilities: Achieving Global Justice*, Malden: Blackwell Publishing: 29–47.

Sen, A. (1999) *Development as Freedom*, New York: Knopf.

Serageldin, M. (2001) 'Preserving a historic city: economic and social transformation of Fez', in I. Serageldin, E. Shluger and J. Martin-Brown (eds) *Historic Cities and Sacred Sites: Cultural Roots for Urban Futures*, Washington, D.C.: World Bank: 237–244.

——(2004) 'Monitoring processes of change in historic centres: a case study from Fes, Morocco', in UNESCO and ICCROM (eds) *Monitoring World Heritage: Shared Legacy, Common Responsibility*, Paris: UNESCO: 53–58.

Simmel, G. (1978) *The Philosophy of Money*, translated by T. Bottomore and D. Frisby, London/New York: Routledge.

Stoler, A.L. (2008) 'Imperial debris: reflections on ruins and ruination', *Cultural Anthropology* 23(2): 191–219.

Touri, A. (1998) 'Fez: The Destiny and Vocation of an Imperial City', in T. Ettayeb (ed.) *International Campaign for Safeguard of the Medina of Fez*, Paris: UNESCO: 8–10.

Tsing, A. (2000) 'The Global Situation', *Cultural Anthropology* 15(3): 327–360.

UNDP (2002) *Human Development Report*, Oxford: Oxford University Press.

UNESCO (1987) *Campagne de Sauvegarde de Fès: Résultats et Recommandations du Projet*, Paris: UNESCO.

——(1993) 'A Network of World Heritage Cities', *The World Heritage Newsletter* 2: 10–12.

Van der Berg, R. and Quarles van Ufford, P. (2005) 'Disjuncture and marginality – towards a new approach in developmental practice', in D. Mosse and D. Lewis (eds) *The Aid Effect: Giving and Governing in International Development*, London: Pluto: 196–212.

Work, M.R. (1993) *The Role of Historic Cities in Sustainable Human Development*, Presented at the 2nd International Symposium of World Heritage Towns, 6–8 September 1993, Fez, Morocco. Provided as Appendix A4-b in *Mission Report: Fès, Morocco, 5–13 September 1993* (S.D. Bronson, Ed.), Rome: ICCROM.

World Bank (n.d.) *World Bank Investment in Cultural Heritage and Development*, Washington, D.C.: World Bank. Available online at <siteresources.worldbank.org/INTCHD/Resources/430063–1095438522099/fes-medina.pdf>

——(1997) *Project Information Document for Fez Rehabilitation Project (Report No. PIC877)*, Washington, D.C.: World Bank.

——(1998) *Project Appraisal Document for Fez Medina Rehabilitation Project (Report No. 18462-MOR)*, Washington, D.C.: World Bank.

——(1999) *Case Study: Fez, Morocco. Rehabilitation of the Fez Medina*, Washington, D.C.: World Bank.

——(2006) *Implementation Completion Report for Fez Medina Rehabilitation Project (Report No. 35074)*, Washington, D.C.: World Bank.

Index

Cultural Diversity, Heritage and Human Rights
Intersections in Theory and Practice
Edited by Michele Langfield, William Logan and Máiréad Nic Craith

Cultural Diversity, Heritage and Human Rights investigates the problematic linkages between conserving cultural heritage, maintaining cultural diversity, defining and establishing cultural citizenship, and enforcing human rights.

Heritage, both tangible and intangible, provides the basis of humanity's rich cultural diversity. Yet conflicts over cultural heritage and cultural identity around the world are the subject of media scrutiny and academic scholarship, from local disputes through to ethnic cleansing over larger regions and to Huntington's grand clash of civilizations. The volume outlines the ways in which the protection and preservation of cultural heritage is especially linked to 'cultural rights' as a form of human rights.

While there is a considerable literature dealing separately with cultural diversity, cultural heritage and human rights, this book is distinctive and has contemporary relevance in focusing on the intersection between the three concepts. *Cultural Diversity, Heritage and Human Rights* establishes a fresh approach that will interest students and practitioners alike and on which future work in the heritage field might proceed.

Hb: 978-0-415-56366-6
Pb: 978-0-415-56367-3

Intangible Heritage

Edited by Laurajane Smith and Natsuko Akagawa

This volume examines the implications and consequences of the idea of 'intangible heritage' to current international academic and policy debates about the meaning and nature of cultural heritage and the management processes developed to protect it. It provides an accessible account of the different ways in which intangible cultural heritage has been defined and managed in both national and international contexts, and aims to facilitate international debate about the meaning, nature and value of not only intangible cultural heritage, but heritage more generally.

Intangible Heritage fills a significant gap in the heritage literature available and represents a significant cross section of ideas and practices associated with intangible cultural heritage. The authors brought together for this volume represent some of the key academics and practitioners working in the area, and discuss research and practices from a range of countries, including: Zimbabwe, Morocco, South Africa, Japan, Australia, United Kingdom, the Netherlands, USA, Brazil and Indonesia, and bring together a range of areas of expertise which include anthropology, law, heritage studies, archaeology, museum studies, folklore, architecture, Indigenous studies and history.

Hb: 978-0-415-47397-2
Pb: 978-0-415-47396-5

Related titles from Routledge

Places of Pain and Shame

William Logan and Keir Reeves

Places of Pain and Shame is a cross-cultural study of sites that represent painful and/or shameful episodes in a national or local community's history, and the ways that government agencies, heritage professionals and the communities themselves seek to remember, commemorate and conserve these cases – or, conversely, choose to forget them.

Such episodes and locations include: massacre and genocide sites, places related to prisoners of war, civil and political prisons, and places of 'benevolent' internment such as leper colonies and lunatic asylums. These sites bring shame upon us now for the cruelty and futility of the events that occurred within them and the ideologies they represented. They are however increasingly being regarded as 'heritage sites', a far cry from the view of heritage that prevailed a generation ago when we were almost entirely concerned with protecting the great and beautiful creations of the past, reflections of the creative genius of humanity rather than the reverse – the destructive and cruel side of history.

Why has this shift occurred, and what implications does it have for professionals practicing in the heritage field? In what ways is this a 'difficult' heritage to deal with? This volume brings together academics and practitioners to explore these questions, covering not only some of the practical matters, but also the theoretical and conceptual issues, and uses case studies of historic places, museums and memorials from around the globe, including the United States, Northern Ireland, Poland, South Africa, China, Japan, Taiwan, Cambodia, Indonesia, Timor and Australia.

Hb: 978-0-415-45449-0
Pb: 978-0-415-45450-6

Available at all good bookshops
For ordering and further information please visit:
www.routledge.com